An Introduction to the Scriptures of Israel

An Introduction to the Scriptures of Israel

HISTORY AND THEOLOGY

Tzvi Novick

William B. Eerdmans Publishing Company
Grand Rapids, Michigan

Wm. B. Eerdmans Publishing Co.
2140 Oak Industrial Drive N.E., Grand Rapids, Michigan 49505
www.eerdmans.com

Published 2018
Printed in the United States of America

27 26 25 24 23 22 21 20 19 18 1 2 3 4 5 6 7 8 9 10

ISBN 978-0-8028-7542-6

Library of Congress Cataloging-in-Publication Data

Names: Novick, Tzvi, author.
Title: An introduction to the scriptures of Israel : history and theology / Tzvi Novick.
Description: Grand Rapids : Eerdmans Publishing Co., 2018. |
Includes bibliographical references and index.
Identifiers: LCCN 2018006910 | ISBN 9780802875426 (pbk. : alk. paper)
Subjects: LCSH: Bible. Old Testament—Criticism, interpretation, etc.
Classification: LCC BS1171.3 .N69 2018 | DDC 221.6/1—dc23
LC record available at https://lccn.loc.gov/2018006910

Contents

Preface vii

Abbreviations ix

1. Three Introductions 1

2. The Wisdom Tradition: Religion without Revelation 15

3. Revelation and Love:
The Patriarchal Narratives and the Song of Songs 29

4. Joseph and Narrative 43

5. The Exodus: Freedom and Sonship 56

6. Sinai: Covenant and Code 66

7. The Problem of Monarchy: Samuel and Kings 77

8. Condemning Israel, Sparing the Nations:
Amos and Jonah 88

9. Eden and the Art of Reading 100

10. Priestly Theology and Holy Space 114

11. Exile and Return: Prophetic Visions 126

12. The Consolidation of Judaism: Temple and Torah 139

13. Violence and Identity: Joshua and Judges 150

14. Jews, Gentiles, and Gender: Esther, Ruth, Ezra, and Nehemiah 159

15. Apocalyptic: Daniel and the Dead Sea Scrolls 169

16. The Israelite at Prayer: The Book of Psalms 180

Subject Index 192

Scripture and Other Ancient Sources Index 198

Preface

This book is designed to serve as a teaching tool, and it has its origins in the classroom. Undergraduates at the University of Notre Dame take a required two-course sequence in theology, and the first of these courses is devoted to "The Foundations of Theology: Scriptural/Historical." The course covers the Old Testament, the New Testament, and the early church; each instructor teaches it with his or her own distinctive set of emphases. The current book derives from my lectures on the Old Testament for this course, but with significant modifications. The book is intended for all readers, of any faith or of none, and for all frameworks, from the theological to the historical.

I would like to thank the undergraduate students that I have taught in the Foundations course, and the graduate students who have helped me teach it. Their engagement with the material has allowed me to appreciate new nuances and clarify claims. Thanks are also due to my colleagues in the Department of Theology at Notre Dame, for whom stewardship of the Foundations course is a weighty and treasured responsibility. Conversations with them in the halls and stairwells of Malloy Hall, in faculty meetings, and elsewhere have shaped my understanding of the Bible. I have drawn inspiration, in particular, from the scholarship of and from conversations with my colleague Gary Anderson. I offer special thanks, too, to the department chairs during my time thus far at Notre Dame: John Cavadini, Matt Ashley, and now Tim Matovina. I hope that this book reflects the culture of inquiry, collegiality, and mission that they have fostered. Despite its genesis, the book, with all of its flaws and idiosyncrasies, is entirely my own.

Because this work is intended as an introductory textbook, I have generally refrained from using footnotes. General background on biblical history and on the dates and composition history of the biblical books can be found, with ample references to secondary literature, in any quality commentary series, such as the Anchor Bible, the International Critical Commentary, or Hermeneia. When I make use of a scholar's work to advance a specific claim, I cite the scholar by name in the body of the chapter and include the relevant secondary literature in the bibliography at the end of the chapter. The bibliography at the end of the chapter also includes scholarly works that inform the chapter in a more general way, as well as literature that addresses aspects of the chapter's topic that I do not take up in the chapter. Where I advance a specific claim without citing previous scholarship, I am not suggesting that the claim is necessarily new, but only that I have not found it in others' work. Because the gestation of this book occurred over many years, it is possible that I have unwittingly drawn, without proper attribution, on the work of another scholar. For any such omission, I apologize at the outset.

Each chapter begins with a list of the "Readings," the primary texts (mostly biblical) to which the chapter is devoted. The discussion in the body of the chapter presupposes a basic familiarity with these texts. Besides the aforementioned bibliography, each chapter concludes with questions "For Further Reflection." Sometimes these questions point the reader in directions that nuance or otherwise supplement the argumentation of the chapter. In other cases, they highlight interesting features of the primary texts that fall outside the chapter's main interests.

Translations from the Hebrew Bible ordinarily draw from the New Jewish Publication Society Version (*Tanakh*), but I have sometimes modified the translations to suit the context (noted as "slightly altered" or "altered"). At times I have cited the New Revised Standard Version (marked as NRSV), especially for translations from the New Testament. For translations from the Apocrypha I draw on *A New English Translation of the Septuagint*, edited by Albert Pietersma and Benjamin G. Wright (Oxford: Oxford University Press, 2007).

A grant from the Institute for Scholarship in the Liberal Arts, College of Arts and Letters, University of Notre Dame, supported the indexing for the book. I would like to thank Christopher Mooney for reading and commenting on a number of chapters. My thanks, too, to Aaron Koller, who read through the entire manuscript and gave valuable feedback. Andrew Knapp, my editor at Eerdmans, offered much helpful advice, especially in the initial stages of the writing. There is no part of my work that is not also the work of my wife, Rachel, and not least this book, which reflects on questions of faith and justice that are our daily discourse. To my parents, for their support and love, I have no words to express my gratitude. And above them all is God, "beyond all blessings and songs."

Abbreviations

COS	*The Context of Scripture.* Edited by William W. Hallo and K. Lawson Younger Jr. 4 vols. Leiden: Brill, 1997–2017
NJPS	New Jewish Publication Society Version (*Tanakh*)
NRSV	New Revised Standard Version

1 | Three Introductions

The Particular and the Universal

On April 3, 1968, the Reverend Martin Luther King Jr. delivered a speech in which he imagined his own death. "I would like to live a long life," he said.

> Longevity has its place. But I'm not concerned about that now. I just want to do God's will. And He's allowed me to go up to the mountain. And I've looked over, and I've seen the Promised Land. I may not get there with you. But I want you to know tonight, that we, as a people, will get to the Promised Land.[1]

To understand what King meant to convey in these sentences, we must appreciate that they allude to the Bible. The prophet Moses took his people, Israel, out of slavery in Egypt and led them to the land of Canaan, the land promised by God to Israel's forefathers. But Moses was not permitted to enter Canaan. God called Moses up to a mountain from which Moses could see the promised land, but Moses died on that mountain, and Israel entered Canaan under the leadership of Moses's successor, Joshua. In the above quotation, King implicitly portrays himself as another Moses. He has seen the "promised land" of racial equality—he calls it "promised" presumably because, as King suggested in his most famous speech, from the March on Washington in 1963, the Declaration

1. A full transcript of the "mountaintop" speech is available online at kingencyclopedia.stanford.edu.

of Independence and the Constitution represent a "promissory note" on which the civil rights movement comes to collect—and so, though he may die before he is able to dwell in it, he can vouch for its reality, and for its proximity.

This book is an introduction to the Old Testament, or the Hebrew Bible, which for our purposes we will, in general, simply call "the Bible." In this book I take my bearings from an assumption implicit in King's use of the Bible. For King, the Bible is a source of moral authority: it underwrites the promises of freedom and equality to which the United States' founding documents give expression. It does so even though the promised land of the Bible is not, of course, racial equality, but a stretch of soil in the Middle East, and even though the promise was made not to human beings as such but to a specific people, Israel, to whom King does not belong ethnically. In other words, King takes the Bible to be generalizable, or universalizable. Even when the Bible speaks about Israel, the particular, it is also speaking about the universal, the human condition.

In relation to the tension between the particular and the universal, for two reasons there is a tendency to situate the Hebrew Bible firmly on the particular side of the ledger. The first reason is that, in the Christian tradition, which has largely determined the reception of the Bible in the Western world, theologians often pit the authority of scripture against the authority of reason. We may consider, for example, a passage from the *Dialogue with Trypho*, written by Justin Martyr, a church father from the second century CE. Born into a pagan family in what is now the city of Nablus, Justin came to Christianity through his study of philosophy. In the following exchanges, from chapters 3 and 7 of his *Dialogue with Trypho*, Justin, at this point not a Christian but a dedicated follower of Plato, encounters a Christian on the shore.

> "What, then, is philosophy?" he [the Christian] says; "and what is happiness? Pray tell me, unless something hinders you from saying."
>
> "Philosophy, then," said I [Justin], "is the knowledge of that which really exists, and a clear perception of the truth; and happiness is the reward of such knowledge and wisdom."
>
> "But what do you call God?" said he.
>
> "That which always maintains the same nature, and in the same manner, and is the cause of all other things—that, indeed, is God."[2]

2. I quote from *The Apostolic Fathers—Justin Martyr—Irenaeus*, vol. 1 of *Ante-Nicene Fathers* (= *ANF* 1), ed. Alexander Roberts and James Donaldson (reprint; Grand Rapids: Eerdmans, 1973), 196.

The Christian then interrogates Justin about the source of his knowledge of God.

> "Some [branches of knowledge] come to us by learning, or by some employment, while of others we have knowledge by sight. Now, if one were to tell you that there exists in India an animal with a nature unlike all others, but of such and such a kind, multiform and various, you would not know it before you saw it; but neither would you be competent to give any account of it, unless you should hear from one who had seen it."
>
> "Certainly not," I said.
>
> "How then," he said, "should the philosophers judge correctly about God, or speak any truth, when they have no knowledge of Him, having neither seen Him at any time, nor heard Him?"
>
> "But, father," said I, "the Deity cannot be seen merely by the eyes, as other living beings can, but is discernible to the mind alone, as Plato says; and I believe him."[3]

Justin insists that philosophers can reason about God, and indeed, that we can only experience God by thinking about him; there can be no direct experience of God. The Christian proceeds to challenge this assumption.

> "There existed, long before this time, certain men more ancient than all those who are esteemed philosophers, both righteous and beloved by God, who spoke by the Divine Spirit, and foretold events which would take place, and which are now taking place. They are called prophets. These alone both saw and announced the truth to men, neither reverencing nor fearing any man, not influenced by a desire for glory, but speaking those things alone which they saw and which they heard, being filled with the Holy Spirit. Their writings are still extant, and he who has read them is very much helped in his knowledge of the beginning and end of things, and of those matters which the philosopher ought to know, provided he has believed them. For they did not use demonstration in their treatises, seeing that they were witnesses to the truth above all demonstration, and worthy of belief; and those events which have happened, and those which are happening, compel you to assent to the utterances made by them. . . . But pray that, above all things, the gates of light may be opened to you; for these things cannot be perceived or

3. *ANF* 1:196.

> understood by all, but only by the man to whom God and His Christ have imparted wisdom."[4]

Justin's dialogue opposes the philosopher to the prophet. The philosopher reasons about God and believes that one has no access to God except through reason. The Christian contends instead that God can be and has been directly experienced, not by philosophers but by prophets, whose writings are preserved as scripture. The philosopher can only demonstrate, but the prophet witnesses.

The Christian concedes, however, that not everyone will find the prophets' witness persuasive. To be persuaded by the prophets' witness is a special endowment, a gift of "wisdom" from God, who opens up the "gates of light"—perhaps, indeed, something akin to prophetic inspiration itself. By contrast, in the above passage and in general, reason is imagined to be the endowment of human beings as such; it is an intrinsically universalist source of authority. Reason purports to offer insight into what is necessarily true, whereas witness appears to concern only what is at best historically true, what is contingently true, what is, in the first instance, directly accessible only to the individuals who happened to be witnesses. From the contrast, then, between the prophet and the philosopher, between scriptural authority and the authority of reason, one naturally emerges thinking of scripture in particularist terms.

A second reason for thinking of specifically the Hebrew Bible or the Old Testament in particularist terms derives from the tendency in some Christian contexts to put the Old Testament in a starkly contrastive relationship to the New. If the New brings good news to all people, then the Old must address Israel alone. But Christianity hardly requires (or arguably even allows for) such a stark contrast, nor does the use of the Old Testament in the above passage from King's "mountaintop" speech—which is deeply informed by King's Christianity—assume it.

Complex interplay between the particular and the universal is a defining feature of the human condition, and of the modern condition. We are all, with the rarest exceptions, born and raised into commitments that define and limit us: commitments to a particular family, to a particular nation, perhaps to a particular religious community or ethnic or racial group. While all of these commitments are negotiable, we have no choice but to negotiate them. Beyond and in relation to particular commitments lies the universal, itself an amorphous boundary. It can encompass the human, in contrast to the nonhuman; or it can

4. *ANF* 1:198.

extend further, as in the case of the environmental framework, to incorporate the earthly—and beyond.

The relationship between the universal and the particular is an abiding concern of Western modernity, whose birth lies in the scientific revolution and the Enlightenment. These developments held out the promise of reason, of universal progress through education and technology. Reality has proven less pliant, and numerous responses to the Enlightenment, some irenic and some very violent, have demonstrated both that a total eclipse of the particular is unlikely, and likely undesirable, and that the Enlightenment's vision of universal progress encoded a very particular and far from perfectly innocuous interpretation of the universal. Without unpacking this dense summary of some three hundred years of human history, we may simply note that the relationship between the universal and the particular will remain a problem far into the foreseeable future.

Following the lead of Justin Martyr, we began by placing the Bible on the particularist side of the ledger, in opposition, at least in the first instance, to universalist reason. We have noted that one might complicate this classification by distinguishing between the Old Testament and the New, and placing the Old Testament in the particularist column, as the story of the people Israel, and the New Testament in the universalist column, as the collection of books that expand God's covenant beyond Israel to the world as a whole. It is one of the burdens of this book to show that this distinction is also far too simplistic. Not only in the relationship between the Old Testament and the New but in the Old Testament itself, the Bible grapples with the problem of the universal and the particular. My purpose in advancing this thesis is not to defend the Bible, specifically the Old Testament, against the charge of particularism by showing that it features universalistic elements. Indeed, I see in neither particularism nor universalism an unadulterated good. My purpose is rather to expose the complex operation of the dichotomy within the Bible.

The Traditional-Canonical and Historical-Critical Methods

Scholars generally recognize two major ways of reading the Bible. The first is often dubbed the *traditional-canonical*. To read the Bible in this way is to read it according to the assumptions of a particular religious tradition, whether Jewish or Christian. These traditions share numerous basic assumptions, first and foremost that because the books of the Bible are, in one way or another, the living word of God, they together form a correct, coherent, and relevant whole. Correct, and therefore if something in the Bible appears to be wrong, whether factually, morally, or in any other way, it must be interpreted otherwise. Coherent, and hence any apparent contradictions between different books in the Bible must be in one way or another reconciled. Relevant, and so every part of the Bible must, in principle, speak to the reader. The religious tradition's accumulated history of interpretation and practice supplies the content of the criteria of correctness, coherence, and relevance.

The *historical-critical* method, by contrast, reads the Bible for what it meant in its original historical context. It does not concern itself with whether this meaning is, by modern standards, factually or morally wrong. Nor does it matter for the historical-critical method whether different passages utterly disagree. On the contrary, disagreement is to be expected, given that the biblical books (and parts thereof) were composed by different individuals and under different historical circumstances. Nor is it a problem if the issue that a biblical text addresses is one of little or no contemporary moment.

As the religious reader of the Bible must confront the challenges that reason (or philosophy) poses to the Bible's claims, so must she grapple with the results of the historical-critical method. For example, if Jews and Christians alike traditionally took the book of Deuteronomy to be what it represents itself to be, that is, a transcript of a speech delivered by Moses to the Israelites on the Jordan plain soon before his death, they are now faced with the fact that Deuteronomy coalesced many centuries after the death of Moses (on the assumption that there was such a figure), that it is the result of multiple revisions, and that it revises earlier parts of the Pentateuch. Likewise, many Christian interpreters take the story of the garden of Eden to describe the origin of the human inclination to sin, even though, as we will see later (in chapter 9), this notion is not to be found in the plain sense of the story.

In the remainder of this section I defend two claims about the relationship between the traditional-canonical and the historical-critical reading methods. The first claim is that they can coexist. The second is that they are indeed mutually reinforcing. We begin with the first claim. It may be difficult, at first glance, to appreciate how the traditional-canonical approach can survive historical criticism. In what sense can an interpretation of a biblical text be "true" even though it does not correspond to the text's original meaning?

Two thematically related poems shed light on this question. The first, entitled "An Arundel Tomb," was written by the twentieth-century English poet Philip Larkin.

> Side by side, their faces blurred,
> The earl and countess lie in stone,

Their proper habits vaguely shown
As jointed armour, stiffened pleat,
And that faint hint of the absurd—
The little dogs under their feet.

Such plainness of the pre-baroque
Hardly involves the eye, until
It meets his left-hand gauntlet, still
Clasped empty in the other; and
One sees, with a sharp tender shock,
His hand withdrawn, holding her hand.

They would not think to lie so long.
Such faithfulness in effigy
Was just a detail friends would see:
A sculptor's sweet commissioned grace
Thrown off in helping to prolong
The Latin names around the base.

They would not guess how early in
Their supine stationary voyage
The air would change to soundless damage,
Turn the old tenantry away;
How soon succeeding eyes begin
To look, not read. Rigidly, they

Persisted, linked, through lengths and breadths
Of time. Snow fell, undated. Light
Each summer thronged the glass. A bright
Litter of birdcalls strewed the same
Bone-riddled ground. And up the paths
The endless altered people came,

Washing at their identity.
Now, helpless in the hollow of
An unarmorial age, a trough
Of smoke in slow suspended skeins
Above their scrap of history,
Only an attitude remains:

Time has transfigured them into
Untruth. The stone fidelity
They hardly meant has come to be
Their final blazon, and to prove
Our almost-instinct almost true:
What will survive of us is love.[5]

Larkin describes the experience of viewing the medieval tomb of an earl and countess. The stone images of the couple lie recumbent, side by side, he depicted in armor, she in pleats. But our eye is arrested by a singular detail: the earl's left gauntlet clasps his right, but the gauntlet is empty. His left hand is withdrawn from the gauntlet, and instead holds the countess's hand.

The sculptor, according to the poem, introduced this feature for a very practical reason. By having them hold hands, he was able to widen the tomb, and thereby made room for the Latin inscription around the circumference of the base. The original "meaning" of the hand-holding lay, then, in the Latin inscription. But the passage of time brings a new audience, different in two important respects. First, it no longer knows Latin: the people "begin to look, not read." Second, it lives in an "unarmorial age," a different era with a different conception of love. This new audience ignores the Latin inscription, and takes the meaning of the sculpture to reside in the hand-holding, construed as a gesture of eternal love. The new "meaning" of the tomb is: "What will survive of us is love."

The poet is half-attracted to this interpretation, but ultimately denies it as "untruth," and not only relative to the sculptor's intent but in absolute terms. Indeed, crucially, its distance from the sculptor's intent is something of a proxy for or a sign of its basic wrongheadedness. Larkin thus describes a gap between the original meaning and subsequent interpretation, and uses this gap to condemn the latter.

A very different evaluation of this gap occurs in the following poem, "Ozymandias," a sonnet written by the nineteenth-century English poet Percy Bysshe Shelley.

I met a traveler from an antique land
Who said: Two vast and trunkless legs of stone
Stand in the desert. . . . Near them, on the sand,

5. "An Arundel Tomb" from *The Complete Poems of Philip Larkin* by Philip Larkin, edited by Archie Burnett. Copyright © 2012 by the The Estate of Philip Larkin. Reprinted by permission of Farrar, Straus and Giroux. Digital rights by permission of Faber and Faber, Ltd.

> Half sunk, a shattered visage lies, whose frown,
> And wrinkled lip, and sneer of cold command
> Tell that its sculptor well those passions read
> Which yet survive, stamped on these lifeless things,
> The hand that mocked them, and the heart that fed.
>
> And on the pedestal these words appear:
> "My name is Ozymandias, king of kings:
> Look on my works, ye Mighty, and despair!"
>
> Nothing beside remains. Round the decay
> Of that colossal wreck, boundless and bare
> The lone and level sands stretch far away.

Like "An Arundel Tomb," Shelley's poem revolves around a sculpture of an elite figure with an inscription. In this case the sculpture is of a forgotten king, Ozymandias. Like Larkin's, Shelley's sculpture undergoes changes over time. In "Ozymandias," time ravages the sculpture, leaving only "two vast and trunkless legs of stone" upon a pedestal, and beside them, part of the head. But in contrast with Larkin's case, where the changes wrought by time lead to disregard of the inscription, time in Shelley's poem exposes a new truth in the inscription. In its original context, the inscription was a boast: You who think you are powerful, look on my far more powerful works, and despair of besting me. But with the devastation of the statue and the disappearance—presumably under the sand—of Ozymandias's architectural achievements, the inscription takes on a very different meaning: You who take pride in your power, see how my mighty works have decayed, and despair of any hope of permanence in your own status.

Larkin's later poem appears to know Shelley's. (Note especially how the concluding turn in Shelley's sonnet, "nothing beside remains," seems to echo in the hinge that introduces Larkin's conclusion: "Only an attitude remains." Both, too, appear to pun on the two senses of the word *lie*, namely, to be recumbent and to be speak falsely.) In any case, Larkin reverses Shelley's perspective on secondary meaning. For Larkin, that an interpretation diverges from its original sense is a reason to suspect that it is "untruth." For Shelley, by contrast, it is possible for the secondary meaning to be truer than the original. In "Ozymandias," the passage of time, wearing away the sculpture and covering the surrounding structures, exposes a new and more accurate meaning in the inscription on the pedestal.

It may be helpful to think of the traditional-canonical approach along the lines of Shelley's poem. The original meaning, that is, the meaning of the biblical text in its original historical context, has its own integrity. But in light of the changed circumstances of later readers, new meaning can emerge that is no less true—indeed, that is possibly even more true—than the original meaning.

This defense of the claim that the traditional-canonical method can coexist with the historical-critical method is far from complete. Indeed, it addresses only one half of the problem. For the two methods can diverge in two entirely different ways: the traditional-canonical method can interpret a biblical text against its plain sense (as in the Eden example above), or it can uphold the plain sense of the biblical text as historical fact even when historical criticism tells us that the biblical text does not correspond to historical fact (as in the Deuteronomy example above). Shelley's poem offers a framework for addressing the first divergence, but its applicability to the second is less certain. We merely flag this gap here; to enter into the second divergence would carry us rather too far afield.

We turn now, more briefly, to the second claim about the relationship between the traditional-canonical and the historical-critical reading methods: they are, in part, mutually reinforcing. If we think of the different books of the Bible as independent entities, gathered together for extrinsic reasons, then the two methods have almost nothing to say to each other. The historical-critical method considers the given book in its original isolation, while the traditional-canonical method reads it in conversation with the other biblical books. But the books of the Bible are not, in fact, independent entities. Historical criticism itself reveals the dense interconnections among the biblical books in their original contexts, both insofar as the books emerge from a common cultural context, and insofar as later books respond to earlier ones. In other words, historical criticism shows that, by and large, the biblical books themselves embody a tradition. Or, in still other words, it shows that the traditional-canonical method is not an imposition out of the blue upon the biblical collection, but, at least in part, a perpetuation of the practices that yielded the biblical books themselves. We will see this process at work in a number of the following chapters.

Some Biblical Basics

This third and final introduction to the book aims to orient the reader by providing a brief overview both of the narrative thread of the biblical books and of the structure of the Bible. The books that make up the Bible were composed over a millennium, between roughly the twelfth century BCE and the second century BCE. The Bible purports to span the entire history of the world, from its creation to roughly the fifth century BCE. (Thus, even though some parts of the Bible were written after the fifth century BCE, the events that they depict do not postdate this century.) At the center of the historical narrative is the people Israel, whose story begins with its founding figure, Abraham, around the beginning of the second millennium BCE.

The geographical setting for the story of Israel is the Near East, especially two regions therein, both characterized by access to water, hence by agricultural fertility and civilization. The first is Mesopotamia, watered by the Tigris and Euphrates rivers. At different periods pertinent to the biblical record, two great empires emerged out of Mesopotamia: Assyria (with successive capital cities at Assur, Calah, and Nineveh) and Babylonia (with the capital city Babylon). The second important region for our purposes is Egypt, watered by the Nile. Ancient Israel is sandwiched precisely between these two civilizations: just southwest of Mesopotamia, and just northeast of Egypt. The complex history of Israelite thought, some of which we will trace in this book, owes much to its intersectional location.

Abraham is said to emigrate from Mesopotamia, in particular the city of Ur, to the land of Canaan. His descendants find their way into Egypt and are enslaved there; but, under the leadership of Moses (around 1300 BCE), they escape to the wilderness of Sinai, where they enter into a covenant with God and receive his law. They make their way back to Canaan—but not before Moses dies in the wilderness, as noted at the very outset of this chapter—and take it by war from the native Canaanites.

What do modern historians make of this biblical narrative, in which the people Israel is not native to Canaan but comes to it through Mesopotamia, via Egypt? While the details are much debated, historians agree that, like many ancient (and not-so-ancient) narratives, this one simplifies what was historically a much messier reality. In particular, there are good reasons to see the Israelites, or some part thereof, not as foreign interlopers to Canaan but as native inhabitants of Canaan or its immediate environs. Most importantly, the Israelites' and Canaanites' languages are extremely similar; indeed, the Hebrew of the Bible is simply a dialect of Canaanite. The decision to portray Israel as foreign to Canaan thus looks like part of a theological strategy designed in part to construct Israel as a nation utterly dependent on God, a nation whose very birth and home come from him. As the beginning of the Bible—Genesis 1—depicts the world as God's work, so likewise is Israel God's work.

Before around 1000 BCE, the tribes that would become Israel were affiliated with one another to varying degrees, in some cases quite loosely. We might with due caution compare these circumstances to those of the postrevolutionary United States of America, where thirteen distinct states formed a country, under the Articles of Confederation, but lacked a strong central government. The United States went on, under the Constitution, to strengthen its central government, but sectional divisions remained and eventually found expression in civil war. The Bible tells a similar story, and again, its relationship with historical fact is a matter of degree. According to the book of Samuel, the tribes came to be unified under a king, Saul, of the tribe of Benjamin, and afterward under a different king, David, of the tribe of Judah. David's son Solomon carried forward the dynasty and built a temple to God in Jerusalem. At Solomon's death, under his son Rehoboam, the fractures reemerged, and the nation split into a northern kingdom (Israel), and a southern (Judah), the latter centered around Jerusalem.

The northern kingdom was conquered by the Assyrian Empire near the end of the eighth century BCE, and its inhabitants either fled to Judah or were exiled to Assyria. The southern kingdom survived until the beginning of the sixth century BCE, when Babylonia invaded, destroyed the temple in Jerusalem, and exiled much of the population. After Persia, under Cyrus, conquered Babylonia half a century later, Jews in Babylonia were given license to return to Judah and rebuild the temple. Some—very far from all—did so and rebuilt the temple some years later (hence it is called the Second Temple). The period in between the destruction of the temple and the return to Judah is known as the exilic period, which separates the First Temple period from the Second Temple period.

We turn now, finally, to a brief review of the biblical canon: the books of the Bible, and their arrangement. It is possible to study ancient Israel from a purely historical perspective, but it is impossible, in a strict sense, to study the Bible outside the framework of a religious tradition, because the very subject in question—the Bible—is defined by that tradition; the tradition determines which books belong to the Bible and which do not, and how the books in the Bible are arranged. Judaism and Christianity differ on these questions.

In the Jewish tradition, the Bible divides into three sections. The first consists of the five books (whence the term *Pentateuch*) from Genesis through Deuteronomy, which ends with Moses's death. Judaism calls these five books the Torah (Hebrew *torah* means "instruction"); we will return to this term in chapter 12. The next section is called the Prophets (Hebrew *nevi'im*). It begins with the books that describe the history of Israel from the death of Moses to the Babylonian exile and just beyond, then continues with books attributed to prophets who lived during the final two hundred years of this period, like Isaiah and Amos. The third section, the Writings (Hebrew *ketuvim*), is a miscellany that includes prayers (the book of Psalms) and wisdom literature (Proverbs), among other types of literature. The Jewish Bible goes by the name *Tanak*, an acronym from the first letters of its three parts (*torah, nevi'im, ketuvim*). As an historical matter, the organization of the Tanak reflects in part the growth of the canon, and in part the texts' internal chronology. But according to Jewish tradition, authorship and inspiration determine the threefold division. The Torah is most authoritative, because the tradition attributes it to the greatest prophet, Moses. The Prophets have secondary authority, because lesser prophets authored them. The Writings, according to Jewish tradition, were written under the inspiration of the Holy Spirit, which is inferior to prophetic inspiration, and hence are less authoritative still.

In the Christian Bible, the Old Testament is also organized into three parts, but according to a different organizing principle, time. The first section is composed of the historical books (the past), from the beginning of the world until the Babylonian exile. The second section consists of timeless material (the present), preeminently the books of Psalms and Proverbs. The third section consists of the prophetic books, which in a Christian context furnish the promises for the coming of Jesus. Most versions of the Christian Bible also include books omitted from the Tanak (known as the Apocrypha or deuterocanonical books), such as the book of Ben Sira (or Sirach), which we will encounter later (chapter 12).

For Further Reflection

1. As noted above, the dichotomy of universalist and particularist involves in the first instance an analytical distinction, not a value judgment. That is, it does not imply the superiority of one pole over the other. When the dichotomy is instantiated in the conflict between loyalty to one's own in contrast with service to the world, some of us tend to privilege one pole of the dichotomy over the other. Reflect on which pole you privilege, and formulate arguments against that pole.

2. Above I explained (or gestured toward an explanation of) how a traditional-canonical interpretation of a text can diverge from the originally intended sense—the meaning of the text from an historical-critical perspective—and nevertheless be true. What of the case when the tradition asserts the truth of the plain sense, and the historical-critical method shows that the plain sense cannot be true? I flagged one example above: the book of Deuteronomy attributes itself to Moses, but historical criticism shows that it was written many centuries after Moses lived. How can a religious reader hold together the Bible's plain sense, affirmed by tradition, and the conclusions of historical-critical analysis?

Bibliography

Fitzmyer, Joseph A. *The Interpretation of Scripture: In Defense of the Historical-Critical Method.* New York: Paulist Press, 2008.

Levenson, Jon D. *The Hebrew Bible, the Old Testament, and Historical Criticism: Jews and Christians in Biblical Studies.* Louisville: Westminster John Knox, 1993.

MacIntyre, Alasdair C. *After Virtue: A Study in Moral Theology.* Notre Dame: University of Notre Dame Press, 1981.

Sternhell, Zeev. *The Anti-Enlightenment Tradition.* Translated by David Maisel. New Haven: Yale University Press, 2010.

2 | The Wisdom Tradition: Religion without Revelation

READINGS

Proverbs 1; 6–8; 15–17; 22:17–24:22; 30–31

Instruction of Amenemope, especially Teaching One (col. 3) and Teaching Thirty (col. 27) (see the translation of Miriam Lichtheim, "Instruction of Amenemope," *COS* 1:115–22)

Job 1–14; 29–31; 38–42

Introduction

We begin our survey of the Bible not at the beginning, with the book of Genesis, but with the book of Proverbs. The explanation for this starting point lies in the fact that Proverbs offers arguably the most universalist perspective in the Bible. In terms of Justin Martyr's contrast of philosophy with prophecy, Proverbs has in it a great deal more of the former than of the latter. After examining, in this chapter, the contours of a paradigmatically universalist worldview and some developments within the tradition chartered by it, we will be in a position to reflect, in the next chapter, on the implications of the particularist perspective that is characteristic of most of biblical literature.

What Is Wisdom?

The book of Proverbs announces itself as a practical book, with a specific purpose:

> For learning wisdom and discipline;
> For understanding words of discernment;
> For acquiring the discipline for success,
> Righteousness, justice, and equity;
> For endowing the simple with shrewdness,
> The young with knowledge and foresight. (Proverbs 1:2–4)

This passage defines the book's aim as instruction in wisdom (Hebrew *hokmah*), and Proverbs is the paradigmatic instance of "wisdom literature" in the Bible. But what is wisdom?

The above passage associates wisdom with success, but does not specify the sort of success envisioned. Two of the initial references to wisdom in the Bible indicate that wisdom and success are, or at least can be, very mundane categories. First, a government bureaucrat who can manage the complex logistical tasks involved in gathering and distributing grain surpluses—Joseph, whom we will encounter later (chapter 4)—is ipso facto "a man of discernment and wisdom" (Genesis 41:33). Second, the goldsmiths, weavers, and other skilled workers, male and female, whom Moses tasks with constructing God's dwelling, the tabernacle, are "wise of heart" (as in Exodus 28:3 NJPS, slightly altered).

If wisdom in these contexts refers to the ability to succeed at the task at hand, then wisdom in general describes the skills and habits essential for success in life, for material gain, for social standing, and so on. Many parts of Proverbs read like a self-help book.

> Do not be of those who guzzle wine,
> Or glut themselves on meat.
> For guzzlers and gluttons will be impoverished,
> And drowsing will clothe you in tatters. (23:20–21)
>
> The lips of a forbidden woman drip honey;
> Her mouth is smoother than oil;
> But in the end she is as bitter as wormwood,
> Sharp as a two-edged sword. (5:3–4)
>
> How long will you lie there, lazybones;
> When will you wake from your sleep?
> A bit more sleep, a bit more slumber, . . .
> And poverty will come calling upon you. (6:9–11)

The book warns against laziness, drunkenness, gluttony, and pursuit of married women, cautioning that no good can come of these things, but only poverty and death. It is clear that these admonitions envision a male audience, and specifically an audience of young men; let us recollect the reference to the "young" in the opening passage above, and note that the speaker of Proverbs regularly addresses "my son," but never "my daughter." We will return later in this chapter to aspects of gender in the book of Proverbs.

The criterion of worldly success means that wisdom can even involve shunning certain actions that one might be inclined to praise as generous or selfless. Thus the book counsels against serving as surety for one's neighbor, that is, acting as guarantor so that one's needy neighbor can borrow money. To do so is to be "trapped by the words of your mouth" (Proverbs 6:2). To one so reckless as to have been thus trapped, Proverbs counsels doing whatever possible to extricate oneself.

Wisdom of the sort described above is pragmatic. It represents prudent counsel. And yet wisdom is bound up not only with success but with "righteousness, justice, and equity" (1:3). The book regularly warns against oppression of the poor: "Do not rob the wretched because he is wretched; do not crush the poor man in the gate" (22:22). But if wisdom is a pragmatic category, how can such counsel amount to wisdom? What profit lies in refraining from taking advantage of the weak? Or, put differently, how does Proverbs hold together prudence and piety under the category of wisdom?

One might venture that Proverbs prescribes piety as a check on pragmatism: one should be sober, industrious, even self-regarding, so as to prosper in the world, but not so self-regarding as to oppress the poor. However, Proverbs conceives of piety as itself an expression of prudence. Why should one not "rob the wretched" or "crush the poor man in the gate"? "For the LORD will take up their cause, and despoil those who despoil them of life" (22:23). One should act justly toward the vulnerable out of fear of God, which is to say, out of fear that God will avenge them. It is this consideration that the book has in mind when it asserts that "the fear of the LORD is the beginning of knowledge" (1:7). Appealing to the threat of divine punishment—an eminently pragmatic consideration—to support moral exhortations is a characteristic feature of Proverbs. Likewise: "Do not encroach upon the field of orphans, for they have a mighty Kinsman, and He will surely take up their cause with you" (23:10–11).

Wisdom and the World

It follows, then, that in the worldview of Proverbs, there is no categorical difference between being practical and being righteous, or between prudence and piety. The wise person, the person who wishes to succeed in the world, will act rightly; and conversely, worldly success is proof of piety. One might say, then, that Proverbs offers a utilitarian defense of righteousness: Be good, because it will make you successful.

One might object to this claim from a moral perspective: Should good deeds not be performed for their own sake, rather than for the sake of reward?

A second, more concrete objection also naturally arises: Is Proverbs' claim not patently falsified by experience? Do we never see the wicked succeed, or the righteous suffer? Is it really fair to suppose that the wealthy are righteous, and that the poor suffer deservedly? Both of these objections—from moral theory and from experience—will trouble later products of the wisdom tradition embodied by the book of Proverbs, and below we will take up one such product, the book of Job. But here let us reflect on why Proverbs appears to be untroubled by the objection from experience. How can Proverbs boldly insist that God dispenses rewards and punishments in the world? Why does it not adopt what looks to us like the easier strategy of allowing the wicked to prosper and the righteous to suffer in this world, so long as God squares accounts in the afterlife?

We may note first that the notion of an afterlife in which the righteous and the wicked can receive their just deserts emerges in a substantial sense only toward the end of the biblical period, during the Second Temple era. Earlier books do have some conception of an afterlife: the dead persist in pallid, ghostlike form underground, in a place called Sheol, and those who die happily and righteously appear to enjoy the company of their deceased kin. But this afterlife serves, at best, only a very limited theological function. Thus the option of postponing reward and punishment to the afterlife is not available in any robust way to the authors of the book of Proverbs.

How, nevertheless, can the perspective of Proverbs, that God dispenses reward and punishment in the form of worldly success, enjoy even superficial plausibility? How is it not patently falsified by experience? The theology of Proverbs depends in part on a conception of human identity different from the one that prevails in the modern West. According to this conception, which is characteristic of the classical biblical world (albeit with important qualifications, some of which we will discuss in chapter 6 in connection with the covenant at Sinai), a person is defined less by his or her own personality and experiences, and more by the family or clan to which he or she belongs. One lives a fulfilling life not by finding one's true self, or by constructing a self, but by wisely executing the duties within the family unit into which one was born. Like identity itself, virtue is determined and reward is dispensed at the familial level. Hence the existence of the righteous sufferer is not a decisive refutation of the principle of worldly divine recompense. Perhaps he suffers because of his parents' sins, or perhaps his reward will become manifest among his children.

The worldliness of Proverbs—its insistence on a strict correlation between prudence and piety, and between being practical and being righteous—means that for Proverbs the principles of reward and punishment are, as it were, programmed into the operation of the world. The drunkard sobers up and finds that he can now make a living, and the wicked landowner suffers from a crop failure after having withheld wages from a poor farmworker; both cases simply illustrate how the world works. There is thus an automaticity in the dispensation of divine justice, so that the book can claim (1:18–19) that the wicked "lie in ambush for their own blood; they lie in wait for their own lives. Such is the fate of all who pursue unjust gain; it takes the life of its possessor."

The book gives mythic expression to this understanding of the nature of the world by making wisdom a goddess, Wisdom with a capital *W*, who existed before the world and accompanied God in his creative undertakings.

> The Lord created me at the beginning of His course,
> As the first of His works of old.
> In the distant past I was fashioned,
> At the beginning, at the origin of earth.
> There was still no deep when I was brought forth,
> No springs rich in water. . . .
> When He assigned the sea its limits,
> So that its waters never transgress His command;
> When He fixed the foundations of the earth,
> I was with Him as a confidant [or: constantly],
> A source of delight every day,
> Rejoicing before Him at all times,
> Rejoicing in His inhabited world,
> Finding delight with mankind. (8:22–24, 29–31)

Like many other creation accounts in the ancient Near East, including the one preserved in Genesis 1, to which we will turn later (chapter 10), this one involves, at its core, the delimitation of the sea. Wisdom says that she existed before the sea, was at God's side when he bounded it, and now rejoices in the world that thus came into being, especially in human beings. By having Wisdom precede and accompany the creation of the world, the book of Proverbs implicitly asserts that the world is harmonious and ordered, that it is structured by the principles of wisdom. The task of human beings is to recognize that wisdom (Wisdom) is their friend, to discern the world's structuring principles and live according to them; and those who do so—the sages—will be successful in the world, because they have conformed themselves to it.

One might wonder why Wisdom is a goddess and not a god, female rather than male. Grammar offers one answer: in Hebrew, (almost) every noun is either masculine or feminine, and the Hebrew word for wisdom, *hokmah*, is feminine. But the more important factor is the gender coding of the book. As noted above, Proverbs addresses itself chiefly to the young man, whom it calls upon to cultivate wisdom. By imagining wisdom as a woman, the book can, in a more rhetorically engaging way, characterize the young man's task as the passionate pursuit of Lady Wisdom. Chapters 7–8 indeed carefully contrast the dangerous allure of the adulterous woman and the welcome temptations of Lady Wisdom. The first leads the young man to his death, while the latter leads him to life.

> Then a woman comes toward him,
> decked out like a prostitute, wily of heart.
> She is loud and wayward;
> her feet do not stay at home;
> now in the street, now in the squares,
> and at every corner she lies in wait.
> She seizes him and kisses him, . . .
> "Come, let us take our fill of love until morning;
> let us delight ourselves with love.
> For my husband is not at home;
> he has gone on a long journey.
> He took a bag of money with him;
> he will not come home until full moon." . . .
> Right away he follows her,
> and goes like an ox to the slaughter. . . .
> He is like a bird rushing into a snare,
> not knowing that it will cost him his life. (7:10–13, 18–20, 22–23 NRSV)

Wisdom, too, goes out in the street to lure lovers, but to a decidedly different end.

> Does not wisdom call,
> and does not understanding raise her voice?
> On the heights, beside the way,
> at the crossroads she takes her stand;
> beside the gates in front of the town,
> at the entrance of the portals she cries out:
> "To you, men, I call,
> and my cry is to sons of man.
> O simple ones, learn prudence;
> acquire intelligence, you who lack it. . . .
> I love those who love me,

and those who seek me diligently find me.
Riches and honor are with me,
enduring wealth and prosperity.
My fruit is better than gold, even fine gold,
and my yield than choice silver.
I walk in the way of righteousness,
along the paths of justice,
endowing with wealth those who love me,
and filling their treasuries." (8:1–5, 17–21 NRSV, slightly altered)

A later passage in the book sums up this contrast succinctly: "A man who loves wisdom brings joy to his father, but he who keeps company with harlots will lose his wealth" (29:3).

What does it mean to love wisdom, or to love Wisdom? It means, first and foremost, to behave wisely: to make prudent decisions, to act toward the vulnerable in ways that show cognizance of the fact that God is their protector. But it also means, as importantly, to participate in the study of wisdom, and to take joy in the memorization, recitation, and formulation of well-wrought sayings. There is, in short, a prominent intellectual aspect to the love of wisdom: it involves, in the most literal sense, philosophy (from Greek *philo-*, "love," and *sophia*, "wisdom"). Within this framework, the pragmatic aspect of wisdom recedes into the background; while the wise man is inevitably successful in the world, his worldly success is not the aim but only a corollary of the true object of desire, wisdom itself (or Wisdom herself).

God's role in the world imagined by Proverbs is relatively limited. He is the creator of the world and the guarantor of its just operation, but in a rather impersonal way. One hardly needs to posit a vividly engaged God to explain why the drunkard who sobers up can now hold down a job. And if it is with the same inevitability, and by the same principle, that the wicked oppressor gets his comeuppance, then the dispensation of punishment and reward also does not call for a terribly intimate God. The foundation of wisdom is, as noted above, fear of God, not love of God. The sage loves wisdom, but God is for him an object of fear.

The Universalism of Proverbs

Love of God and God's love for others are central ideas in other books of the Bible, especially in connection with the people Israel and their ancestors. It is not surprising, then, that, as love of God is absent from Proverbs, so likewise is Israel itself. Elsewhere in the Bible, God's relationship with Israel is worked out in history, through a sequence of specific, unique interventions; but history, too, is missing from Proverbs. God's relationship with the world is instead constant, unchanging, and undifferentiated. It is also silent: prophets, who serve as the agents and mouthpieces of God in history, play no role in the book. Proverbs, in short, makes claims about how the world as a whole works, and it attaches no importance, for its purposes, to differences among peoples.

The relevant unit is rather the family, and the key authority figure is not the prophet but the parent. The maxims that make up the bulk of the book occur in the voice of the father or mother, or of the sage who stands in loco parentis: "Hear, my son, your father's instruction, and do not reject your mother's teaching" (Proverbs 1:8 NRSV, slightly altered). (The inclusion of the mother is no mere rhetorical flourish; the book includes [31:1–9] an extensive rebuke of a certain King Lemuel—on whom more below—by his mother.) The authority of parents, and more generally, of age, is a reflex of Proverbs' refusal to attribute significance to particular historical events. The things that matter are not events, but age-old truths that have not changed and indeed cannot change.

The universalism of Proverbs is reflected in the substantially similar collections of maxims that were produced by other contemporaneous societies, including Israel's neighbors in Egypt and Mesopotamia. Indeed, the very category of wisdom, in Israel as in the ancient Near East in general, was cosmopolitan, easily crossing borders; and the Bible was prepared to recognize wisdom in nations outside Israel.

The Bible's characterization of King Solomon, to whom the book of Proverbs is attributed, illustrates the cosmopolitan character of wisdom. The attribution is not historical in the straightforward sense. It is certainly not the case that the entire book was authored or authorized by Solomon; the book itself attributes some teachings to the court of King Hezekiah of Judah (Proverbs 25:1), who lived long after Solomon. The attribution of the book to Solomon is rather a reflection of his great reputation for wisdom. And when the Bible wishes to describe Solomon's wisdom, it does so in relation to that of other nations.

> God gave Solomon very great wisdom, discernment, and breadth of understanding . . . so that Solomon's wisdom surpassed the wisdom of all the people of the east, and all the wisdom of Egypt. . . . His fame [or: name] spread through all the surrounding nations. . . . People came from all the nations to hear the wisdom of Solomon. (1 Kings 4:29–34 NRSV)

While the wisdom of the Israelite Solomon is unsurpassed, the very baseline for defining wisdom is cosmopolitan: to be very wise is to be wiser than the wise of Egypt and of the east.

The perspective of the book of Proverbs extends beyond Israel not only in virtue of the cosmopolitan character of wisdom generally, but more strikingly in its dependence on specific non-Israelite works of wisdom literature. Most importantly, scholars have long recognized that at least one section of the book, Proverbs 22:17–24:22, and especially the first part thereof, 22:17–23:11, draws, sometimes verbatim, on a work of Egyptian wisdom literature probably written in the twelfth or eleventh century BCE, the Instruction of Amenemope.

The arguments for Proverbs' dependence on this work are complex, but perhaps the most striking point of contact is this. Near the very beginning of the unit in question, the speaker in Proverbs declares: "Have I not written for you *sh-l-sh-w-m* [or in a different version: *sh-l-y-sh-y-m*] of admonition and knowledge?" (22:20 NRSV). The word *sh-l-sh-w-m* long puzzled commentators. It seems to have something to do with the Hebrew word *shalosh* ("three") or *sheloshim* ("thirty"), but there is no relevant group of three or thirty maxims or groups of maxims in the vicinity. The solution to this puzzle lies in the fact that the Instruction of Amenemope is divided into thirty chapters, and indeed speaks self-referentially of its "thirty chapters [or: teachings]" (27:7). Nor is this a coincidence: the number thirty is typologically significant in Egyptian culture, but not in Israelite culture, which instead prefers forty. The word *sh-l-sh-w-m* in Proverbs 22:20 is evidently a garbled echo of the thirty teachings of the Egyptian wisdom text.

Nor is the Instruction of Amenemope the only foreign wisdom collection incorporated into Proverbs. Recall King Lemuel, whose mother's rebukes are recorded in Proverbs 31:1–9. There is no Israelite king by the name of Lemuel. Most likely, Lemuel was a king of a nearby, non-Israelite land, around whom a collection of maxims coalesced. This collection evidently circulated among Israelites too and found its ways into Proverbs.

A final indication of the universalism of Proverbs comes from its reception in the New Testament. Because the New Testament generally presents Jesus as the source of salvation for everyone, not just for Israel, it often draws upon parts of the Old Testament that concern human beings as such, rather than Israel specifically. For example, the apostle Paul interprets Jesus in relation to the first human being, Adam (Romans 5, 1 Corinthians 15). In this light, let us turn to the famous opening of the Gospel of John. "In the beginning was the Word, and the Word was with God, and the Word was God" (John 1:1). In the continuation (1:14–17), this Word takes on flesh, in the form of Jesus; but what is "the Word," and where does John get this concept from?

Undoubtedly, John draws on the creation story in Genesis 1, to which we will turn later (chapter 10), wherein God creates by means of speech, or words.

Genesis 1 also furnishes the phrase "in the beginning." But whence John's notion that the Word was a distinct entity that dwelled with God? This notion comes from Proverbs 8, quoted above, which depicts personified wisdom as God's companion prior to the creation of the world. In the universalist outlook of the book of Proverbs, the Gospel of John finds one framework for understanding the universalist mission of Jesus.

The Book of Job: Beyond the Universal

The Bible includes three major challenges to the theology of the wisdom tradition as expressed in the book of Proverbs, all three of which appear to have been composed in the early Second Temple period. I will briefly summarize the challenge posed by the book of Ecclesiastes, then turn at greater length to the challenge posed by the book of Job. We will take up the Song of Songs in the next chapter. All three of these challenges to traditional wisdom as embodied in the book of Proverbs occur in that tradition's native universalist idiom. None features Israelite history or specific Israelite figures (other than Solomon, to whom the book of Proverbs is also attributed), nor does any have use for divine revelation. We will have occasion subtly to complicate this characterization in relation to the Song of Songs in the next chapter, but as a general matter, these books critique the wisdom tradition from within its universalist framework.

The book of Ecclesiastes is an extended monologue attributed to "Ecclesiastes son of David, king in Jerusalem" (Ecclesiastes 1:1, slightly altered), just as the book of Proverbs is attributed to King Solomon, son of David. This book takes issue with traditional wisdom for the shortness of the temporal horizon: "The wise man, just like the fool, is not remembered forever; for, as the succeeding days roll by, both are forgotten. Alas, the wise man dies, just like the fool!" (2:16). Even if the wise man does win fame and fortune, as Proverbs promises, he can enjoy them only for a brief time, before death and human forgetfulness erase his memory. Then what advantage has the wise man over the fool?

The book of Job complicates the core assumption of traditional wisdom that God's world operates in such fashion that the righteous will inevitably prosper. Job is a pious and upright man, but he suffers the loss of his property, the deaths of his children, and bodily afflictions. Most of the book is taken up by exchanges between Job and his friends in which Job challenges God's justice, and his friends speak in God's defense. The series of exchanges culminates in a one-sided conversation between Job and God himself, to which we will return momentarily. The exchanges between Job and his friends, and between God and Job, are written in a high, poetic style that contrasts sharply with the prose passages that enclose the book, the first of which (Job 1–2) describes Job's descent into misery, and the second of which (42:7–17) tells how Job regains his wealth and fathers more children. As Carol Newsom has observed, the challenge to the wisdom tradition is embedded in the book's structure. The prose of the bookends is self-consciously simple, especially by comparison with the dense poetry of the book's interior, and implicitly conveys that the easiest solution to the problem of the suffering of the righteous, the solution that is embedded in the prose frame (namely, that they will get their reward in the end), is a facile one, too convenient to be credible.

It is far from clear what the book of Job means to proffer as its own, more complex solution to the problem of righteous suffering, but the essence of its solution must lie somewhere in God's response to Job. In Job 38:1, God speaks "out of the tempest," and his words are themselves tempestuous.

> Who is this who darkens counsel,
> Speaking without knowledge?
> Gird your loins like a man;
> I will ask and you will inform Me. (38:2–3)

What follows is a sublime description of the cosmos that underscores the pitiful limits of human knowledge and power.

> Where were you when I laid the earth's foundations?
> Speak if you have understanding. . . .
> Onto what were its bases sunk,
> And who set its cornerstone
> When the morning stars sang together,
> And all the divine beings [or: sons of God] shouted for joy? (38:4, 6–7)

God proceeds, in the same vein, to describe, among other natural wonders, the dawn, the deep, the snow, the hail, the rain, the constellations, the clouds, the lion, the wild ass, the wild ox, the ostrich, the horse, the hawk, the eagle, Behemoth (literally "animals," perhaps the hippopotamus), and Leviathan (perhaps the crocodile). Job's response is muted:

> Indeed, I spoke without understanding
> Of things beyond me, which I did not know. . . .
> I had heard You with my ears,

> but now I see You with my eyes;
> Therefore, I recant and relent,
> Being but dust and ashes. (42:3–6)

In the face of God's rhetorical onslaught, Job cannot but concede defeat.

What are we to make of this exchange? To what end does God batter Job with his questions about and descriptions of natural phenomena? A consolation one often hears in the aftermath of an apparently senseless tragedy is that the tragedy must play a role in a divine plan whose wisdom we are incapable of understanding. It is tempting to read God's speech from the tempest along these lines: God means, on this approach, to rebuke Job for having the presumption to question God, for lacking faith that Job's suffering serves a larger purpose. But there is no positive evidence for this explanation—no reference in God's speech to such a purpose, still less to a role for Job's suffering therein—nor can it account for the length of God's speech or for the specific details on which it focuses.

A different interpretation of God's speech would make it a power play. God, on this approach, is telling Job: I am so much more knowledgeable and so much more powerful than you that I need not entertain your complaint. This interpretation has a better foundation in the text; God does set his own knowledge of and control over natural phenomena in contrast to human ignorance of and powerlessness before them. But, as Newsom notes, this interpretation, too, does not account for a crucial fact about God's speech: God manifests admiration or even affection for the elements and animals that he details, and often specifically for those features in them that oppose the ordered, civilized world administered by human beings.

For example, in God's speech in the book of Job, just as in Proverbs 8, the sea is the epitome of the primordial chaos that God must constrain in order to have room to create; but in his speech to Job, God speaks tenderly of "swaddling" the sea (Job 38:9). Likewise, God highlights that the rains fall "on uninhabited land, on the wilderness where no man is" (38:26). God seems to wish to underscore that the rain does not fall for humankind's benefit. Again, God details, with apparent admiration, the habits of the wild ass, "whose home I have made the wilderness," and who "scoffs at the tumult of the city" (39:6–7). God's description of the eagle ends with the eagle spying out its food from afar, and conveying it to its young, who "gulp blood." This blood, we immediately learn, is that of "the slain," that is, human corpses (39:30). From the perspective of humankind, this scene is a harrowing one, but God adopts the perspective of the eagle, for whom it is an achievement of flight and sight. This rhetorical strategy reaches its zenith at the beginning of God's description of Behemoth, whom, God says, "I made as I did you" (40:15). Humankind loses its privileged place in God's catalog of the world and its animals.

Leviathan, whom God turns to at the end and on whom he lavishes the most attention, is a monster of the sea, and thus harks back to the first feature of nature in God's speech, the sea itself. As we will see in chapter 10 when we examine Genesis 1 and related texts, Leviathan serves in some mythic accounts of creation as the embodiment of the sea, and God must defeat it before he can bind the sea and build the world. God does imply that Leviathan is his creature and thus subject to his control, but God is far more interested in describing Leviathan's great power. The bookends of God's speech thus underscore the persistence of chaos, and God's affection for it, his identification with it.

God's point, then, is not simply that he is more powerful than Job, and it is certainly not that Job's suffering can be justified by its place in a larger plan. It is rather, at least in part, that chaos persists in God's world. God did order the world and did set human beings atop that order, but he reserves a place, alongside and within that order, for the sublime, for the powerful, for the violent, for the wilderness. If personified wisdom in Proverbs 8 makes human beings her delight, then the book of Job suggests that to God belongs a higher wisdom that delights as much in animals that no human being can defeat, even in animals that eat human corpses.

The book of Proverbs is universalist in relation to the major, Israelite story line of the Bible, but the book of Job might be understood, on the approach developed by Newsom and summarized above, as challenging Proverbs to be more universalist still. The problem of righteous suffering compels the book of Job to conceive of God as the God not only of order but also of chaos. And yet one might also say that this movement beyond the universalism of Proverbs turns out to be a particularist movement. Only after the analysis in the next chapter can we appreciate how this is so, but we may note preliminarily that the book of Job, in sharp contrast with the book of Proverbs, features divine revelation.

Conclusion

If scripture and reason are the two (or two of the) major sources of authority in theological reflection, then scripture falls naturally on the particularist side of the ledger, and reason on the universalist. But there are universalist strains in scripture, and nowhere more so than in Proverbs. Proverbs makes no distinctions among peoples and attributes no fundamental importance to history (Israelite or otherwise) or to prophetic revelation. By beginning our analysis of the Bible with Proverbs, we are now in a position to ask: What is at stake in the particularist perspective? How does revelation, how does history, challenge, and how are they challenged by, the coherent, world-centered, universalist perspective of Proverbs? We begin to address these questions in the next chapter. Near the end of the next chapter we will also return to the book of Job.

For Further Reflection

1. The book of Proverbs concludes with a song praising the "woman of valor" or "capable wife" (31:10–31). What does the woman of valor do? How does the portrayal of the woman of valor correlate with the representation of women elsewhere in the book?

2. In this chapter I describe Proverbs' portrayal of the wise man in general terms: he is prudent, pious. How, in greater detail, does the wise man behave? How, by contrast, does the foolish man behave? What are the chief virtues and vices that they embody? In addition to the excerpts listed in the "Readings" at the beginning of the chapter, consider Proverbs 25–29.

3. Besides God and Job, the main actor in the prose frame of the book of Job is "the Adversary [or: Satan]." How does his role in the book compare with portrayals of this figure in the New Testament and elsewhere? Consult the overview by T. J. Wray and Gregory Mobley, *The Birth of Satan*.

Bibliography

Cohen, Yoram, ed. *Wisdom from the Late Bronze Age*. Atlanta: Society of Biblical Literature, 2013.

Fox, Michael V. *Proverbs: A New Translation with Introduction and Commentary*. 2 vols. Anchor Bible. New York: Doubleday, 2000–2009.

Lichtheim, Miriam. "Instruction of Amenemope." *COS* 1:115–22.

Newsom, Carol A. *The Book of Job: A Contest of Moral Imaginations*. New York: Oxford University Press, 2009.

Steiner, Richard C. *Disembodied Souls: The Nefesh in Israel and Kindred Spirits in the Ancient Near East, with an Appendix on the Katumuwa Inscription*. Atlanta: SBL Press, 2015.

Wray, T. J., and Gregory Mobley. *The Birth of Satan: Tracing the Devil's Biblical Roots*. New York: Palgrave Macmillan, 2005.

3 | Revelation and Love: The Patriarchal Narratives and the Song of Songs

READINGS
Genesis 11:10–28:9
Deuteronomy 21:15–17
Song of Songs 1; 2; 5; 8

Introduction

The patriarchal narratives in the book of Genesis describe the origins and early history of the covenant through which, by the very end of the book and at the beginning of the next book (Exodus), the people of Israel will eventually emerge. We come to these narratives from the book of Proverbs, a work that has no place for the notion of divine covenant or revelation, a work that speaks of human beings generally, and not of Israel in particular. To what extent does the particularist perspective of the patriarchal narratives take account of the universalist perspective of Proverbs? We will discover that it not only acknowledges this perspective but defines itself in relation to it.

Israel's story begins with Abraham. It is to Abraham (then named Abram) that God appears, promising him that, should he leave his homeland and travel to the place that God will show him, Abraham will become a great nation.

> I will bless those who bless you
> And curse him that curses you,
> And all the families of the earth
> Shall bless themselves by you. (Genesis 12:3)

The last clause is ambiguous. As translated here, it indicates that the families of the earth—other nations—will refer to Abraham in blessing their own. The clause might also be translated: "and in you all the families of the earth shall be blessed" (NRSV), so as to convey that, through Abraham, God will bless all the world. The latter notion is present, at least conditionally, in the preceding clause, "I will bless those who bless you." In any case, it is notable that here, at the very outset of Israel's story, we find recognition of the interplay of particular and universal to which God's election of Israel gives rise.

Election and Illegality

Despite God's promise that he will make Abraham a great nation, Abraham remains childless for a long time—so long that his wife Sarah (then named Sarai) proposes that Abraham marry her Egyptian maidservant Hagar, so that Sarah and thus Abraham can have children through her (Genesis 16:1–2; Rachel, wife of Jacob, will adopt the same strategy later; see 30:3). This union does bear fruit, in the form of Ishmael; but soon after, Sarah herself bears a child, Isaac. God's promise to Abraham passes not to both of his sons, but to Isaac. Again, in the next generation, Isaac's wife Rebekah bears twins, Esau and Jacob; and again, only one, Jacob, is chosen as the vehicle of the promise.

Both cases are marked by irregularity and pain. Isaac's very birth is miraculous, as Sarah bears him past the age of ninety (Genesis 17:17; 18:9–15; 21:1–7). As importantly, while the firstborn is ordinarily the privileged heir, it is Isaac the younger rather than Ishmael the elder who inherits God's blessing. The election of Isaac entails, for Sarah, the expulsion of Ishmael; and while Abraham recoils from this course of action, God endorses it (21:9–12). In the case of Esau and Jacob, too, the promise ends up falling to the younger. And just as Sarah pushes Abraham to expel Ishmael, so Rebekah persuades Jacob to steal the blessing from Esau (27:5–15). The Bible does not shy away from depicting the anguish occasioned by the spurning of the elder brothers. Having been expelled from Abraham's household and finding herself and her child without water in the wilderness, Hagar "lifted up her voice and wept" (21:16–17 NRSV); and Esau, too, upon discovering that Jacob had stolen his blessing, "lifted up his voice and wept" (27:38 NRSV).

The pattern of the election of the younger recurs in subsequent generations. Jacob's firstborn is Reuben, the offspring of his "hated" or "unloved" wife, Leah (Genesis 29:31–32); but his favored son, and the one whose descendants will dominate the northern kingdom that is named after Jacob, is Joseph, the first child of Rachel, his wife whom "he loved" (29:18, 20, 30). Again, in the case of Joseph himself, the younger son Ephraim receives the blessing that ought by right to go to the older son Manasseh (45:17–19). Election consistently runs counter to birth and to the natural right of the firstborn.

The anomalous, even illegal character of election becomes clear by the light of a law detailed in Deuteronomy 21:15–17.

> If a man has two wives, one hated and one beloved, and if both the hated and the beloved have borne him sons, the firstborn being the son of the hated, then on the day that he wills his possessions to his sons, he is not permitted to treat the son of the loved as the firstborn in preference to the son of the hated, who is the firstborn. He must rather acknowledge as firstborn the son of the hated, giving him a double portion of all that he has; for he is the first sign of his [father's] strength; the right of the firstborn is his. (NRSV, slightly altered)

The law speaks to the situation of the patriarchal narratives, and even more specifically to the situation of Jacob: the younger is better loved than the elder. But the law, unlike the patriarchal narratives, recognizes birth, not love. The elder son must be acknowledged as the firstborn.

It is emphatically not the case that the patriarchal narratives are ignorant of or reject the Deuteronomy law. On the contrary, these narratives make no sense except against the background of the normative expectation to which the Deuteronomy law gives expression. The text's sensitivity to the distress of Hagar and Esau underscores this normative expectation: they have suffered an injustice, precisely the injustice that Deuteronomy means to combat. The economy of election in Genesis works through persistent violation of the norm. Or, because the norm is that which is generally the case, or the universal, we may say that the economy of election runs counter to the universal. Election recognizes the beloved status of the younger rather than the legal right of the elder. The Deuteronomy passage teaches us that the economy of election in Genesis represents the realization of transgressive love.

Arguably, the exceptional character of election is also expressed through the integral role of women in the victory of the younger over the elder. As noted earlier, it is Sarah and not Abraham who pushes for the expulsion of Ishmael. Even as Isaac favors Esau, Rebekah favors Jacob (Genesis 25:28) and orchestrates Jacob's theft of the blessing. If we suppose, plausibly for a patriarchal society, a link between the normative and patriarchy, then the prominence of the matriarchs in driving forward the election narrative is a mark of its antinomian character.

The normative is the universal; it is that which holds in general. Election is the particular, the exception to the general. There is a sense in which this dynamic is inevitable, or so argues Søren Kierkegaard, the nineteenth-century existentialist philosopher from Denmark, in his book on Abraham, *Fear and Trembling*. A relationship with God that is universal, that is mediated by a set of exceptionless norms, is not a fully realized relationship, precisely because it is mediated, indirect. There is something impersonal about it. (By analogy: We should be perplexed by someone who loves his family no more than and no differently than he loves all human beings. Nor is it even clear that one *can* love humanity as a group in the way that one loves a particular person; or to put the point differently, the gesture of exclusion may be a defining element of love.) The only way to penetrate the universal, to create a real encounter, is by violation of the norm, by an event that is in one way or another irregular, even illegal. There is a sense in which Israel's salvation history is constitutively at odds with the universal.

Election in Universalist Terms

There is a danger in this perspective. The norm describes what is fair, what is just, even what is moral. To valorize oneself as the exception, the particular, is to come close to situating oneself beyond good and evil. The Bible is acutely aware of this temptation; the book of Amos, which we shall examine at length later, offers nothing less than a critique of precisely this drift. The patriarchal narratives, too, offer a partial check against the danger of the particular by grounding the dynamic of election, to a certain extent, not in violation of the norm but in fulfillment thereof. That is, there is a strain in the patriarchal narratives that suggests that Israel's patriarchs were chosen not by an act of unmotivated divine fiat, made visible by running counter to the norm, but because they were especially moral, because they, to a greater degree than others, fulfilled the norm. For example, Jacob comes across as a more pleasant character, even a better person, than the wild, uncouth Esau, who can sell his birthright for soup (Genesis 25:29–34), and who, discovering that Jacob has cheated him, turns immediately to thoughts of fratricide (27:41).

More importantly, Abraham is portrayed as a righteous man, most explicitly in Genesis 18:16–33. At the beginning of this unit, God decides to reveal to Abraham that he is going to destroy the city of Sodom.

> The LORD said: Shall I hide from Abraham what I am about to do? Abraham will surely become a great and mighty nation, and through him all the nations shall be blessed. For I have chosen him, that he will instruct

> his children and his household after him to keep the way of the LORD by doing righteousness and justice; so that the LORD may bring about for Abraham what he has promised him. (18:17–19 NRSV, slightly altered)

God's reasoning is not altogether transparent. Why should the fact that God has chosen Abraham, or that Abraham will instruct his offspring in righteousness and justice, lead God to inform Abraham of his plans for Sodom? In any case, there is a connection between this preface and the subsequent conversation between God and Abraham, in which Abraham boldly calls God to task for his apparent willingness to annihilate all of Sodom, the righteous inhabitants with the wicked.

> Will you indeed sweep away the righteous with the wicked? . . . Far be it from you to do such a thing, to slay the righteous with the wicked, so that the righteous fare as the wicked! Far be that from you! Shall not the judge of all the earth do what is just? (18:23, 25 NRSV)

Abraham's argument with God operates entirely in universalist terms, familiar from the world of Proverbs. God is the engine of reward and punishment, rewarding good and punishing evil, and he acts in relation to the world as a whole—in this case, to the city of Sodom—rather than to Israel in particular. The basis for the election of Abraham, in this chapter, is likewise universalist: he is righteous, he is just, in an exemplary way.

There is, of course, also a danger in election framed in universalist terms, election grounded in the moral heroism of the elect. Election so conceived licenses conceit or smugness among the elect. This danger is probably less acute, and evidently of less concern to the biblical authors, than the danger that follows from election conceived of as the exception, but it still lurks; election is a fraught category, however it is understood.

Election and Divine Will

If Genesis 18 rests Abraham's election on universalist considerations of righteousness and justice, then both at the beginning of the story of Abraham (Genesis 12) and near the end (Genesis 22) a different, particularist account of his election comes to the fore. In both cases, God appears to Abraham and bids him each time to "go" (or "take yourself") to an unspecified location: "to the land that I will show you" (12:1), and "to one of the mountains that I will show you" (22:2 NRSV). In the first case, Abraham must abandon his father's house, that is, his familial past; while in the second, he must sacrifice his son, that is, his familial future. In these chapters, Abraham's election rests not on his adherence to a universalist standard of justice to which God himself is beholden, as in Genesis 18, but on the demonstration of his intense personal loyalty to God, a loyalty that compels obedience even when the destination is left unstated, a loyalty capable of overcoming even the bonds of family. The notions of loyalty and obedience have no place in the universalist framework of Proverbs, where God issues no specific commands, and where communication from parent to child is the very matrix of divine wisdom. The conception of election in Genesis 12 and 22 is thoroughly particularist.

Genesis 22 is among the most famous chapters in the Bible. Abraham's willingness to sacrifice "your son, your only son Isaac, whom you love" (22:2 NRSV), becomes, in the New Testament, one template for understanding Jesus's crucifixion. According to John 3:16, God "so loved the world" that, like Abraham, "he gave his only [or: only begotten] Son" for its sake. In Judaism, this event, called "the binding [Hebrew *'aqedah*] of Isaac," is the ultimate sign of the patriarchs' piety, and serves as a storehouse of merit, on some views infinite, for Abraham's descendants.

The chapter is also famous in the history of modern literary criticism. One of the most important essays in this field, "Odysseus' Scar," by Erich Auerbach, uses Genesis 22 to contrast the biblical way of representing reality with the ancient Greek way. What interests Auerbach about the chapter is its reticence. We are told what Abraham does, we hear his laconic conversation with Isaac, but we do not get inside his head. The questions that so weigh on the mind of the reader (including many an ancient reader) are left unaddressed: What was Abraham thinking? Was he angry with God? Did he hold out hope that God would stay his hand? How did he feel when God *did* stay his hand? The narrative is thus, in Auerbach's trenchant formulation, "fraught with background." By leaving important things unsaid, Scripture compels the reader to interpret. The reader cannot merely witness the story; she must inevitably try to make sense of it. For Auerbach, the authority of the Bible is not merely an artifact of its God-centered plot or of its reception. It makes demands upon the reader by virtue of the very way in which it tells stories.

Be that as it may, our main interest here lies in the demand described in the plot itself, God's demand that Abraham sacrifice Isaac, and what it tells us about the logic of Abraham's election. To a modern sensibility, like Kierkegaard's, God's demand seems outrageous; it is an order to commit murder outright. This sensibility is not so very modern, as we shall see momentarily. But what differentiates the perspective implicit in Genesis 22 from our own is the social framework described in the last chapter, in which one's identity is defined first and foremost within the framework of the family. The minor child, in this framework, is not an independent person, but at once the prize possession and extension of the father. And just as God is entitled to gifts from the best of one's crops and one's flocks, so too is he entitled to the best of one's sons, the firstborn.

> Do not hold back offerings from your granaries or your vats. You must give me the firstborn of your sons. You shall do the same with your cattle and with your sheep: seven days it shall remain with its mother; on the eighth day you shall give it to me. (Exodus 22:29–30 NRSV, slightly altered)

From the law code given at Sinai, it is unclear what, precisely, this general demand for the firstborn son entails. Is human sacrifice in view? More likely, does it envision these firstborn sons serving in the cult?

In *The Death and Resurrection of the Beloved Son,* Jon Levenson enters into these and related questions with subtlety and in detail; but for our purposes, two interrelated insights are critical. First, in the social framework that can generate laws like Exodus 22:29–30, the sacrifice of the firstborn to God is not an absolute evil. The firstborn does belong to God by right. But second, God does not, in the ordinary course of things, insist on his right, nor, in the ordinary course of things, is it even desirable to offer the firstborn to God. The sacrifice of the firstborn is an exceptional, terrible thing, but also one that is effective in winning God's favor. The exceptional character of the firstborn sacrifice is nicely conveyed by the concluding passage of the narrative of the war of Israel, Judah, and Edom against Moab in 2 Kings 3:26–27.

> When the king of Moab saw that he was being overpowered in the battle, he took with him seven hundred sword-drawing men to break through to the king of Edom, but they were unable. So he took his firstborn son, who was to reign after him, and he offered him up on the wall as a burnt offering. A great wrath came upon Israel, so they withdrew from him and returned to the land. (NRSV, slightly altered)

The sacrifice of the Moabite king's son is a last-ditch measure, only undertaken after the failure of a desperate attempt to turn the battle by going after a tightly protected, high-value target. But this measure yields results: God appears to intercede, in response, on the king's behalf.

God's demand in Genesis 22 is, in short, justifiable but exceptional. The dynamic of this chapter is thus similar though not identical to the dynamic of election in the patriarchal narratives as a whole. In the latter, God becomes manifest in his person, as a personality, in the violation of the universal norm of primogeniture. Ordinarily God upholds the way of the world, as its creator and guarantor; but to break through the universal, he breaks the norm and chooses the younger. With respect to Genesis 22, too, while God is entitled to the firstborn, he does not ordinarily demand him. Ordinarily, the righteous man will live to see his firstborn become a father in his own right; and while this too is God's doing, in this respect God operates through the mediation of universal norms. When he demands the firstborn sacrifice, he presents himself as an individual, capable of loving and being loved.

Song of Songs: Human Love and the Particular

Love, not divine per se but human, is the subject of perhaps the most unusual book in the Bible, the Song of Songs. In the preceding chapter, we mentioned this book as one of three biblical books that belong, with Proverbs, to the wisdom tradition, but that also challenge the wisdom tradition in one way or another. Against the background of our analysis above, we are in a position to understand the nature of the challenge that the Song of Songs poses.

Like Proverbs and Ecclesiastes, the Song of Songs is attributed to Solomon. But very much unlike these books, it contains no maxims, nor does it address the reader. It consists, instead, of dialogue, mainly in the form of a series of poetic exchanges between two young lovers, a man and a woman. Each seeks the other and fondly details the other's body. The natural setting for their love is the garden, the forest, the earth, populated by fragrant trees and grazing animals. The city, by contrast, is a more troublesome place, where the woman must confront the skepticism and stares of the "daughters of Jerusalem" (Song of Songs 1:5; 2:7; 5:8–9) and the violence of the watchmen (5:7).

The book comes closest to traditional, axiomatic wisdom literature near the end, where the woman offers a rousing paean to love.

> For love is fierce as death,
> Passion is mighty as Sheol;
> Its darts are darts of fire,
> A blazing flame.
> Vast floods cannot quench love,

Nor rivers drown it.
If a man offered all his wealth for love,
He would be laughed to scorn. (8:6–7)

The passage describes intense love of a sort that cannot be purchased; one who attempts to purchase it would only earn ridicule. As Michael Fox has noted, this passage is in conversation with Proverbs' condemnation of the foolish man who would spend all his money on prostitutes (Proverbs 6:20–35). The Song of Songs implicitly critiques Proverbs for setting up a false dichotomy. Yes, such a man is foolish, but this does not mean that he should instead devote his attention to Lady Wisdom, in the hope of gaining further wealth. He should rather pursue the love of a woman, the passionate love whose value exceeds the material success promised by Proverbs to the wise. If the book of Proverbs finds wisdom first and foremost in the prudence of age, then the Song of Songs instead uncovers wisdom in the passion of youth.

The analysis in this chapter allows us to appreciate that the Song of Songs' departure from Proverbs is no mere quibble. Love is the very thing that pierces the universal, that leads to the counternormative election of the younger over the elder. Of course, the love that orchestrates election in the patriarchal narratives is God's, but God's love is intimately bound up with human love, such as Abraham's for Isaac and Jacob's for Rachel. Likewise, the paean to human love in the above passage from Song of Songs 8:6–7 includes numerous references to divine figures: "death," in Hebrew *mavet,* is also the Canaanite god of death, Mot; "darts," in Hebrew *reshafim,* is the plural form of the Canaanite god of plague, Reshef; and the "blazing flame" is literally a "flame of Yah," where "Yah" is a shortened form of the name of Israel's God. This concentration of divine names suggests that human love has in it something of divine revelation.

A topic much debated in scholarship on the Song of Songs is whether the book was meant to be read, as it has indeed been read by generations of Jewish and Christian readers, as an allegory for the relationship of love that binds God (or more specifically, in the Christian case, Christ), represented by the man, to the people of God (Israel, the church), figured by the woman. There is no doubt that, as Fox has shown, the poems in the book depend on and perhaps were originally composed as love songs, designed for performance at weddings (among other contexts), to celebrate the love, physical and otherwise, that weddings are part culmination of and part prelude to. But whether the biblical book, as edited and as received in more or less its current form by its earliest readers, was understood allegorically remains an open question. Without attempting to answer this question, we may simply note that the allegorical interpretation is continuous with the "plain-sense" interpretation, not only because both revolve around love, but also because, in the Israelite context, the workings of human love and of divine love are not altogether separable.

At the end of our analysis of the book of Job in the previous chapter, we observed that while it is more universalist than Proverbs in the sense that it expands outward from it, to encompass under God's purview not only order but chaos, not only justice but injustice, the book of Job might also be construed as particularist. It features divine revelation. God's speech describes the forces of chaos in what we can reasonably call loving detail. Nor is a noncombative relationship with chaos possible in any terms other than love; surely justice, a creature of order, has no place in this relationship. God's speech in the book of Job shares with the Song of Songs a preference for nature (albeit of a very different, more predatory sort than the forms of nature prominent in the Song of Songs) over human civilization. It also shares with it, albeit more subtly, an embrace of love.

Addendum: Source Criticism in the Pentateuch

This chapter represents our first exposure to the Pentateuch, and hence also an opportunity to introduce one of the important achievements of modern scientific study of the Bible: source criticism. We will enter into this topic by means of two case studies, two pairs of stories within the patriarchal narratives. The first pair of stories involves Abraham's travels outside Canaan. Abraham twice leaves Canaan on account of famine, the first time to Egypt (Genesis 12:10–21) and the second time to Gerar (20:1–18). In each case, concerned that the local king might, on account of Sarah's beauty, seize her and kill him, Abraham passes Sarah off as his sister. The king indeed seizes Sarah, only to be chastised and, upon discovering the truth, to return Sarah to Abraham.

The second pair of stories involves the departure of Hagar. In the first case (16:4–14), because, after conceiving a child, Hagar treats Sarah lightly, Sarah torments her, to the point that she flees. An angel finds Hagar, informs her that God has heard her cries, promises her that her son will become a great nation, and directs her to return. In the second case (21:8–21), again ultimately at Sarah's impetus, Hagar is expelled together with Ishmael, and they wander in the wilderness, where an angel encounters them and informs them that God has heard Ishmael's cry and that he will become a great nation.

Pairs of similar stories like the "wife-sister" stories and the "Hagar in the wilderness" stories are called *doublets*. Such doublets have long aroused suspicion among biblical scholars. The problem is not so much that it is historically implausible that two such similar events should happen twice; most biblical scholars are disinclined to treat the patriarchal narratives as straightforward historical records in any case. The problem is rather that doublets seem literarily inelegant: Why should an author repeat the same plot event, with so little variation?

A closer look at these doublets reveals that certain features distinguish one member of each doublet from the other member. First, and at least at first glance most superficially, God is named in one way in the first wife-sister story and in the story of Hagar's first departure (for the sake of convenience: "the first departure story"), but in another way in the second wife-sister story and in the story of Hagar's second departure ("the second departure story"). In the first wife-sister story and the first departure story, God is always "Lord." (The English word corresponds to the proper name of God in the Hebrew text, a name consisting of four consonants, *Y-H-W-H,* thought to be pronounced "Yah-weh." From a very early date, pious readers replaced this proper name of God with "Lord": *'adonai* in Hebrew, *kyrios* in Greek.) In the second wife-sister story and the second departure story, God is rather "God" (which translates the generic Hebrew noun *'elohim*).

Substantive differences correlate with the difference in divine name. Abraham comes off better in the second wife-sister story than in the first, and in the second departure story than in the first. In the second wife-sister story, Abraham is able to defend himself against the charge that he lied in claiming Sarah as his sister. "In fact," says Abraham in Genesis 20:12 (slightly altered), "she is the daughter of my father, though not the daughter of my mother," that is, Sarah *is* his sister or at least his half-sister. In the first wife-sister story, by contrast, Abraham has no answer to Pharaoh's gruff criticism of Abraham's mendacity. In the second departure story, Abraham is reluctant to expel Hagar and Ishmael, doing so only after God insists (21:11–12), whereas in the first departure story, Abraham readily agrees to allow Sarah to do what she will with Hagar (16:6).

The same pattern holds with reference to the mode of divine revelation. In the first departure story, an angel of the Lord "finds" Hagar (Genesis 16:7), evidently while circumambulating in ordinary, human fashion. In the second departure story, the angel of God calls to Hagar "from the heavens" (21:17, slightly altered). The ethereal mode of revelation in the latter echoes in the second wife-sister story, where God speaks to King Abimelech not in person but in a dream. This difference in mode of revelation resonates with the difference in characterization of Abraham. The second wife-sister story and the second departure story alike seem to manifest a certain theological anxiousness that is missing from their corresponding pairs. It is important in these two stories, but not in the two stories with which they pair, that the patriarch come out well and that God be distinguished from human beings.

How are we to make sense of patterns like these? Beginning in earnest in the nineteenth century, some biblical scholars came to appreciate that they can be accounted for by supposing that the patriarchal narratives and other parts of the Pentateuch came about through the merger of originally independent or partially independent versions of the same narrative. Thus, out of a mass of fluid oral traditions about Abraham passing his wife off as his sister in a foreign court to which he had traveled in a time of famine, and about Hagar departing Abraham's home, two different fixed textual versions emerged, one in which Abraham went to Pharaoh's court and in which Hagar left while pregnant, and another in which Abraham's travels took him to Gerar and in which Hagar was expelled after Ishmael's birth. The first version referred to God as *Y-H-W-H* (translated "LORD") and espoused certain theological views, while the second referred to God as *'Elohim* ("God") and was committed to other theological views. We may think, by analogy, of the different versions of Jesus's life preserved in the canonical Gospels, each telling of Jesus's miracles and crucifixion in its own way, and with its distinctive terminology. But while the New Testament preserves each of the different versions of Jesus's life as a separate work, the story of Abraham in the book of Genesis is the work of an editor or redactor who combined the different accounts of Abraham's life into a single, continuous account. It is this combination process that produced the doublets.

Because the foundational scholarship on this approach to the biblical text was German, and because in German it is the letter *J* that gives the sound /y/, the first source was christened the Jahwist source, or J. The second source is the Elohist source, or E. Using reading strategies like the ones above and others, biblical scholars have identified other pentateuchal texts, especially from Genesis, Exodus, and Numbers, that belong to these sources. They have also identified other sources. The two most important additional sources are the Priestly source, or P, which occurs in texts from Genesis through Numbers, including almost all of Leviticus, and the Deuteronomist source, or D, which consists of most of Deuteronomy. These posited sources are the basic elements of the Documentary Hypothesis, which contends that the Pentateuch is the result of the stitching together of distinct sources, first and foremost J, E, P (together with P-like sources), and D.

This approach to the biblical text is called *source criticism*, because its aim is to identify the textual sources drawn upon by the editors of the biblical text that we now possess. The account of the Pentateuch's sources that I have sketched above is one among a number of alternatives. Other accounts make different assumptions about the number and interdependence of the sources. Still others eschew the identification of distinct, independent narrative threads in favor of models that envision something more like a single, fluid textual entity supplemented over the course of centuries by discrete accretions. However we adjudicate among these accounts, they enable us to appreciate that even an apparently continuous narrative like the Pentateuch did not emerge all at once but over a long period of time. We realize, in their light, that the Pentateuch is not only the foundation of a tradition but the result of a tradition, a negotiation over time among theologically distinct voices.

In this book, we will hew more or less to the traditional source-critical approach of the Pentateuch introduced above. The analysis above of the two wife-sister stories and the two departure stories serves us chiefly as a methodological exercise, with limited theological payoff, but later we will identify very theologically meaningful differences among sources.

For Further Reflection

1. I have suggested that the Sodom episode figures in the Abraham story as something like a universalist interlude, wherein questions of righteousness and justice figure centrally. Support for this interpretation comes from the fact that the Sodom story resembles that of the flood, also a universalist story in that it affects the entire world. Identify parallels between the story of Sodom in Genesis 18:16–19:38 and the story of the flood in Genesis 6:9–9:29. (We will turn to the flood story in detail in chapter 10.)

2. How do the patriarchal narratives describe the relationship between Abraham's family and the people and land of Canaan and its environs? Consider, among other things: the possibility of intermarriage, as it arises in Genesis 24; 26:34–35; 27:46; 28:1–9; the purchase of a family burial plot in Genesis 23; and the appearance in the patriarchal narratives of Edom, Ammon, and Moab, all of them characters in the patriarchal narratives whose descendants populate lands just to the east and south of Canaan.

3. How do the man and the woman in the Song of Songs differ in the ways in which they speak and act, in the ways in which they situate themselves in relation to society, in their understanding of love and of the other? For careful and creative treatment of these questions, see J. Cheryl Exum's commentary on the Song of Songs.

Bibliography

Auerbach, Eric. *Mimesis: The Representation of Reality in Western Literature.* Translated by Willard R. Trask. 1953. Reprint. Princeton: Princeton University Press, 1968.

Baden, Joel S. *The Composition of the Pentateuch: Renewing the Documentary Hypothesis.* New Haven: Yale University Press, 2012.

Carr, David M. *The Formation of the Hebrew Bible: A New Reconstruction.* New York: Oxford University Press, 2011.

Cover, Robert M. "The Supreme Court, 1982 Term—Foreword: Nomos and Narrative." *Harvard Law Review* 97 (1983–84): 4–68.

Exum, J. Cheryl. *Song of Songs: A Commentary.* Old Testament Library. Louisville: Westminster John Knox, 2005.

Fox, Michael V. *The Song of Songs and the Ancient Egyptian Love Songs.* Madison: University of Wisconsin Press, 1985.

Kierkegaard, Søren. *Fear and Trembling/Repetition.* Edited and translated by Howard V. Hong and Edna H. Hong. Princeton: Princeton University Press, 1983.

Levenson, Jon D. *The Death and Resurrection of the Beloved Son: The Transformation of Child Sacrifice in Judaism and Christianity.* New Haven: Yale University Press, 1993.

4 | Joseph and Narrative

READINGS

Genesis 28:10–33:20; 35; 37–46; 48–50

Introduction

The readings for this chapter focus on the careers of Jacob and his son Joseph. The plot, in brief, is as follows. Jacob, after impersonating his brother Esau and stealing the blessing that their father Isaac intended to bestow on Esau, flees his brother's anger and betakes himself to the home of his mother's brother Laban in Haran, in modern Syria. There he encounters Laban's daughter Rachel, whom he eventually marries, together with Rachel's sister, Leah. Jacob works for Laban as a shepherd, eventually accumulating two more wives (the maidservants of Rachel and Leah), twelve sons, and much wealth. He returns to Canaan, where the favor that he shows Rachel's firstborn, Joseph, arouses the jealousy of Joseph's brothers, who conspire to sell him as a slave to Egypt. In Egypt, Joseph rises to become second in command after Pharaoh and directs Egypt's affairs during seven years of plenty and seven subsequent years of famine. The famine, which also affects Canaan, leads Joseph's brothers down to Egypt and thus eventually to a reunion with Joseph. Jacob's entire family relocates to Egypt, where it will become a nation and endure slavery.

Our analysis begins with and focuses on the Joseph story, but returns toward the end to the Jacob story to highlight aspects of the latter that enable the transition from the family intrigues of Genesis to the national narrative that begins in Exodus. The Joseph story is often characterized by biblical scholars as a didactic tale or a wisdom tale, that is, a narrative that illustrates and animates the principles espoused in wisdom texts like Proverbs. One of our goals in the discussion below is to support but also to nuance this position, and to situate the Joseph story in relation to the universalist perspective of Proverbs and the predominantly particularist perspective of the other patriarchal narratives. The other, related goal is to describe the distinctive literary aspects of the Joseph story, which is one of two stories in the Bible that, in length and psychological complexity, resemble the modern novel. (The other is the story of David in the book of Samuel.)

Divine Action in the Joseph Story

The most distinctive feature of the plot of the Joseph story, relative to the stories that were the subject of the previous chapter, is the almost total absence therefrom of God. God never appears to or speaks to Joseph or to any other character, nor does he perform any concrete act, with two exceptions to which we will turn below. In the earlier patriarchal narratives, God is a character much like any other. He appears to Abraham in Genesis 12, for example, to direct him to go to Canaan. God, or an angel of God, engages Hagar in conversation in Genesis 16, and in Genesis 21 speaks to her from heaven and opens her eyes so that she can take note of a well. In his flight from Esau, Jacob overnights at Bethel and has a dream (28:10–17) in which God appears to him and reassures him that God will keep watch over him. God rains fire and brimstone upon Sodom (19:24) and closes the wombs of the women in the household of Abimelech, king of Gerar (20:18). Such things do not happen in the Joseph story. God speaks to no one and does no specific deed.

God is nowhere in the Joseph story, but he is at the same time everywhere. The reader, alongside the characters themselves, comes to appreciate that it was God's plan to raise Joseph to a position of authority in Egypt, and eventually to have his family join him there. The entire arc of the plot makes manifest the designs of God. We will specify later precisely how the reader and the characters come to appreciate God's presence, but for now our interest lies in the fact that this presence is at the same time an absence. In the preceding patriarchal narratives, the author (or narrator) resides by himself above the narrative plane; God toils below him, on the narrative plane, together with the other characters. In the Joseph story, by contrast, God retreats from the narrative plane and joins the author up above.

There is thus an important irony in the retreat of God to the author's position. In the earlier narratives, because God is a character, his influence is limited to his person, to the words that he speaks and the actions that he performs. But when he absents himself, he becomes an invisible presence pervading and guiding all events. It is not altogether unprofitable to compare the phenomenon to that of the "force ghost" in the *Star Wars* movies. Obi-Wan Kenobi tells Darth Vader that if Vader strikes him down, Obi-Wan will become more powerful. Loosed from his body, the Jedi, as a ghost, can more easily intervene anywhere and everywhere. Likewise, God, disembodied in the Joseph story, becomes pervasive. Or, from a more "elevated" cultural register and even more aptly, we may note Gustave Flaubert's famous characterization of the author: "An artist in his book must be like God in the universe, present everywhere, and visible nowhere."[1] In the earlier patriarchal narratives, God is seen and therefore not everywhere felt: he exerts influence as far as he acts, but beyond his sphere of action, human beings do as they will. It is only in the Joseph story that the biblical God becomes Flaubert's God, and Flaubert's author.

The two blatant exceptions to the generally invisible character of divine action in the Joseph story are exceptions that prove the rule. First, God appears to Jacob in a "vision by night" when he sets out for Egypt (Genesis 46:1–4), to reassure him that he will be with him in Egypt and that he will return to Canaan. This exception proves the rule because it is not, in essence, part of the Joseph story but an intrusion from the Jacob story, which shares with the preceding patriarchal narratives a very different way of representing divine action. Indeed, the night vision on the road to Egypt is the bookend to the night vision that a much younger Jacob experienced at Bethel, on the road from Canaan to Laban's home (28:10–17). In that dream, too, God promises Jacob that he will be with him on his journey and return him to Canaan. The second exception comes in 38:7, 10, where the narrator reports on specific acts performed by God: killing Judah's sons, Er and Onan, on account of their wickedness. Here too the exception proves the rule, for Genesis 38 is a clearly demarcated interlude, an excursus that features only Judah, not Joseph.

How does the biblical text manage the feat of at once concealing and revealing God? We may identify three important tactics, from least to most subtle. First, the narrator does attribute a few actions to God, but nebulous ones. God blesses Potiphar's house on Joseph's account (39:5), acts beneficently toward Joseph in jail, and wins for him the favor of the chief jailer (39:21, 23). While these remarks do unambiguously gesture to God's guiding presence, they leave the precise nature of God's intervention amorphous.

Second, and most importantly, characters have dreams that, properly interpreted, accurately foretell the future. The dreams in the Joseph story come

1. Gustave Flaubert, *The Letters of Gustave Flaubert, 1830–1857*, trans. Francis Steegmuller (Cambridge, MA: Harvard University Press, 1971), 173.

in three pairs: two to Joseph as a young man (37:5–11), anticipating his future elevation; two to the imprisoned officers (40:1–19), which describe their divergent fates; and two to Pharaoh (41:1–32), predicting the seven years of plenty and the subsequent seven years of famine. These dreams differ categorically from the dreams of characters in the preceding patriarchal narratives (and from Jacob's dream in 46:1–4). In the latter dreams, God appears to the characters directly, and either instructs them or informs them of a present or future fact. In the six dreams in the Joseph story, God does not appear, and the meaning is obscure, clouded in symbols. The dreams in the Joseph story require interpretation.

Not only is their meaning unclear; it is not even certain, in the moment, that the dreams are from God. Consider, for example, the reaction of Joseph's family to his dreams. These dreams—in the first, his brothers' sheaves bow to his sheaf; and in the second, eleven stars, together with the sun and moon, bow to him—seem to portend that Joseph will rule over his brothers. The brothers are perturbed by these dreams but hardly resign themselves to such a future. They presumably suppose that the dreams are more likely than not the product of Joseph's own self-aggrandizing imagination. Their father, too, outwardly dismisses the dreams as nonsense (37:10), even if in his heart he reflects upon them (37:11). Only by the end of the story, and perhaps even then only with a measure of hesitation, can the reader be confident that Joseph's dreams were messages from heaven.

The third ambiguous marker of divine presence in the Joseph story is coincidence. Consider, for example, the sequence of events that brings Joseph to Egypt. The brothers are tending Jacob's sheep in Shechem, and Jacob sends Joseph there to bring back a report of their well-being. A man finds Joseph wandering, presumably because Joseph has arrived in the vicinity of Shechem but cannot find his brothers. This man tells Joseph that he overheard his brothers expressing the desire to go to Dothan. Joseph, following this clue, indeed finds them in Dothan (37:12–17). It is out of character for the biblical narrator to enter into such detail about so trivial a thing as Joseph's brief detour; we could as easily have been told simply that Jacob sent Joseph to his brothers and that he arrived at the place where they were pasturing. The details, and especially the coincidental appearance of the mysterious man who just happened to have overheard the brothers, seem designed to suggest God's implicit presence. Again, after the brothers have cast Joseph into the pit and sat down to eat, a caravan of Ishmaelites happens to pass by on its way to Egypt, and the brothers sell Joseph to them (37:25–28). The plot of the Joseph story turns on such apparent coincidences in a way that the preceding patriarchal narratives do not.

Recurrence is a species of coincidence. When two or more independent events occur along the same lines, they suggest the presence of a guiding hand. For example, the Ishmaelite caravan that conveys Joseph to Egypt carries "gum, balm, and ladanum" (37:25); and when the brothers accompany Benjamin, Joseph's brother, down to Egypt, they bring with them the very same items as a gift for the Egyptian ruler (43:11). Again, when the brothers fool Jacob into thinking that Joseph is dead by presenting him with Joseph's cloak, stained with the blood of a goat (37:31–32), they replay Jacob's crime of deceiving his own father Isaac by means of goatskin worn on the arms and neck (27:16). Deception involving clothing recurs in the story of Judah and Tamar in Genesis 38 (on which more below), and again in the story of Joseph and Potiphar's wife in 39:7–20.

Human Action and Divine Action in the Joseph Story

The simultaneous presence and absence of God means that the plot can be accounted for on two distinct levels: God drives events forward, but human beings make their own decisions. It is the brothers themselves who decide to sell Joseph as a slave, and it is Potiphar's wife who slanders Joseph and lands him in the prison where he can encounter the officer who will lead him from the deep pit to the lofty palace. At the same time, these decisions play essential roles in the fulfillment of God's plan to bring Jacob's family to Egypt. We may speak, then, of dual causality, on both the human plane and the divine.

Causality is further complicated by the fact that these planes intersect, if ambiguously, along the three lines described above, and the human characters know this. They know that it is possible, though not easy, to find traces of God's guiding presence by paying careful attention to—by interpreting—dreams, unusual events, coincidences. For example, when confronted with an Egyptian viceroy (really Joseph) who accuses them of being spies and tells them that he will hold one of them ransom until they prove their bona fides by bringing their youngest brother (Benjamin) to Egypt, Joseph's older brothers infer:

> We are guilty on account of our brother, because we saw how his soul was troubled when he pleaded with us, yet we did not heed him. That is why this trouble has come upon us. (42:21, altered)

Thus human beings, in addition to making their own decisions on independent grounds, are also always on the lookout for echoes of the divine orchestrations to which they might attune themselves.

Sorting out causality becomes even more complex because it is possible to game this system: a character can take advantage of the predilection to look for God's hand in human affairs to manufacture circumstances that will encourage others to make precisely such an inference. Some aspect of this dynamic lies behind the entire series of interactions between Joseph and his brothers in Egypt, insofar as the brothers are ignorant of Joseph's machinations: Joseph appears to want the brothers to deduce that the accusations leveled at them by the Egyptian viceroy are God's way of punishing the brothers for their misdeeds. The possibility of subterfuge is realized most explicitly during the brothers' return trip, when they inform the overseer of Joseph's household that they found the money with which they had purchased their grain in the sacks of grain themselves. The overseer attributes this wonder to God (43:23, altered): "Fear not. Your God, the God of your father, placed a treasure in your bags for you. Your money indeed reached me." This claim is, of course, patently false: Joseph had ordered that the money be returned to his brothers' sacks. And yet it is not altogether false, for in the causality framework assumed by the Joseph story, there is no categorical distinction between human and divine action.

As Joseph excels as an interpreter of dreams, so, we are meant to understand, he excels as an interpreter of events. When, therefore, in the latter capacity, he concludes that "it was not you who sent me here, but God" (45:8), we are inclined to agree with him, even if, in light of the above complexities, we necessarily cannot be altogether sure. What the Joseph story loses in clarity it gains in realism, for it describes the conditions of the world that we live in, as the biblical author sees it. The story encourages the reader to take all events as opportunities for interpretation, as potential manifestations of God.

What sort of worldview underlies the complex interaction of divine and human action in the Joseph story? In the preceding two chapters, we described two different and opposing frameworks: one represented paradigmatically by Proverbs, wherein a relatively distant God enforces the norms of justice; and one that prevails in the patriarchal narratives, where a personal God becomes manifest through violation of the norm. The Joseph story is much closer to the Proverbs framework and has indeed been construed as a didactic tale that embodies the teachings of the wisdom tradition. Joseph, the protagonist, is wise in the ways favored by this tradition: He can anticipate what the future will bring. He is skilled at formulating and carrying out prudent plans in service of the government. He resists the advances of a married woman. Joseph's wisdom has nothing particularist about it, but is intelligible and obvious to non-Israelites like Pharaoh, who makes explicit the story's characterization of Joseph when he declares: "There is none so discerning and wise as you" (Genesis 41:39).

But there is a crucial aspect of the Joseph story that distinguishes it from the framework of Proverbs. As in Proverbs, God does not directly guide human affairs; but, unlike in Proverbs, he does intervene indirectly, from behind the scenes, to lead the story toward a specific end. We are witness not simply to the timeless operation of divine justice but to the working out of a plan conceived by a more personal God for the sake of a specific people.

Character Development in the Joseph Story

The departure of God from the plane of the characters, his disappearance behind the scenes, opens up space for character development to a far greater degree than in the preceding patriarchal narratives. The brothers, for example, eventually come to recognize their guilt. Joseph, who as a youth seems happy to bask in his father's favor and to flaunt his dreams of grandeur, matures into a more prudent man. But the most dramatic development occurs in the character of Judah, and a careful study of this dynamic reveals the subtlety of the Bible's characterization techniques.

Judah's first speaking part comes after the brothers have cast Joseph into the pit and sat down to eat. The sight of an Ishmaelite caravan passing by in the direction of Egypt inspires Judah to make a proposal.

> What is the profit if we kill our brother and cover his blood? Come, let us sell him to the Ishmaelites, and let us not send forth our hand against him, for he is our brother, our flesh. (Genesis 37:26–27 NRSV, slightly altered)

What motivates Judah? He voices a moral objection to fratricide. But he also, less nobly, introduces a mercenary consideration—profit. Is Judah's concern for profit genuine, or does he introduce it, indeed lead with it, as a rhetorical tool to win over his brothers, who might be unwilling altogether to release Joseph? Judah's words echo those of the psalmist, who pleads to God in his distress: "What profit is there . . . if I go down to the Pit [i.e., the underworld]? Can dust praise you?" (Psalm 30:9 NRSV, slightly altered). Here too Judah would raise Joseph from the pit for the sake of profit. Does the availability of such profit rhetoric even in a liturgical context allow us to judge Judah less harshly?

In any case, Judah comes off as an ambiguous figure: morally refined enough to recoil from fratricide, morally courageous enough to articulate his objection, charismatic enough to persuade his brothers, but ultimately willing to sell Joseph as a slave. As Joseph heads down to Egypt, in Genesis 38 the narrator diverges from the main thread to take up a series of events in Judah's private life, before returning in Genesis 39 to the scene of Joseph, newly arrived in Egypt. The decision to take this detour is a striking indication of the narrative's interest in Judah, and specifically in the maturation of his character.

The plot of Genesis 38 runs as follows: Judah's son Er marries a woman, Tamar, and dies childless. In such circumstances, it is the duty of the deceased husband's brother to marry the widow, so that they can produce a child who will carry on the name of the deceased. But Onan, Er's brother, knowing that the child would not ultimately be his, refuses to father a child with Tamar. He too dies. Judah has a third son, Shelah, but tells Tamar that her marriage to him should be delayed because he is yet too young. The narrator informs us that Judah was concerned that Shelah too would die if he married Tamar; and indeed, even after Shelah comes of age, Judah does not move forward with the marriage. Taking matters into her own hands, Tamar conceals herself as a harlot and sleeps with Judah, taking his seal and staff as surety until he can deliver her payment. When Judah discovers that Tamar is pregnant, he orders that she be executed, but Tamar brings forward Judah's seal and staff. He recognizes that it is none other than he who impregnated Tamar, and he is compelled to admit that she is more righteous than he, because it was his refusal of Shelah that compelled her to act.

This narrative combines, in different ways, building blocks familiar from the Joseph story: there are fathers and children, there is fraternal conflict, there is deception. Tamar's speech to Judah is especially evocative: "Examine these: whose seal and cord and staff are these?" (38:25). These words echo those of the brothers when they send Joseph's bloodstained coat to Jacob: "Please examine it; is it your son's tunic or not?" (37:32). Possibly recognizing the echo, Judah acknowledges his guilt in relation to Tamar and perhaps, implicitly, his guilt in relation to Joseph. The crimes are, after all, not dissimilar: in the case of Joseph, Judah was unwilling to save his brother; and in the case of Tamar, Judah is unwilling to allow one brother to "save" his brother by raising up children in his place.

In the continuation of the narrative, Judah redeems himself more completely. The brothers descend to Egypt for food and depart from there without Simeon, and with instructions not to return except with Benjamin. Now the scenario of Genesis 38, where Judah refuses to risk the life of his youngest son, Shelah, for the sake of producing a child for the deceased Er, recurs in force: Will Jacob put his youngest son, Benjamin, at risk for the sake of an older son?

Upon their initial return, Jacob refuses (42:38), but after their food runs out, he is left with little choice. Nevertheless, he hesitates (43:6). It is at this point that Judah intervenes decisively.

> And Judah said to his father Israel, "Send the boy with me, and we will arise and go, and we will live and not die—you and we and our children. I will stand surety for him. From my hand you may seek him. If I do not bring him back to you and stand him before you, I shall have sinned against you forever." (43:8–9, altered)

To understand precisely what Judah is committing to in this passage, and how it reverses, as it were, the sin of Joseph's sale, we must appreciate the relationship between Judah's words and an earlier declaration by his father, Jacob. The setting for Jacob's declaration is his conflict with Laban. Jacob worked for Laban as a shepherd for many years, before departing with his family. Laban pursues Jacob to lay claim to his daughters and because he suspects that someone in Jacob's camp stole his household gods. Laban searches through the camp but finds nothing. Indignant at Laban's apparently false accusation, Jacob then angrily notes that, during his employment with Laban, it was Laban who dealt craftily, and Jacob who was scrupulously honest: "That which was torn by wild beasts I did not bring to you; I bore the loss of it myself; of my hand you required it, whether stolen by day or stolen by night" (31:39 NRSV).

Jacob's claim is that, as Laban's shepherd, he did not ask Laban to cover the cost of animals torn by wild beasts or of stolen animals, but bore the loss himself. Judah employs the same terminology in the above passage. He will bear the loss of Benjamin and consider himself the sinner if Benjamin is lost. Earlier, Judah, together with his brothers, denied responsibility for the torn and stolen "animal," Joseph. Judah was the bad shepherd; indeed, he was the very wolf who compelled Jacob to conclude that "Joseph was torn by a beast" (37:33), and the very thief whose actions led Joseph to describe himself as having been "kidnapped from the land of the Hebrews" (40:15). What Judah takes up, in his pledge to Jacob, is the mantle of the good shepherd.

Joseph contrives events so that Judah must make good on his pledge. After Joseph frames Benjamin as a thief and threatens to constrain him as a prisoner while allowing the other brothers to leave, Judah approaches to insist that he take Benjamin's place.

> Let your servant [i.e., me, Judah] remain as a slave to my lord instead of the boy, and let the boy go back with his brothers. For how can I go

> back to my father unless the boy is with me, lest I see the woe that would overtake my father? (44:33–34, slightly altered)

It is Judah's intervention that compels Joseph finally to reveal himself to his brothers and thus to reconstitute the brothers as a unified whole.

While the Joseph story is a family drama that precedes the birth of the nation—more on this dichotomy below—it also encodes a conception of Israelite politics. The two characters around whom it centers, Joseph and Judah, are figures, respectively, of the northern kingdom of Israel and the southern kingdom of Judah. In the tension but eventual reconciliation between these protagonists, the Bible projects a vision of political coexistence.

Jacob and the Transition from Genesis to Exodus

Let us return now to the story of Jacob's youth, and through it, to the ways in which the biblical narrative pivots from the patriarchal narratives, which center on a family, to the subject of the next chapter, the book of Exodus, where the major protagonist is now a nation. We will focus in particular on Jacob's journey to his uncle Laban in Haran and more particularly still on the two events that bookend that journey, each of which raises questions. First, upon Jacob's arrival in the area of Haran, he enters into an exchange with some local shepherds whom he finds gathered around the well.

> He said, "Look, much daylight remains; it is not time to gather the flocks. Give drink to the sheep, and go and pasture." But they said, "We may not until all the herds gather, and they roll the stone from the mouth of the well. Then we will give drink to the sheep." (29:7–8 NRSV, altered)

This exchange plays no apparent role in the narrative; it seems simply to mark the time between when they inform Jacob that Laban's daughter is approaching (29:6) and when she arrives (29:9). Why, then, must we hear this exchange? What narrative purpose is served by Jacob's critique or the shepherds' response? It does convey Jacob's industriousness, and it also informs us about the stone on the well's mouth, which Jacob will gallantly remove upon Rachel's arrival; but these considerations still leave the exchange rather underdetermined.

Before attempting an explanation for the exchange, let us turn to the final incident from Jacob's journey to Haran. After Jacob's departure from Laban's home and the tense confrontation between Jacob and Laban that follows, the two men agree to enter into a nonaggression pact.

> Jacob took a stone and set it up as a pillar. And Jacob said to his brothers: "Gather stones." And they gathered stones, and made of it a heap, and they ate there by the heap. And Laban called it Jegar-sahadutha [Aramaic for "witness heap"], and Jacob called it Galeed [Hebrew for "witness heap"]. (31:45–47 NRSV, slightly altered)

In this closing incident, as in the opening incident, Jacob moves a stone. The details of this incident, too, are somewhat puzzling. In particular, why do Jacob and Laban assign the heap—the witness to or sign of their covenant—different names, Jacob a Hebrew one and Laban an Aramaic one? It is hardly surprising that Jacob, from Canaan, should favor Hebrew, while Laban, from the Aramaic-speaking regions of Syria, should favor Aramaic; but why should this language difference surface precisely now, and nowhere else in the story?

I suggest that the answer to this question, as to the question about the incident with which Jacob's sojourn in Haran begins, is that this sojourn plays a determinative role in an important dynamic in the book of Genesis. We have already discussed one fundamental dynamic in the book around election, and in particular the election of the younger. It is through this dynamic that Isaac is chosen among Abraham's children, and Jacob among Isaac's. But there is a second and more immediately germane dynamic, involving the demarcation of Abraham and his descendants as a distinct group, separate from his pagan past. How are the ties that bind Abraham to his family ultimately to be severed? Abraham departs from his family, but both Abraham's servant, on behalf of Isaac, and afterward Jacob himself return to find wives.

Consider the modern experience of someone who moves away from the town in which she grew up. She retains fond memories of it and may even still think of it as her true home. Perhaps she even imagines returning to live there some day. Then she does return to visit. She finds that the town is not quite as she had remembered it. Some aspects of the town, she now realizes, had been idealized in or overlooked by her memory. Other things have genuinely changed. She herself is a changed person, different now from when she lived there. The experience of returning to the town makes her appreciate that the town is no longer home. It will remain part of her past, but only of her past.

The same dynamic appears to be at work in the patriarchal narratives, albeit over multiple generations. Abraham is the one who leaves his home, but continues to think of it as home. Isaac remains in the land of Canaan and thus establishes it as the new home, but the possibility of a return still lingers. Jacob does return, but he is immediately confronted by the place's foreignness: he does not know its herding customs. The purpose (or one of the purposes) of the exchange with the shepherds of Haran is to underscore that Jacob is, and now recognizes himself to be, a foreigner in his grandfather's home. The same narrative strategy recurs later in the same chapter (29:26), when Jacob again finds himself ignorant of local practices, in this case that of marrying off the younger sister only after marrying off the elder. These two incidents, by constructing Haran as alien territory at the outset of Jacob's sojourn thereto, foreshadow the final break between Abraham's descendants and his ancestral family that will occur in the covenant between Jacob and Laban. The Bible reports that Jacob assigned the stones a Hebrew name, and Laban an Aramaic one, in order to convey that the two sides are now separate peoples. Jacob, with his family, now belongs to Canaan and speaks Hebrew, the language of Canaan. Laban's people are Arameans and speak Aramaic.

In the figure of Jacob, both of the principal dynamics of Genesis—the winnowing dynamic of election, and the weaning dynamic of separation from Abraham's family—reach their end. All of his children are Israel, and they are categorically distinguished from Abraham's ancestral family. They will not return to their ancestral home for wives and will no longer think of it as their home. Here, then, with the conclusion of these two family dynamics, is the decisive shift from Genesis to Exodus, to the birth of the nation of Israel.

For Further Reflection

1. In the two cases discussed above where Judah decisively intervenes in the Joseph plot—to propose that Joseph be sold, in Genesis 37:26–27, and to stand as surety for Benjamin, in 43:8–9—he does so directly after attempted interventions by Jacob's eldest son, Reuben, in 37:21–22 and 42:37, respectively. How might one explain this pattern? Consider literary and source-critical solutions. On the latter, see the introduction to Joel Baden's book, *The Composition of the Pentateuch* (pp. 1–12).

2. Jacob's ladder (Genesis 28:10–22) is among the most famous images in the Bible. What is the significance of the ladder according to the plain sense of the text? Consider the ways in which the ladder was understood by some of the Bible's earliest readers, whose work is summarized and analyzed in the second chapter of James Kugel's book, *Ladder of Jacob* (pp. 9–35).

Bibliography

Alter, Robert. *The Art of Biblical Narrative.* New York: Basic Books, 1981.

Baden, Joel S. *The Composition of the Pentateuch: Renewing the Documentary Hypothesis.* New Haven: Yale University Press, 2012.

Berlin, Adele. *Poetics and Interpretation of Biblical Narrative.* Sheffield: Almond Press, 1983.

Kawashima, Robert S. *Biblical Narrative and the Death of the Rhapsode.* Bloomington: Indiana University Press, 2004.

Kugel, James. *The Ladder of Jacob: Ancient Interpretations of the Biblical Story of Jacob and His Children.* Princeton: Princeton University Press, 2006.

Leuchter, Mark. "Genesis 38 in Social and Historical Perspective." *Journal of Biblical Literature* 132 (2013): 209–27.

Zakovitch, Yair. *Jacob: Unexpected Patriarch.* Translated by Valerie Zakovitch. New Haven: Yale University Press, 2012.

5 | The Exodus: Freedom and Sonship

READING
Exodus 1–17

Introduction

As the second book of the Pentateuch opens, Jacob's offspring are in Egypt. If the beginning of the first book (to which we will turn in chapter 9) has God, in a universalist mode, bestow upon human beings the blessing of reproduction—"Be fertile and multiply, fill the earth and master it" (Genesis 1:28, slightly altered)—then the beginning of Exodus finds this blessing made manifest particularly in the family of Jacob: "But the Israelites were fertile and prolific; they multiplied and increased very greatly, so that the land was filled with them" (Exodus 1:7). Noting this demographic development, the new pharaoh is fearful for Egypt's security, and not without cause; after all, Genesis 1:28 identifies "filling the earth" as an immediate prelude to "mastering" it.

Pharaoh implements policies of enslavement and infanticide. One Israelite, Moses, a descendant of Jacob's son Levi, is chosen by God to liberate Israel from Egypt. After ten plagues, culminating in the death of the Egyptian firstborn, the Israelites exit Egypt. The Egyptian army pursues them but meets its end at the Red Sea, which God first parts to allow the Israelites to cross, then hurls back upon the pursuing Egyptians.

We may begin our analysis with a simple question: Why does God take Israel out of Egypt? The first stirring of Israel's redemption comes with a cry.

> The Israelites were groaning under the bondage and cried out; and their cry for help from the bondage rose up to God. God heard their moaning,

> and God remembered His covenant with Abraham and Isaac and Jacob. God looked upon the Israelites, and God took notice of them. (Exodus 2:23–25)

In a passage dense with sonic terms, the narrator details two aspects of God's response to the Israelites' cry, hearing and recalling: he hears the Israelites' cry and recalls his covenant with the patriarchs. While these two aspects clearly work together, they have rightly been distinguished, to different degrees and in different ways, by generations of readers. The first aspect is universalist: God rescues the victimized. The second is particularist: he acts to fulfill the covenantal promises that he made to Israel's forefathers.

The Exodus in Universalist Terms: Freedom

The notion that God heeds the cry of the oppressed is familiar to us from Proverbs. Recall, for example, the injunction: "Do not encroach upon the field of orphans, for they have a mighty Kinsman, and He will surely take up their cause with you" (Proverbs 23:10–11). God defends the weak against their oppressors. The law code that God will convey to Moses at Sinai soon after the exodus from Egypt highlights the role of the cry in this dynamic.

> You shall not abuse [or: ill-treat] any widow or orphan. If you do abuse them, I will heed their outcry as soon as they cry out to me; and my anger shall blaze forth and I will put you to the sword, and your wives shall become widows and your children orphans. (Exodus 22:22–24 NRSV, altered)

While it is incidental to our immediate purposes, we may note that the attention devoted in 22:22–24, as in 2:23–25, to the cry casts God in rather anthropomorphic terms. God does not respond to the mistreatment immediately; his attention must, as it were, first be drawn to the mistreatment by means of the cry of the victim.

Besides the fact that God heeds the cry of the oppressed, what, more specifically, does the Bible take to be the universalist expression of the exodus event? Or put differently, what sort of oppression does the exodus story condemn? One answer that springs to the mind of the modern reader familiar with the role of the exodus narrative in American history, from the American Revolution to the struggle for civil rights, is: denial of freedom, or enforced servitude to a tyrant.

The original plan for the Great Seal of the United States included a detailed depiction of the crossing of the Red Sea surrounded by the motto, "Rebellion to Tyrants is Obedience to God." Enslaved blacks and abolitionists before the Civil War found comfort and support in the exodus paradigm, even as secessionists in the southern states also invoked it to frame their actions as justified resistance against alleged northern tyranny. We noted the use of the exodus paradigm by Martin Luther King Jr. at the beginning of this book.

The Bible itself sometimes interprets the exodus story along similar lines. It is likely not a coincidence that in the aforementioned law code that Moses will receive at Sinai (Exodus 21–23), and to which we will turn in detail in the next chapter, the first set of laws (21:2–11) concerns slaves and begins with the rule that an Israelite slave must be allowed to go free after six years of labor. More strikingly, there is reason to think that the very prominence of the exodus story in Israel's national self-consciousness is owed, in part, to the use of the story to justify the secession of the northern kingdom, Israel, from its southern neighbor, Judah.

In support of this theory, Karel van der Toorn and, following him, John Collins have taken note of the following facts. First, among the earliest prophets whose oracles have been collected in books, it is specifically prophets active in the north, like Hosea (2:17; 11:1; 12:10, 14; 13:4) and Amos (2:10–11; 3:1; 9:7), who invoke the exodus from Egypt. (We will return to Amos's invocation of the exodus in chapter 8.) Second, the book of Kings describes the origin of the kingdom of Israel—the fracture of the Solomonic kingdom and the emergence of an independent northern kingdom—in terms that vividly recall the book of Exodus. Solomon is pharaonic: having married Pharaoh's daughter (1 Kings 3:1), he is Pharaoh's son-in-law, and he acquires from Egypt its characteristic military trappings, the horse and chariot (10:28). Solomon, like Pharaoh, engages in massive building projects. Notable especially are Solomon's storehouses (9:19); the only other storehouses built in the Bible are the work of the Israelite slaves in Egypt (Exodus 1:11). Solomon's construction program depends on regular levies that impress Israelites into labor gangs (1 Kings 5:13–17); and when the northern tribes eventually rebel against Solomon's son, Rehoboam, they will name this hard labor as the cause of their dissatisfaction (12:4). The seeds of revolt begin in Solomon's own reign around the figure of Jeroboam. Solomon attempts to kill Jeroboam in order to suppress the incipient revolt, but Jeroboam flees to Egypt (11:40), just as Pharaoh attempted to kill Moses, only to be foiled by Moses's flight to Midian (Exodus 2:15). When Jeroboam returns and founds the kingdom of Israel, he associates the golden calves that he erects with the exodus: "Here are your gods, O Israel, who brought you up out of the land of Egypt" (1 Kings 12:28 NRSV).

These salient points of contact between the origin story of the northern kingdom in 1 Kings and the story of Israel's servitude in and liberation from Egypt in the book of Exodus suggest that the exodus story served as what van der Toorn calls a "charter myth" for the northern kingdom, one that justified its separation from the house of David. The dynamic of oppression that this use of the exodus story highlights is that of the tyrant who enslaves his subjects, more or less as in the cases of the American Revolution and the antebellum south.

The concretization of the circumstances of oppression within a national narrative introduces a different and important dimension to the dichotomy of the universal and the particular. In our analysis of Proverbs, we noted that the book has no interest in revelation, in history, in the sorts of categories that structure most of the other biblical books. In turning to the patriarchal narratives, we asked how revelation and history become manifest in relation to the universal and found that, for the most part, they do so as the exception, as the antinomian. God "punctures" the universal and engages with specific people through violation of the norm. But the exodus story offers a different answer to this question. History intersects with the universal, in this case not by violating the universal but by concretizing the universal within the national narrative. The Israelites, as a people, should be especially sensitive to the possibility of abuse of power. Solomon is worse than the average oppressive king, and the slaveholder who refuses to release his Israelite slave after six years is worse than the typical slaveholder, because he imitates the posture of Israel's historic oppressor, Pharaoh. The universal thus becomes the responsibility of the particular.

The Exodus in Quasi-universalist Terms: The Stranger

When the Bible explicitly dwells on the lesson to be learned from the experience of oppression in Egypt, it takes a somewhat different direction from that implicit in the slave law in Exodus 21–23 and in the northern kingdom's origin story. Immediately prior to the law against oppression of widows and orphans in Exodus 22 appears another prohibition, also designed to protect the vulnerable: "You shall not wrong or oppress a resident alien [or: stranger], for you were aliens [or: strangers] in the land of Egypt" (22:21 NRSV). The stranger of whom this verse speaks is a non-Israelite who resides among the Israelites in their land. The same injunction against oppressing the stranger, again rooted in Israel's experience in Egypt, occurs elsewhere in the Pentateuch (Exodus 23:9; Leviticus 19:34; and Deuteronomy 10:19; but see Deuteronomy 24:22).

It is important to appreciate how different such a lesson is from a lesson like: do not oppress the underclass—the widows and orphans and the poor—because you were the underclass in Egypt and suffered oppression; or, do not take advantage of your power so as to enslave, because you were enslaved in Egypt. The categories at work in these alternative possible lessons—the second of which is present implicitly at the beginning of the law code in Exodus 23 and in the northern kingdom's origin story—are perfectly universal. By contrast, the category of the stranger, as Michael Walzer notes in his brilliant reflection on the exodus story, *Exodus and Revolution*, is a political category, one that is intelligible only within the framework of an Israelite polity or, in other words, within a particularist framework. The stranger is a universalist category not because there is nothing specifically Israelite implicit in it but because the category of stranger encodes a contrast with the Israelite. The notion of not oppressing the stranger is thus both less and more universalist than the notion of not oppressing the vulnerable: less universalist, because it assumes the opposition between Israelite and non-Israelite, and more universalist, because it directs its concern specifically to the latter.

We cannot ignore the fact that the slaves protected by the first passage of the law code in Exodus 21–23 and pitied in the northern kingdom's origin story are specifically Israelite. The lesson that these passages teach looks more like "do not oppress other Israelites" than "do not take advantage of your power" per se. A categorically universalist lesson against oppression can easily turn wholly particularist—from "do not oppress the vulnerable" to "do not oppress the vulnerable of your own people"—in a way that the more structurally nuanced lesson against oppressing the stranger cannot.

The Exodus in Particularist Terms: The Birth of God's Son

To this point, we have considered the exodus from Egypt in more or less universalist terms: it is a story about oppression and about God's attentiveness to the cry of the oppressed. We have seen that even as the Bible endorses this perspective, it complicates it by highlighting the oppression specifically of the non-Israelite stranger. But the events surrounding the exodus can also be conceived of in wholly particularist terms. Recall Exodus 2:23–25, quoted above. In these verses, God's intervention does not come solely in response to the Israelites' cry. Their cry moves God to recollect his covenantal promise to Israel's forefathers. The exodus is thus a story about God's intervention in history on behalf of his chosen people.

As a next step in the national narrative that begins in Genesis, the exodus story both propagates certain motifs from the patriarchal narratives and departs from them. There is something like a patriarchal figure in the exodus story, namely, Moses. Like Isaac, Jacob, and Joseph, Moses is a younger brother who comes to be exalted above his older brother (Aaron). Like Jacob, he flees for his life to a foreign country (Midian), and there he finds a wife (Zipporah) at the well, and becomes a shepherd in his father-in-law's employ. But in the case of Moses, these patriarchal elements are not "weight bearing"; that is, the narrative does not rest on them. We meet Aaron only after we encounter Moses, and there is no overt tension between the two brothers, or at least not any that arises from the fact that Moses is the younger. Likewise, the biblical text makes almost no attempt to individuate Zipporah. At the well, she is unnamed, no more than one of Jethro's seven daughters.

The continuities with Genesis thus ultimately underscore that we are no longer in Genesis. The dynamic has fundamentally changed with the introduction of the people Israel. In Genesis, the crucial relationship is between God and the patriarch. This is not a fatherhood relationship, wherein God takes the patriarch as his son. The only father in the picture is, on the contrary, the patriarch himself, and he enters into the covenant with God on behalf of his own son(s). In the book of Exodus, by contrast, God enters into a father relationship with the people Israel: "Thus says the LORD: Israel is my firstborn son" (Exodus 4:22 NRSV). God thus displaces the human father; one might even say, indeed, that God is the true patriarch in Exodus. Moses is Israel's leader, but not its father.

The significance of this development is worth underscoring. While the Bible often speaks of God acting on Israel's behalf for the sake of their fathers (in Exodus 2:23–25, the passage quoted at the outset of this chapter, and also, for example, in Leviticus 26:42; Jeremiah 33:26), there are other ways in which Israel's relationship with God is more intimate than the patriarchs' relationship with God. When God calls upon Abraham to leave his father, Terah, he does not promise to take Terah's place as Abraham's father, but to make Abraham himself a father to many children. Isaac, likewise, is not God's son but Abraham's, and Jacob is Isaac's son. It is only Israel the people that becomes God's son. The difference between God's relationship with the patriarchs and his relationship with the people Israel finds expression in another way in the exodus story, in the notion that God's proper name, Y-H-W-H, was unknown to the patriarchs and revealed only to Israel.

> God spoke to Moses and said to him, "I am Y-H-W-H. I appeared to Abraham, Isaac, and Jacob as El Shaddai, but I did not make myself known to them by My name Y-H-W-H." (Exodus 6:2–3)

God thus commits himself to Israel in a new and more thoroughgoing way.

Within this framework, the election of Israel can be conceived of as another iteration of the elevation of the younger, where God, the creator and thus the father of all the nations, constructively makes Israel, the youngest nation, his firstborn. For the Bible portrays Israel as a latecomer, a nation that emerges on the scene after the other nations in the midst of whom the patriarchs wander. Israel is, as it were, the beloved child of God's old age.

Insofar as the exodus narrative constructs Israel as God's son, it is not surprising that it dwells on Israel's birth. Birth is indeed the major preoccupation of the first two chapters of Exodus. In chapter 1, Jacob's descendants multiply inexorably, and the pharaoh's oppressive policies only fuel their birth rate. The next chapter turns to the birth of a particular Israelite, Moses. As Ilana Pardes has noted, Moses's infancy narrative anticipates a second expression of Israel's birth. Moses is pulled from the water, and likewise Israel, with the parting of the Red Sea, will come through the water into safety. In light of the fact that one of the dominant metaphors for the womb in the ancient Near East is the sea, we should take Israel's passage through the Red Sea as, among other things, a metaphorical birth.

Another womb image, also noted by Pardes, occurs in the context of the plague of the firstborn. In this plague, the last of the ten that the Egyptians must endure, God lets loose a destructive angel at midnight to go throughout Egypt to kill its firstborn sons. In advance of the plague, God commands the Israelites to smear their doorposts and lintels with the blood of a sacrifice called the *pesah* (in English: Pesach or Passover), and reassures them that, seeing the blood there, he will protect the entrance and not allow the destroyer to enter. Here, in a house whose entrance, like that of the womb at birth, is bathed in blood, another moment of birth occurs: the Egyptian firstborn will die, and Israel will emerge as God's firstborn.

Birth constitutes the beginning of time for the newborn, and for Israel, too, the exodus becomes a temporal point of origin:

> The LORD said to Moses and Aaron in the land of Egypt: This month shall mark for you the beginning of the months; it shall be the first of the months of the year for you. (Exodus 12:1–2)

The month in which the exodus occurs—Nisan, according to the naming system that the Jews would acquire from Babylonia, and which Judaism maintains even today—becomes the first month of Israel's year, because it marks its beginning. As this month represents the beginning of the spring (13:4), its status as marker of the new year is wholly explicable in natural terms: it is the moment of rebirth, the moment at which the earth wakes from its winter slumber. But the Bible resists this universalist account of the Nisan new year and links it instead to the particular, not to the eternal cycle of natural rebirth but to a singular, historical moment of national birth. The time that Israel keeps is its own.

The same turn is evident in the festival sequence that celebrates the exodus. God instructs Moses that the exodus event is to be marked annually by a lamb sacrifice (the Passover) and by a seven-day grain celebration (the Feast of Unleavened Bread). The pastoral and agricultural roots of these festivals, in the springtime birthing of lambs and in the sprouting of the new grain crop, are patent. The exodus story integrates the natural elements into an historical narrative and thus transforms the festival sequence from a celebration of nature into a celebration of history.

The exodus must thus be read from (at least) three perspectives. First, it marks the beginning of Israel's history as a nation. Recalling his promises to Abraham, Isaac, and Jacob, God adopts their descendants as his firstborn and bestows upon them knowledge of his name. Second, the exodus is a concretization of the book of Proverbs. The victimized calls out to the God of justice to save him from the hand of his oppressor, and God heeds this call. Third, the exodus coordinates the relationship between the particular and the universal: the Israelites, living on their land, must recollect their experience as strangers in Egypt and act protectively toward the strangers in their midst.

Moses

Let us conclude this chapter by reflecting briefly on the main character in the exodus narrative and indeed in the remainder of the Pentateuch. As the subject of the birth narrative of Exodus 2, threatened by the Egyptians but ultimately pulled through and from the water to safety, Moses stands for Israel. But he is also, as Israel's savior, a stand-in for God. And just as God acts both as the God of justice and as the God of Abraham, Isaac, and Jacob, so Moses, in the same chapter, is moved by considerations universal and particular.

After being raised in Pharaoh's palace, Moses one day "went out to his kinsfolk" (Exodus 2:11). He immediately becomes witness to their suffering, in the form of an Israelite whom an Egyptian, presumably a taskmaster, is beating. Moses kills the Egyptian and conceals the body, in an act that both foreshadows his role as Israelite leader and represents a symbolic burial of the Egyptian element of his identity. This confrontation is starkly defined by the dynamic of identification. Moses does not simply intervene on behalf of a victim; he allies himself with a particular group.

When Pharaoh learns of Moses's crime and seeks to kill him, Moses flees to Midian and rests by the well. There he once again confronts a scene of oppression and saves the oppressed.

> Now the priest of Midian had seven daughters. They came to draw water, . . . but shepherds came and drove them off, and Moses rose and saved them. (2:16–17)

This second confrontation replicates the first but is stripped entirely of considerations of identity. The oppressors and the oppressed are alike Midianites, strangers to Moses. Moses does not even appear as an Israelite; the daughters of the Midianite priest tell their father that "an Egyptian rescued us from the shepherds" (Exodus 2:19). In this second confrontation, then, a universalist dimension of Moses's motivation comes to the fore: he intervenes not only as an Israelite, and on behalf of the oppressed Israelite, but as a man, on behalf of the oppressed per se.

For Further Reflection

1. The plagues that God visits upon the Egyptians are typically characterized as signs of God's might. In some cases—see in particular Exodus 15:26 and Deuteronomy 7:15—they are characterized as illnesses and situated in a medical framework. What if anything is the relationship between these two apparently different ways of thinking about the plagues?

2. We noted that Jethro's daughters identify Moses as an Egyptian. In what other ways does Moses come across as an Egyptian? What is the significance of Moses's Egyptian aspects in the narrative? Sigmund Freud famously reflected on this question in his book *Moses and Monotheism*. For a more recent treatment that takes its bearings in part from Freud, see Jan Assmann, *Moses the Egyptian*.

Bibliography

Assmann, Jan. *Moses the Egyptian: The Memory of Egypt in Western Monotheism*. Cambridge: Harvard University Press, 1998.

Collins, John J. "The Development of the Exodus Tradition." Pages 144–55 in *Religious Identity and the Invention of Tradition.* Edited by Jan Willem van Henten and Anton Houtepen. Assen: Van Gorcum, 2001.

Freud, Sigmund. *Moses and Monotheism.* Translated by Katherine Jones. New York: Vintage Books, 1967.

Langston, Scott M. *Exodus through the Centuries.* Malden: Blackwell, 2006.

Pardes, Ilana. *The Biography of Ancient Israel: National Narratives in the Bible.* Berkeley: University of California Press, 2000.

Toorn, Karel van der. "The Exodus as Charter Myth." Pages 113–27 in *Religious Identity and the Invention of Tradition.* Edited by Jan Willem van Henten and Anton Houtepen. Assen: Van Gorcum, 2001.

Walzer, Michael. *Exodus and Revolution.* New York: Basic Books, 1985.

6 | Sinai: Covenant and Code

READINGS

Exodus 19–24

Laws of Hammurabi (see the translation of Martha Roth, "The Laws of Hammurabi," *COS* 2:335–53)

Deuteronomy 1:1–3; 4; 6

Introduction

Some three months after the exodus from Egypt, the Israelites arrive at the Sinai desert and encamp at Mount Sinai (Exodus 19:1–2). At Sinai, God appears to the people and enters into an agreement or covenant with them. Most of the terms of the covenant are detailed in two passages. First comes a series of injunctions in Exodus 20 that God afterward inscribes on tablets given to Moses. Deuteronomy 10:4 calls these the "ten utterances," and we know them as the Ten Commandments or the Decalogue. After a brief narrative interruption, Exodus 21:1 introduces a series of laws that run through 23:33. This second unit is known in biblical scholarship as the Covenant Code.

Why does God appear to Israel at Mount Sinai specifically? The Exodus passage offers no explanation; the mountain simply looks like a convenient stopping point in the trek through the wilderness from Egypt to Canaan. But various biblical texts suggest that the link between God and Sinai is more significant. In Deuteronomy 33:2, for example, a poem attributed to Moses speaks of God coming *from* Sinai. Underlying this text and others is the conception of Sinai as the ancient mountain home of Israel's God, Y-H-W-H. He resides upon Mount Sinai just as, for example, Zeus makes his home on Mount Olympus. In the course of time, Israel's God came to be associated with a different mountain home, in the land of Israel: Mount Zion, according to the canonical biblical narrative. The narrative in Exodus 19–24 preserves an echo of the earlier tradition.

Sinai and Law

The Sinai event is many things: a theophany, or manifestation of the Divine; a covenant, or agreement; and a legislative moment, a moment of law-giving. The latter aspect becomes ever more important in the Second Temple period, and afterward in both Judaism and Christianity; and we can enter into our interpretation of the Sinai event by reflecting, in very general terms, on the nature of law at Sinai and in the Bible more generally.

A legal scholar well known for his contributions to the study of law and narrative, Robert Cover, wrote an essay on this topic entitled "Obligation: A Jewish Jurisprudence of the Social Order." In this essay, Cover reflects on two different ways of giving legal expression to a social order: through a discourse of rights, and through a discourse of obligations. At first glance, rights and obligations look like mirror images. One can say that individuals have a right to private property, and one can express more or less the same thing by saying that individuals are obligated to behave in such a way as not to infringe on others' property. In fact, however, rights and obligations undergird two very different conceptions of society. Modern Western society is rights-centered; in this connection we might think of its flagship document as the Bill of Rights. By contrast, Sinai, on Cover's view, portrays a society that is defined by obligations; its watchword is the Ten Commandments.

How does a discourse of rights differ from a discourse of obligation? Most simply, a right requires only one person, whereas an obligation is always an obligation to another and hence requires two persons. In other words, rights are individual, while obligations are social. It is of course possible to have a society structured by rights. As Cover explains, a society so structured is one that imagines itself as having emerged from a state of nature, or in any case as defined in contrast with a state of nature. In this state, each individual is for herself; she has the right to do anything. But this natural condition is violent and uncertain. And so individuals congregate into a group by means of a social contract in which, for the sake of preventing harm to themselves, they cede their right to cause harm to others. The society thus formed is "thin" in that participation in the society is not a source of meaning or self-definition. Indeed, in such a society, there is hardly such a thing as participating at all; one participates only by not infringing upon the other. Each individual finds meaning for herself.

In a framework defined by obligation, by contrast, society is itself a natural category, rooted in the biological framework of family. Such a society is "thick," a source of meaning and self-definition. Each member of the society—and here it is indeed fitting to speak of members rather than simply individuals—grows into a role that is defined by obligations toward other members of the society. As Cover observes, the difference between this society and the rights-based society emerges clearly in relation to the nature of adulthood. Within the framework of obligation, to become an adult is to become fully responsible toward others. Within the framework of a social contract, an adult is rather someone who is fully capable of exercising her rights.

For Cover, these frameworks are complementary. On the one hand, obligation rhetoric is much better at supporting entitlements like education. The notion that one is obligated to educate one's children, or by extension, that a society is obligated to educate its young, is clear and almost self-executing: it demands that the parent teach the child, or that parent and society pay for the child's education. The notion of a right to education, however, is inert. While intelligible in the abstract, it means nothing in practice unless one can specify who will make good on that right. A relatively recent attempt to tackle the problem of education in the United States went under the banner of "No Child Left Behind." This banner has a military resonance; it imagines children as threatened soldiers whom we cannot leave behind in the field. "No Child Left Behind" thus taps into a nexus of obligation available even in the rights-centered West, namely, the army, whose members are defined first and foremost by their duties or obligations.

On the other hand, a rights framework does certain things that a framework of obligations cannot easily do. A society structured by obligation tends to fix individuals within rigid status categories. It might, for example, claim that a woman's duty is to her family, and so abridge a married woman's property or voting rights. Obligation cements a thick society with a sense of purpose; but taken too far, cemented too thickly, such a society can be stifling and allow no room for freedom. The ideal society is therefore one that produces a coherent or at least stable synthesis of obligations and rights.

When Cover looks to Sinai as a metonym for obligation, he is only in a loose sense commenting on the biblical texts that we will examine below. Indeed, as we will see, contractual and egalitarian elements in the Sinai event anticipate precisely the rights-based framework of the modern West. It is true that the texts associated with Sinai, especially as received in Judaism, assume a thick society bound together by the bonds of obligation; but in this respect they are hardly different from any generically comparable ancient text. All premodern societies are thick. The notion that Sinai is about obligation, that it implicitly critiques the social contract, emerges precisely because social and political changes, especially from the eighteenth century to today, make this aspect of the Sinai story stand out.

Recollect our introductory discussion of Philip Larkin's poem, "An Arundel Tomb." According to the poet, the rise of modern conceptions of romantic love that were largely unknown to the medieval sculptor of the tomb encourages the crowds now visiting it to fixate on the hand-holding depicted on the tomb, even though this gesture was hardly important for the sculptor himself. The passage of time changes how we perceive objects—and how we perceive texts. In a somewhat similar way, the Bible can play the role of cultural critic in the modern world not (or not only) in virtue of the distinctive claims that it makes vis-à-vis the ancient world in which it emerged, but precisely in virtue of the features that it shares with that world.

Law Code and Suzerainty Treaty

We now turn to consider the biblical passages on the Sinai event directly, beginning with the Covenant Code (Exodus 21:1–23:33). The code covers a range of topics in civil and criminal law. It closely parallels and indeed was inspired by similar codes from the ancient Near East, especially the Laws of Hammurabi. Hammurabi, a ruler of Babylon in the eighteenth century BCE, produced a singularly comprehensive code of laws whose popularity is proven by the large number of copies discovered by archaeologists. Fragments of a law code much like Hammurabi's were discovered in 2010 at the site of ancient Hazor in Israel.

We will turn below to some important differences between the Laws of Hammurabi and the Covenant Code, but for now it is important to clarify their fundamental similarity. The following pair of passages illustrates their closeness.

> When a man gives to another an ass, an ox, a sheep, or any other animal to guard, and it dies or is injured or is carried off, with no witness about, an oath before the LORD shall decide between the two of them that the one has not laid hands on the property of the other; the owner must acquiesce, and no restitution shall be made. (Exodus 22:10–11 NRSV, slightly altered)

> If a man rents an ox, and a god strikes it down dead, the man who rented the ox shall swear an oath by the god and he shall be released. (Laws of Hammurabi §249)

In addition to their substantive similarities, these two laws share the same form: first a condition, introduced by "when" or "if," then a consequence. Almost all the laws in both corpora take this conditional form. Many other similarities in substance, form, and sequence, coupled with the great age of the Laws of Hammurabi relative to the Covenant Code, establish that the Covenant Code depends on the Laws of Hammurabi or on another set of laws related to it.

The Laws of Hammurabi, and the Covenant Code following it, inscribe a vision of the just society. Hammurabi indicates at the outset of the prologue that he was called by the gods to his legislative task:

> For the enhancement of the well-being of the people, . . . to make justice prevail in the land, to abolish the wicked and the evil, to prevent the strong from oppressing the weak, to rise like the sun-god Shamash over all humankind, to illuminate the land. (I.27–49)

Hammurabi returns to these themes at the end of the prologue, when he indicates that through the laws that follow, he has "established truth and justice as the declaration of the land," and "enhanced the well-being of the people."

These law codes are, in their essence, universalist. In the preceding chapter we noted that the Covenant Code has subtle traces of the influence of the exodus narrative; but the content of the Covenant Code depends, in the main, not on this narrative but on the Laws of Hammurabi and on the ancient Near Eastern conceptions of justice and law that they reflect. The conditional form—the "if . . . then" sequence—that defines these codes shares with the epigrams of the book of Proverbs a distance from the tone of imperatives or commands. The laws of the Covenant Code, like Proverbs' verses, present themselves as the right responses to the complexities of life in the world.

The Decalogue that precedes the Covenant Code is very different. It is composed exclusively of commands: "You shall not swear falsely by the name of the Lord your God" (Exodus 20:7); "you shall not steal" (20:13); and so on. Indeed, the Decalogue originates in an entirely different social and literary context from the Covenant Code. If the proper genre for the Covenant Code in the ancient Near East is the law code, like the Laws of Hammurabi, then the genre to which the Decalogue belongs is instead the suzerainty treaty.

The suzerainty treaty, a basic tool of ancient Near Eastern imperial politics, defines a relationship between the imperial lord, or suzerain, and the inferior vassal king. The treaty typically begins with a prologue that describes the suzerain's might and recounts the deeds already performed by the suzerain on behalf of the inferior king. This prologue justifies what follows, namely, a series of demands upon the vassal, first and most importantly the demand of exclusive loyalty: the vassal must serve this suzerain alone, and no others. This sequence is precisely instantiated in the beginning of the Decalogue: "I [Y-H-W-H] am your God who brought you out of the land of Egypt, the house of bondage: You shall have no other gods besides Me" (Exodus 20:2). Y-H-W-H is the suzerain, and the vassal in this case is not a king but a nation, Israel. The suzerain describes the benefit he bestowed upon the vassal by taking Israel from Egypt. Israel must therefore have no other god—must worship the god of no other nation—save Y-H-W-H.

In sharp contrast with the Covenant Code, the Decalogue is particularist in its very essence. It describes an historically conditioned relationship of loyalty between the people Israel and the God who acts on their behalf. Its purpose is to distinguish Israel from the other nations and their gods. In the book of Deuteronomy, set in the fortieth and final year of the wilderness sojourn, the suzerainty treaty model comes most prominently to the fore, and with it the repeated injunction to love God. (In this passage as throughout almost all of Deuteronomy, the speaker is Moses.)

> Hear, O Israel, the LORD is our God, the LORD alone. And you shall love the LORD your God with all your heart and with all your soul and with all your might. (Deuteronomy 6:4–5)

The love prescribed here and elsewhere in the book of Deuteronomy undoubtedly has an affective or emotional aspect to it, but it involves, first and foremost, exclusive loyalty.

What is perhaps most striking about the Sinai event, both as told in Exodus and as retold in Deuteronomy, is its synthesis of the particularist (in Exodus, the Decalogue) and the universal (in Exodus, the Covenant Code). Indeed, the Decalogue itself represents something of a synthesis, as it includes stipulations governing not only Israel's relationship with God (in the first half of the Decalogue) but also the Israelites' interpersonal relationships (in the second half). The synthesis is conditioned, in part, by the aforementioned observation that the vassal in this case is not a king but a nation. Because a nation includes many individuals, it is possible for the suzerainty treaty to specify not only the vassals' obligations toward the suzerain but also how the vassals ought to treat one another.

Two important and related consequences follow from the synthesis. First, in Proverbs, one acts justly for the sake of prudence, out of fear of a powerful God who punishes those who abuse the weak. The synthesis of the Covenant Code with the Decalogue means, however, that one can act justly also out of love of God. The God of the book of Proverbs is interested neither in love nor in loyalty; but after Sinai, the Israelite who cultivates wisdom is thereby pledging his loyalty, declaring his love, to God. Mundane acts of interpersonal ethics become expressions of personal love of God; and conversely, to steal from others, to abuse others, is not only imprudently to test the power of the divine judge but ungratefully to betray one's divine patron.

Second, the synthesis of the Decalogue and the Covenant Code sets in motion a conception of wisdom different from the one that prevails in Proverbs. In Proverbs, wisdom is our inheritance from the ancients, the accumulated deposit of human experience—it is not revealed. But if God's pact with Israel includes the laws, which are nothing other than expressions of wisdom, then wisdom must itself be, at least to some degree, esoteric, concealed. The laws become God's gift to Israel, a privileged path to attaining wisdom. A passage from Deuteronomy articulates this concept.

> See, I have imparted to you laws and rules.... Observe them faithfully, for that will be proof of your wisdom and discernment to other peoples, who on hearing of these laws will say, "Surely, that great nation is a wise and discerning people." (Deuteronomy 4:5–6)

The nations have wisdom enough to appreciate the supreme wisdom of God's laws, but not enough to have arrived at those laws themselves; God is the source for this special wisdom. (Compare Genesis 41:38–39, from the Joseph story.)

The Covenant Code and the Laws of Hammurabi

Despite the close dependence of the Covenant Code on works belonging to the genre instantiated by the Laws of Hammurabi, or even on the Laws of Hammurabi themselves, there are important differences between the two compositions. The first and most obvious concerns the promulgator of the laws. As noted above, the Laws of Hammurabi begin with a prologue written supposedly by Hammurabi, in the first person; and he presents himself as the legislator. The Covenant Code, by contrast, is attributed to God. The displacement by God of what would otherwise be a royal Israelite legislator in the Covenant Code corresponds with the displacement by the people Israel of an Israelite vassal king in the Decalogue. God (from one direction) and Israel (from the other direction) squeeze out monarchy, and leave no room for an Israelite king interposing between God and his people.

We will return to the problem of a king in the next chapter, but for now let us take note of other differences between the Covenant Code and the Laws of Hammurabi. In the two passages quoted below, the first on the goring ox and the second on the death of a fetus, the Covenant Code and the Laws of Hammurabi are so similar that the differences emerge particularly clearly.

Exodus 21:28–32 NRSV, slightly altered	Laws of Hammurabi §§250–252
[28] When an ox gores a man or a woman to death, the ox shall be stoned and its flesh shall not be eaten, but the owner of the ox is not to be punished.	[250] If an ox gores to death a man while it is passing through the streets, that case has no basis for a claim.
[29] If, however, that ox has been in the habit of goring, and its owner, though warned, has failed to guard it, and it kills a man or a woman—the ox shall be stoned, and its owner, too, shall be put to death.	[251] If a man's ox is a known gorer, and the authorities of his city quarter notify him that it is a known gorer, but he does not blunt(?) its horns or control his ox, and that ox gores to death a man of the *awīlu*-class, he (the owner) shall give 30 shekels of silver.
[30] If ransom is laid upon him, he must pay whatever is laid upon him to redeem his life.	
[31] So, too, if it gores a son or a daughter, [the owner] shall be dealt with according to the same rule.	
[32] But if the ox gores a slave, male or female, he shall pay thirty shekels of silver to the master, and the ox shall be stoned.	[252] If it is a man's slave (who is fatally gored), he [the ox's owner] shall give 20 shekels of silver.

Exodus 21:22–25 (slightly altered)	Laws of Hammurabi §§209–210
[22] When men fight, and one of them pushes a pregnant woman and her fetus comes out, but there is no calamity, the one responsible shall be fined according as the woman's husband may exact from him, the payment to be based on reckoning.	[209] If an *awīlu* strikes a woman of the *awīlu*-class [literally "the daughter of an *awīlu*"] and thereby causes her to miscarry her fetus, he shall weigh and deliver 10 shekels of silver for her fetus.
[23] If there is a calamity, you shall pay life for life, [24] eye for eye, tooth for tooth, arm for arm, leg for leg, [25] burn for burn, wound for wound, bruise for bruise.	[210] If that woman should die, they shall kill his daughter.

One of the important differences between the two sets of rules is that the Laws of Hammurabi recognize a distinction among social classes: the Laws of Hammurabi legislate mainly for the *awīlu* or landowning class. The Covenant Code does not recognize any class distinction other than that between free and slave.

A related but subtler difference arises from close consideration of Exodus 21:31. According to this verse, if a man's son or daughter is gored by a habitual gorer, then the same law applies as in the case in which the man himself is the victim, that is, the ox is to be stoned and the owner either executed or ransomed. What is the purpose of such a statement? Would it have occurred to anyone that the consequence should be different just because the victim is an adult male's son or daughter rather than the adult male himself?

Clarification comes with the second set of laws, on the case of a man who causes a woman to miscarry. Here the Covenant Code distinguishes between a case in which there is a miscarriage but no "calamity," and a case in which there is also a calamity. The term *calamity* is ambiguous, but most likely it refers to the death of the woman herself. This interpretation is supported by the parallel in the Laws of Hammurabi, which likewise distinguishes between a case where the woman miscarries and a case where the woman dies.

In the first scenario, of miscarriage alone, both compositions demand monetary compensation alone. In the second scenario, according to the Covenant Code, the man must die. The Laws of Hammurabi rather surprisingly dictate that not the man himself should die but his daughter. With this decision, the Laws of Hammurabi recognize the family structure as determinative. The man who kills the woman has killed not a person so much as the daughter of an *awīlu*, and therefore it is not he who dies but his own daughter, in tit-for-tat fashion. The Covenant Code never makes family structure legally relevant in this way. The man who kills the woman is himself killed. Likewise, when Exodus 21:31 specifies that the law of the goring ox is no different when a son or daughter of a man is the victim rather than the man himself, it means to exclude the view—evidently familiar to the author of the Covenant Code—that when a man's son or daughter dies, the son or daughter of the ox's owner must die in the victim's place.

We have noted three major differences between the two codes: the Laws of Hammurabi give legal recognition to the king, to an upper class, and to the family structure. In short, they envision, as the reality within which they intervene, a whole series of articulated human relationships. In the Covenant Code, by contrast, with the important exception of the free/slave distinction, human society becomes flattened, as all are equally subordinate to God. Of course, this differences between the Laws of Hammurabi and the Covenant Code at least in part reflect the different social contexts in which they were composed. The Israelite society addressed by the Covenant Code was less complex, less ramified, than the Babylonian one underlying the Laws of Hammurabi. This does not, however, make the deviations of the Covenant Code from the Laws of Hammurabi any less momentous. For the Covenant Code transforms the relative egalitarianism of Israelite society from social fact to theological truth. The proximity of God should indeed render apparently important internal social differentiations irrelevant.

Conclusion

But for whom should society be flat? Which group is supposed to be without a king? The Covenant Code is part of God's covenant with Israel, and it is Israelite society specifically, in the first instance, that the Decalogue and the Covenant Code regulate. The biblical text portrays it as Israel's unique privilege to be subject directly to Y-H-W-H's rule. But in an intellectual context in which henotheism (the notion that there are many gods, and that Y-H-W-H is only one among them) is rapidly giving way to monotheism (the notion that there is only one god, in this case, Israel's), the flat society of the Covenant Code and (to a lesser extent) of the Decalogue naturally becomes a model for human society generally. But whatever the scope of this social model, the Bible generally portrays Israelite society as distinctive in its suspicion of kingship. In the next chapter we examine biblical texts that explicitly articulate and partly allay this suspicion.

For Further Reflection

1. The Ten Commandments rank among the most famous of biblical texts. What is the basis of this special status? Why do they loom so much larger in the history of the Bible's reception than the other legal passages in the Pentateuch? Consider the commandments in themselves. Do you count ten? How might one explain the selection and sequence of the commandments?

2. What if any are the implications of Exodus 21:22–25—the passage on accidental miscarriage quoted above—for abortion? In this connection, there is an important divergence between the Hebrew text of the Bible (which is determinative for Judaism) and the ancient Greek translation (which has played an especially important role in the history of Christianity). The Hebrew word *ason*, rendered above as "calamity," is translated in the Greek *exeikonismenon*, "having been fully formed."

Bibliography

Alt, Albrecht. "The Origins of Israelite Law." Pages 101–71 in *Essays on Old Testament History and Religion*. Translated by R. A. Wilson. Garden City, NY: Doubleday, 1967.
Berman, Joshua A. *Created Equal: How the Bible Broke with Ancient Political Thought*. New York: Oxford University Press, 2008.
Cover, Robert M. "Obligation: A Jewish Jurisprudence of the Social Order." *Journal of Law and Religion* 5 (1987): 65–74.
Greenberg, Moshe. "Some Postulates of Biblical Criminal Law." Pages 25–41 in *Studies in the Bible and Jewish Thought*. Philadelphia: Jewish Publication Society, 1995.
Horowitz, Wayne, Takayoshi Oshima, and Filip Vukosavoivić. "Hazor 18: Fragments of a Cuneiform Law Collection from Hazor." *Israel Exploration Journal* 62 (2012): 158–76.
Levenson, Jon D. *Sinai and Zion: An Entry into the Jewish Bible*. Minneapolis: Winston Press, 1985.
Roth, Martha. "The Laws of Hammurabi." *COS* 2:335–53.
Weeks, Noel. *Admonition and Curse: The Ancient Near Eastern Treaty/Covenant Form as a Problem in Inter-Cultural Relationships*. London: T&T Clark, 2004.
Wright, David P. *Inventing God's Law: How the Covenant Code of the Bible Used and Revised the Laws of Hammurabi*. New York: Oxford University Press, 2009.

7 | The Problem of Monarchy: Samuel and Kings

READINGS

1 Samuel 8–10; 16–17
2 Samuel 5–7; 11–12
1 Kings 16:29–21:29

Introduction

In the previous chapter we learned that at Sinai, God covenants with his people Israel and furnishes them with a law code. In comparing this law code—the Covenant Code—with the Laws of Hammurabi, we found that, relative to the latter, the former downplays status distinctions among people. The Covenant Code does not distinguish between elite and commoner, nor between the family patriarch and the members of his household. Most importantly, for our immediate purposes, there is no human king: the lawmaker is not a Hammurabi, but God. God alone is king, and in his presence status differences among humans become insignificant.

Likewise, we noted that the Sinai covenant itself, concretized in the Decalogue, is modeled on the suzerainty treaty, wherein the suzerain, the great king, makes a pact with a lesser king, his vassal. While God at Sinai easily fills the role of the great king, there is no vassal king at Sinai. It is the people Israel, directly, with whom God covenants. Thus the Sinai event, both as a covenant and through the Covenant Code, leaves no room for human kingship.

But Sinai is a utopia, in the literal sense of the word: a no-place, a wilderness that is neither here (Egypt) nor there (Canaan). When Israel enters and conquers the land of Canaan, monarchy arises almost inevitably, together with other social demarcations. In this chapter we consider how the Bible confronts the reality of monarchy. We will find that the Bible is suspicious of monarchy, both on universalist grounds and on particularist grounds, but that it is willing to endorse, even exalt, a king who humbles himself before God. It is from this foundation that the concept of the messiah, so central for Judaism and especially for Christianity, will emerge.

Kings and God

The books of Samuel and Kings (each conventionally divided in our Bibles into two parts, 1 and 2 Samuel, and 1 and 2 Kings) represent the last two books of a longer, continuous narrative that begins in Genesis with the creation of the world, and ends at the conclusion of Kings with the destruction of the Jerusalem temple by the Babylonians in 586 BCE and the simultaneous exile of many inhabitants of Judah. While this narrative is the product of many centuries and many hands, scholars have detected numerous links in thought and vocabulary between the last book of the Torah, Deuteronomy, and the subsequent books in this narrative, that is, Joshua (on the conquest of the land of Canaan), Judges (on the period of Israelite habitation before the rise of the monarchy), Samuel (on the emergence of the monarchy), and Kings (on the kings of Israel and Judah until the Babylonian exile). On the consequent assumption that a school of scribes connected with Deuteronomy was responsible for the editing of Joshua, Judges, Samuel, and Kings, these four books (or, including Deuteronomy, five) have been dubbed by some scholars the Deuteronomistic History. This chapter concerns Samuel and Kings; Joshua and Judges are the subject of chapter 13 below.

Samuel comes at the end of the line of "judges," the charismatic leaders who succeeded in occasionally and temporarily unifying this or that group of Israelite tribes in the face of a foreign enemy. Samuel is both a judge and a prophet. In his old age, the Israelites approach him to seek a king.

> All the elders of Israel assembled and came to Samuel at Ramah, and they said to him, "You have grown old, and your sons have not followed your ways. Therefore appoint a king for us, to govern us like all other nations." Samuel was displeased that they said "Give us a king to govern us." Samuel prayed to the LORD, and the LORD replied to Samuel, "Heed the demand of the people in everything they say to you. For it is not you that they have rejected; it is Me they have rejected as their king. Like everything else they have done ever since I brought them out of Egypt to this day—forsaking Me and worshiping other gods—so they are doing to you. Heed their demand; but warn them solemnly, and tell them about the practices of any king who will rule over them." (1 Samuel 8:4–9)

God characterizes the desire for a king as a rejection of God. In what sense is this so? First, and most obviously, to desire a human king is to wish for a less direct relationship with God, for it is the king and not God who will immediately rule over the people. Of course, even before the Israelites had kings, they were guided by leaders, such as Samuel. What distinguishes kingship from the ad hoc leadership system that preceded it is kingship's dynastic element. Because a king is succeeded automatically by his son, kingship limits God's ability to choose or confirm the Israelites' leaders, and so distances God from them.

But there is a second and subtler way in which the desire for a king represents a rejection of God, and it comes across in the final words of the Israelites' request: "to govern us like all other nations." To request a king is to seek to be like other nations and thus to reject the yoke of election. This concern is a matter not merely of principle but also of practice. A king is inevitably a cosmopolitan figure, an international player, one among many kings. Hence he will naturally enter into treaties and marriages with foreign monarchies and thus entangle Israel with the nations and with their gods. It is for this reason that God, in the above passage, compares the request for a king to past crimes involving "worshiping other gods."

We may think of the first aspect of rejection of God as vertical: the human king usurps God's position as leader over Israel. The second aspect of rejection is horizontal, directed at the gap that separates Israel from the other nations: the king narrows this gap and becomes a conduit through which the practices of those nations can be introduced into Israel. The vertical threat is universalist, in that it centers on the categories of human and divine (even if it is Israel's unique privilege, among humans, to be directly subject to God), while the horizontal threat, centered on the distinction between Israel and the nations, is particularist.

Corresponding to these two theological problems with the institution of kingship are two paradigmatic royal crimes. The second problem—the refusal of Israelite election—finds its expression in idolatry. We will note below some instances in which the royal court becomes a center of foreign worship. Corresponding to the first problem—the displacement of God by the king—is the sin of oppression. The king, imagining himself as godlike, lords it over the people. In the continuation of the above passage, Samuel tells the Israelites that the king whom they wish for will conscript their sons and daughters into his service.

> He will take a tenth part of your grain and vintage and give it to his eunuchs and courtiers. . . . He will take a tenth part of your flocks, and you

> shall become his slaves. The day will come when you cry out because of the king whom you yourselves have chosen. (1 Samuel 8:15, 17–18)

According to biblical law (e.g., Leviticus 27:30, 32), the tithe of grain, grapes, and flocks belongs by right to God. But according to Samuel's warning, the king will usurp them.

The critique of kingship in the Bible can thus be analyzed into universalist and particularist dimensions. The universalist critique, a critique not specific to Israelite kingship, is bound up with the elevated stature of the king. He is godlike and so can easily come to displace God and to set himself above the people as a tyrant. The Bible levels the same critique against other non-Israelite kings, for example, the king of Tyre, whom Ezekiel condemns for saying, "I am a god; I sit enthroned like a god" (Ezekiel 28:2). The particularist critique, by contrast, is specific to Israelite kingship and follows from Israel's election. Because Israel is duty-bound to worship God alone, it should stand apart from other peoples and from their gods. An Israelite king, however, will inevitably make alliances that entwine Israel with other peoples and thus with their gods.

The Rise of David

Despite his reservations, God accedes to the people's request, and instructs Samuel to appoint Saul, of the tribe of Benjamin, as king. Saul is possessed of one distinctive physical feature: "he was a head taller than any of the people" (1 Samuel 9:2). Height is a physical representation of the king's elevated status and thus intrinsically kingly; ancient Near Eastern art typically depicts kings towering over their attendants. But what is quite common among other nations is, for the Bible, quite inappropriate in the Israelite context, insofar as the king exalts himself over the people and interposes between them and God. Indeed, Saul is a failure as a king, and through his failure, the Bible conveys a lesson about Israelite monarchy: if it is to succeed, it must violate convention to make room for God.

God confirms this lesson when he instructs Samuel in the selection of Saul's successor. Samuel is directed to the family of Jesse, from Bethlehem, of the tribe of Judah, to anoint one of his sons—secretly, because Saul remains on the throne—as Israel's future king. When Samuel sees Eliab, evidently Jesse's eldest, some unidentified aspect of his appearance impresses Samuel, and he thinks: "Surely the LORD's anointed stands before Him" (16:6). That it is Eliab's height that impressed Samuel becomes clear from God's response: "Pay no attention to his appearance or his stature, for I have rejected him. For not as man sees [does the LORD see]; man sees only what is visible, but the LORD sees into the heart" (16:7). Samuel ends up anointing Jesse's seventh and last son, David, in another instance of the election of the younger.

While the Bible never suggests that David is particularly short, his height is unremarkable; and the Bible highlights this fact in the very next chapter, through the famous story of David and Goliath (1 Samuel 17). The Israelites are warring with the Philistines, a non-Semitic people that dwelled in and around modern-day Gaza. A Philistine giant, Goliath, armed with a bronze helmet, a breastplate, and a spear (17:4–7), emerges from the Philistine ranks to challenge the Israelites to produce a hero willing to fight Goliath man-to-man. David volunteers for the task. Since, as a shepherd, he lacks armor, Saul offers him his own: a bronze helmet, a breastplate, and a sword (17:8–9). Both through their height and through their armor, the Bible establishes a relationship between Goliath and Saul. David will reject both. Finding that he cannot move well in Saul's war gear, David doffs it and confronts Goliath with his stick, his sling, and some stones—but also with God: "I come against you in the name of the LORD of Hosts, the God of the ranks of Israel" (17:45). David kills Goliath and cuts off his head (17:51). On Saul's shoulders, the head is a marker of superlative height. What David symbolically slays is a certain kingly ideal, embodied both by Saul and Goliath, according to which the king exalts himself above his people. David is short enough—self-effacing enough—to make room for God.

Saul immediately and correctly perceives David as a rival, whom he attempts alternately to absorb, by giving him the hand of his daughter Michal, and to overcome. After a long series of struggles with the house of Saul, David finally emerges as king over all Israel. He later conquers Jerusalem, which had been inhabited by a Canaanite tribe, the Jebusites, then orchestrates a ritual procession by which the ark of the covenant is conveyed to the city.

> When the bearers of the Ark of the LORD had moved forward six paces, he sacrificed an ox and a fatling. David whirled with all his might before the LORD. . . . Thus David and all the House of Israel brought up the Ark of the LORD with shouts and with blasts of the horn.
>
> As the Ark of the LORD entered the City of David, Michal daughter of Saul looked out of the window and saw King David leaping and whirling before the LORD, and she despised him for it. (2 Samuel 6:13–16)

When David returns to his house, Michal offers a biting and sarcastic critique:

> Didn't the king of Israel do himself honor today—exposing himself today in the sight of the slavegirls of his subjects, as one of the riffraff might expose himself! (6:20)

Michal, looking on the procession from above, from a height, represents the Saulide position, and it is no coincidence that the Bible identifies her in this incident not as David's wife but as Saul's daughter. For Michal, the king must be set apart from the people. But David, the slayer of the giant Goliath, the displacer of the tall Saul, thinks otherwise.

> David answered Michal, "It was before the LORD who chose me instead of your father and all his family and appointed me ruler over the LORD's people Israel! I will dance before the LORD and dishonor myself even more, and be low in my own esteem; but among the slavegirls that you speak of I will be honored." (6:21–22)

David appreciates the two flaws in the Saulide position of kingly elevation over Israel. First, such elevation is incompatible with the king's obligation to humble himself before God. Second, the people above whom Michal would station the king is no ordinary people but the Lord's, and thus themselves exalted. The brief and devastating conclusion of this episode affirms the correctness of David's position: "So to her dying day Michal daughter of Saul had no children" (6:23). Since dynasty is constitutive of kingship, Michal's infertility is an expression of God's rejection of her father as king.

The rise of David culminates in a covenant. The immediate impetus is David's desire to build a temple for God.

> When the king was settled in his palace and the LORD had granted him safety from all the enemies around him, the king said to the prophet Nathan: "Here I am dwelling in a house of cedar, while the Ark of the LORD abides in a tent!" (7:1–2)

God endorses David's desire, but with a caveat: not David, but David's son, will build God's house. Thus Nathan reports:

> The LORD declares to you that He, the LORD will establish a house for you. When your days are done and you lie with your fathers, I will raise up your offspring after you, one of your own issue, and I will establish his kingship. He shall build a house for My name, and I will establish

> his royal throne forever. . . . I will never withdraw My favor from him as I withdrew it from Saul. . . . Your house and your kingship shall ever be secure before you; your throne shall be established forever. (7:11–16)

Why is it that God permits only David's son, and not David himself, to build the temple? The passage does not answer this question explicitly, but it seems implicitly to insist on a link between God's house and David's "house," that is, his dynasty. Only with the establishment of David's dynastic house, through succession, can God's house be built. The connection forged, through the figure of the house, between the royal line and the temple is another way in which the Bible conveys that the successful Israelite king must make room for God.

The Fall of David

Even David is not immune to the temptations of kingship, and not long after God declares his eternal fidelity to David's line, David sins (2 Samuel 11). David's general, Joab, is off besieging Rabbah of the Ammonites, but David remains in his palace. Strolling on his roof one late afternoon—thus from a position of height, from which no good can come—he spies Bathsheba, the wife of Uriah, one of his soldiers, bathing. He sends for her and sleeps with her. Soon afterward, she informs David that she is pregnant. David then calls for Uriah to return from the war camp, ostensibly so that David can have a report about the progress of the siege, but really so that Uriah can sleep with his wife and thus allow Bathsheba to attribute the child's paternity to her husband and avoid scandal.

After reporting on the siege, however, Uriah upsets David's plan by refusing to return to his home. "The Ark and Israel and Judah are located at Succoth [or: in booths; the word is the same], and my master Joab and Your Majesty's men are camped in the open; how can I go home and drink and sleep with my wife? As you live, by your very life, I will not do this!" (11:11). Uriah's objection closely parallels David's own expression of discomfort about living in a house of cedar while God resides in a tent (7:2). The ironic echo highlights the extent to which David, in rising to the roof, has fallen far from the kingly ideal. He has become the oppressive king of whom Samuel warned from the first.

With plan A foiled, David hatches a nefarious plan B. He dispatches Uriah back to Rabbah bearing his own death warrant, in the form of instructions to Joab to station Uriah in the front lines and draw his men back in the midst of battle so as to leave Uriah utterly exposed to enemy fire. Sure enough, Uriah falls in battle, and David marries Bathsheba, who soon afterward bears a son.

God's condemnation comes in the next chapter (2 Samuel 12), through the mouth of the prophet Nathan. Nathan comes to David with the story of two fellow citizens, a rich man and a poor man. The rich man owned large flocks, and the poor man had only a single ewe, whom he treated like a daughter. One day, the rich man entertained a traveler; but, unwilling to take from his own flocks, he seized and slaughtered the poor man's ewe. David angrily condemns the rich man, only to be told that he is none other than that man, for God gave him possession of Saul's house and wives, yet David insisted on taking Uriah's wife and having him "killed by the sword of the Ammonites" (12:9). David repents and wins partial forgiveness: he will go unharmed, but his son, the product of the adulterous union, will die. While we noted in the previous chapter that biblical law leaves no room for the punishment of a child for its parent's crime, this law has in mind only the operation of a human court and does not limit the prerogative of God, acting on his own initiative, to punish children for the sins of their parents.

King and Prophet

Reflecting on the texts that we have examined, we may identify three ways in which the Bible sets a divine limit to kingly power. First, the king must be humble or, metaphorically, short. Second, the Bible coordinates the dynasty with the temple: the king's house is bound up with God's house. Third, and perhaps most importantly, the king is confronted by God's messenger, the prophet. As Nathan rebukes David for his crimes, so other kings, and other members of the royal household, face prophetic rebukes. If the king threatens to arrogate to himself godlike power, or to bind Israel too closely to other nations, then the prophet works to remind the king of his mortality and of Israel's unique bond with God. The prophet speaks truth to power. This is not the prophet's only function, but it is one that the Deuteronomistic History highlights. As we move forward into the book of Kings, we will focus on confrontations between king and prophet.

Upon David's death, his son Solomon emerges as his successor. As we noted in our discussion of Proverbs (chapter 2), Solomon is a truly international figure. Not surprisingly, he is also the first Israelite king said to worship foreign gods, for, having married into other royal households, he comes inevitably to support his wives' cultic practices.

> Solomon built a shrine for Chemosh the abomination of Moab on the hill near Jerusalem, and one for Molech the abomination of the Am-

> monites. And he did the same for all his foreign wives who offered and sacrificed to their gods. (1 Kings 11:7–8)

After Solomon dies, the kingdom splits. The Davidic dynasty continues to rule in the southern kingdom of Judah, while other dynasties arise in the northern kingdom of Israel. We rejoin the narrative in the northern kingdom of Israel, in the first part of the ninth century BCE, under the reign of Ahab. Ahab is implicated in both of the characteristic crimes of kings, oppression and foreign worship. In both cases, Ahab's wife, Jezebel, the daughter of the king of Sidon, a city-state in what is now Lebanon, plays a major role; and in both cases, it is a prophet who opposes the royal couple.

As a worshiper of Baal, Jezebel, like Solomon's wives, brings her cultic practices with her to Israel. At least in part through her influence, Baal worship becomes more popular in the northern kingdom. But we should not think of Baal worship, and more generally the foreign cults condemned by the Bible, as entirely foreign imports. It is important to keep in mind that, from an historical perspective, the notion that Y-H-W-H is the only God (monotheism), and even the notion that the people of Israel ought to worship Y-H-W-H alone (monolatry), are ideas with a history, the results of theological reflection and sociocultural changes, and not least, as we shall see momentarily, of troublingly violent repression.

The prophet who rebukes the king and the queen and the Baal worshipers, the prophet who defends exclusive worship of Y-H-W-H, is Elijah, a miracle worker and healer from Gilead, in modern-day Jordan, then the home of the Transjordanian Israelite tribes. Elijah engineers a showdown on Mount Carmel, around modern-day Haifa, with four hundred and fifty prophets of Baal "who eat at Jezebel's table" (1 Kings 18:19). Both they and he pray to their respective divine patrons to consume a sacrifice. Elijah is a hard man, a harsh man, and as he attacks the people of Israel for swerving from the Lord, so, in his prayer, he appears to attack the Lord himself: "Answer me, O LORD, answer me, that this people may know that You, O LORD, are God; for You have turned their hearts backward" (18:37). God indeed answers, with fire from heaven that consumes the sacrifice. The people, spurred by Elijah, kill all the prophets of Baal.

The second major confrontation between prophet and king revolves around the other paradigmatic royal sin, oppression, and reads like an almost slavish sequel to the Bathsheba episode. At its center is Naboth, who, like Uriah, resides, to his eventual misfortune, near the king's palace. Like Nathan's rich man, Ahab, though possessed of many vineyards, wants to own Naboth's vineyard as well. He offers to purchase it; but Naboth, like Uriah, refuses the king's bid on pious grounds and with an emphatic oath: "The LORD forbid that I should give up to you what I have inherited from my fathers!" (21:3).

The king returns to his palace to sulk, and Jezebel, finding him thus, calls him out: "Now is the time to show yourself king over Israel. Rise and eat something, and be cheerful; I will get the vineyard of Naboth the Jezreelite for you" (21:7). According to the view implicit in these words—which the Bible clearly discredits by associating it with the foreign queen Jezebel—to be a king is to take what one wishes. While far from a positive character, Ahab is nevertheless Israelite and hence, as the Bible would have it, more constrained by conscience: he wishes to be a king in the foreign sense, but does not quite have the resolve to pull it off. So Jezebel does his dirty work for him. As David schemes to bring about Uriah's death, so Jezebel arranges Naboth's, on false charges of blasphemy and treason; and because he dies an enemy of the state, his vineyard becomes forfeit to the king. Elijah, following in Nathan's footsteps, rebukes Ahab and forecasts his utter destruction. Like David, Ahab confesses his guilt and thus wins forgiveness for himself, but not for his offspring.

Conclusion

The Bible flags the institution of monarchy as dangerous on both universalist grounds, that is, because the king displaces God, and on particularist grounds, insofar as the king narrows the gap that ought to separate Israel from the other nations. While the prophet serves as a check against these dangers, ultimately it rests upon the king himself to make monarchy work by humbling himself before God and maintaining a distance from foreign kings. David of Bethlehem, of the tribe of Judah, accomplishes this feat; and while far from perfect, he wins God's eternal love. Indeed, as we noted in discussing the exodus (chapter 5 above), if Israel is God's son, then the Davidic king enjoys the same status: "I will be a father to him, and he shall be a son to Me" (2 Samuel 7:14); "You are My son, I have fathered you this day" (Psalm 2:7).

The exaltation of the Davidic king has no little role to play in the history of Judaism and Christianity. We will turn later (see chapter 11) to the rise of messianism in the Second Temple period, but for now we may note that the word *messiah* is the anglicized form of Hebrew *mashiakh*, which means "one who is anointed" and which refers, in the first instance, to the king, whom the priest invests in his role by anointing him with oil. When we speak of the messiah, we speak of the Davidic king. The word *christ*, in turn, is nothing other than the Greek translation of Hebrew *mashiakh*. Roughly a millennium after David, when followers of Jesus came to think of him as Christ, they were taking him to be the rightful heir of David and thus the son of God. Judaism does not recognize Jesus as Christ, but continues to look forward to a *christ*, a Davidic king, to the point that the renewal of the moon each month is taken as a sign, according to the Talmud, that "David, king of Israel, lives and endures."

For Further Reflection

1. While mention of Saul's height almost inevitably condemns him, the specific transgression that leads to his downfall seems, on the contrary, to stem from his meekness. Reread 1 Samuel 9:21 and 10:22–23, and read 1 Samuel 15. How are we to make sense of this? Compare Saul's meekness and David's expressions of lowliness. Are they meaningfully different?

2. Read 1 Kings 14:21–28 and 16:1–14. How does God act in these passages (which are typical of the book of Kings)? Compare the ways in which God acts in these passages—his presence in the world—with our analysis of the ways in which he acts in the Joseph story.

Bibliography

Halpern, Baruch. *David's Secret Demons: Messiah, Murderer, Traitor, King.* Grand Rapids: Eerdmans, 2001.

Jacobs, Mignon R., and Raymond F. Person Jr., eds. *Israelite Prophecy and the Deuteronomistic History: Portrait, Reality, and the Formation of a History.* Atlanta: Society of Biblical Literature, 2013.

Noth, Martin. *The Deuteronomistic History.* Translated by J. Doull. 2nd ed. Sheffield: JSOT Press, 1991.

Wright, Jacob L. *David, King of Israel, and Caleb in Biblical Memory.* New York: Cambridge University Press, 2014.

8 | Condemning Israel, Sparing the Nations: Amos and Jonah

READINGS
Amos
Jonah

Introduction

In the preceding chapter we examined two confrontations between a prophet and a king, one set in the reign of David, from the beginning of the monarchic period, and another featuring Ahab, leader of the northern kingdom of Israel in the ninth century BCE. From roughly one century later, during the reign of Jeroboam II of Israel, we read of another confrontation, in this case between a prophet, Amos, and the king's priest, Amaziah.

> Amaziah, the priest of Bethel, sent this message to King Jeroboam of Israel: "Amos is conspiring against you within the House of Israel. The land cannot endure all his words. For Amos has said, 'Jeroboam shall die by the sword, and Israel shall be exiled from its soil.'" (Amos 7:10–11, slightly altered)

The immediate continuation furnishes a narrative that seems intended to clarify the circumstances that led to Amaziah's missive.

> Amaziah said to Amos: "Seer, off with you to the land of Judah! There eat bread, and there do your prophesying. But don't ever prophesy again in Bethel; for it is a king's sanctuary and a royal place." And Amos answered and said to Amaziah: "I am not a prophet nor am I a prophet's disciple. I am a cattle breeder and a tender of sycamore figs. But the LORD took me

> away from following the flock, and the LORD said to me: Go, prophesy to my people Israel. And so, hear the word of the LORD: You say, 'Do not prophesy about Israel, and do not preach about the House of Isaac.' Hence, thus says the LORD: 'Your wife shall play the harlot in the town, and your sons and daughters will fall by the sword. And your soil shall be divided up by a measuring line. And you shall die on unclean soil. And Israel shall be exiled from its soil.'" (7:12–17, slightly altered)

The exchange between Amaziah and Amos assumes the existence of two different sorts of prophets: on the one hand, the professional prophet, who receives wages ("bread") for his work and cultivates prophetic disciples; and on the other hand, the charismatic prophet, who makes his living some other way and has no affiliation with prophetic networks but conceives of himself as called by God to speak God's word. Amaziah wishes to discredit Amos by characterizing him as a professional prophet, a prophet perhaps motivated less by religious fervor than by base political considerations. Amos counters by insisting that he is the second kind of prophet. Notably, even as the exchange assumes the distinction between the two sorts of prophets, the debate between Amaziah and Amos concerning what sort of prophet Amos is suggests that the distinction was likely often fuzzy in practice.

In this exchange, the transgression of the king (or his representative) lies in his refusal to accept prophecy as a genuine check, which is a form of self-aggrandizement. On Amaziah's view, if Amos speaks against the king, then he has shown himself to be no true prophet. For Amaziah, prophetic critique must reduce to treason. Nor, from the perspective of realpolitik, is Amaziah wrong; prophets do assert a limit to the power of the throne.

In this chapter we reflect further on the figure of the prophet, and specifically on the prophet in relation to the universal, through the lens of two prophets, first the aforementioned Amos and then Jonah. The books named for them constitute two of the twelve short prophetic compositions in the edited collection known as the "Book of the Twelve" (also called the "Minor Prophets" because of the books' brevity).

Prophecy in an Age of Empire

In the century from Ahab to Amos, momentous changes began to take root in the environs of the Israelite kingdoms. Among other factors, the Neo-Assyrian Empire's westward expansion, which would ultimately spell the end of the northern kingdom, led to the broadening of Israel's economic and political horizons, and to the augmentation of bureaucratic and scribal institutions. One manifestation of these changes was the emergence, with Amos and some rough contemporaries—Hosea, Isaiah, and Micah—of the literary prophet. Of prophets earlier than Amos no oracular pronouncements are preserved. Nathan and Elijah figure as characters in narratives, but there is no work that collects their words. With Amos, the prophet becomes a producer of texts. This development represents an important step in the emergence of the notion of scripture, of a fixed collection of texts encompassing divine revelation. We will examine this notion in depth in chapter 12.

The appearance of the expansionist Assyrian Empire on the scene also raised the stakes of confrontations between prophet and king. Nathan and Elijah, whose encounters with their kings may well have been constructed retrospectively on the model of the sort of confrontation described in the seventh chapter of Amos, predict only the downfall of the sinning monarch. Amos, by contrast, foretells not only Jeroboam's death—"Jeroboam shall die by the sword"—but also the end of the kingdom itself: "and Israel shall be exiled from its soil" (7:11).

Amos is a prophet of doom, and even if, as is likely, a hopeful undercurrent runs beneath his words—the very purpose of foretelling Israel's downfall is at least in part to inspire changes that will avert such a future—it is hardly surprising that his bleak oracles encountered resistance; bearers of bad news are famously unwelcome. In Amos 2:11–12, set within a passage to which we will return, the prophet accuses the kingdom of Israel of the same offense with which he charges Jeroboam in the aforementioned confrontation, namely, that of suppressing prophets: "And I raised up prophets from among your sons. . . . But you . . . ordered the prophets not to prophesy."

In the face of such opposition, a natural response is silence, or the course of action urged by the priest Amaziah: flight. But Amos conceives of himself as compelled to prophesy: "A lion has roared, who can but fear? My Lord GOD has spoken, who can but prophesy?" (Amos 3:8). The association of prophecy with the terrifying roar of the lion reflects the negative content of Amos's message. We now turn in more detail to the content of this message.

Israel and the Nations in Amos

After a brief introduction, the book of Amos begins with a series of judgments condemning the nations roundabout Israel: the Arameans (Amos 1:3–5), the

Philistines (1:6–8), the Phoenicians (1:9–10), the Edomites (1:11–12), the Ammonites (1:13–15), and the Moabites (2:1–3). Biblical scholarship calls such prophecies "oracles against the nations," and we find them collected in blocks throughout the prophetic corpus, for example, in Isaiah (chapters 13–23), Jeremiah (chapters 46–51), and Ezekiel (chapters 25–32). Two short prophetic books, Obadiah and Nahum, are taken up almost entirely with oracles against the nations. (The same is true, in a very different way, of the book of Jonah, which we will take up in the second half of the chapter.)

Amos's oracles differ from those of other prophets in two ways of special importance for us. First, the other oracles focus their descriptive efforts on the fact and manner of the foreign nation's future destruction. The reason for the destruction is sometimes not given at all. When the prophet does specify the reason, it inevitably revolves around the friend/enemy binary: God's anger burns against the foreign nation either because it has been hostile toward God's people, Israel, or because it has arrogantly asserted itself against Israel's God himself. Scholars have reasonably supposed, on the basis of these features, that the original setting for the genre of oracles against the nations is war: Israel, on the battlefield, finds encouragement in the prophet's condemnation of its enemy.

While Amos's oracles do detail the foreign nations' destruction, they begin, in striking contrast to the other oracles, by specifying each nation's transgression. More importantly, the transgression does not concern hostility toward Israel's God or to Israel, but cruelty in war.

> For three transgressions of Damascus,
> For four, I will not revoke it:
> Because they threshed Gilead
> With threshing boards of iron. . . .
> For three transgressions of Moab,
> For four, I will not revoke it:
> Because he burned the bones
> Of the king of Edom to lime. (Amos 1:3; 2:1)

These two oracles, like all the others in Amos's collection, are unified by the form: "For three transgressions . . . , for four." If the victims in the first instance are presumably Israelites (the inhabitants of Gilead), the victims in the second are Edomites. It thus becomes clear that for Amos, the nations stand condemned not as enemies of Israel, but for their moral failings. From its outset, then, the book of Amos puts forward a universalist framework: God sits in judgment over non-Israelites as much as over Israelites. Moreover, he weighs the deeds not only of individuals, as in Proverbs, but of peoples.

The continuation deepens but also nuances this universalist framework. In a surprising move that marks the second difference between Amos's oracles and those of the other biblical prophets, Amos, after condemning Moab, turns God's anger upon the Israelite kingdoms themselves, first Judah, in a very brief passage (Amos 2:4–5) that some scholars consider the work of a later author, then Israel (2:6–16). This move extends Amos's universalist perspective: because God condemns foreign nations for their lapses, there is an essential similarity between his relationship with them and his relationship with the Israelites, and thus the Israelites can be included among the nations whom Amos condemns in his oracles against the nations.

But a subtle yet important difference also emerges, for, as Shalom Paul among others has noted, the ground for condemnation is not the same in the case of the Israelites. Leaving aside the passage on Judah, which may have been added by a later writer, we will take up Amos's oracle against the northern kingdom.

> For three transgressions of Israel,
> For four, I will not revoke it:
> Because they have sold for silver
> Those whose cause was just,
> And the needy for a pair of sandals.
> They trample the heads of the poor
> and divert the way of the humble. (Amos 2:6–7, slightly altered)

Amos has condemned foreign nations for their behavior toward other nations in war, and in particular for deploying cruel tactics, or what we might today call crimes against humanity. God holds the Israelites to a different standard, indeed a higher one. It is not enough for Israel to refrain from dehumanization of enemies. God calls upon Israel to realize justice in its society and to protect the poor from oppression. To justify this higher standard, God recalls his kindnesses toward Israel.

> Yet I
> Destroyed the Amorite before them,
> Whose stature was like the cedar's. . . .
> And I
> Brought you up from the land of Egypt

And led you through the wilderness forty years,
To possess the land of the Amorite! (2:9–10)

The fate of other nations as nations depends only on their readiness to recognize foreigners as human beings; but because God has attached himself to and bestowed special kindnesses upon Israel, he demands more of it.

This perspective becomes explicit at the beginning of the very next chapter:

Hear this word, O people of Israel,
That the LORD has spoken concerning you,
Concerning the whole family that I brought up from the land of Egypt:
You alone have I singled out
Of all the families of the earth—
That is why I will call you to account
For all your iniquities. (3:1–2)

Again calling to mind the exodus from Egypt as evidence of God's beneficence toward Israel, Amos insists that the Israelites' chosenness does not mean that God will judge their failings kindly. The manifestation of the particular does not, as in the patriarchal narratives, take an antinomian form. On the contrary, the particular becomes manifest as the hypernomian: God will judge Israel more strictly than he does the other nations. Of all the books in the Bible, the prophecies of Amos take squarest aim at the dangers of moral complacency and exceptionalism implicit in the conception of chosenness that predominates in Genesis.

Amos and Jonah

The book of Jonah was composed much later than the book of Amos, likely near the beginning of the Second Temple period; and unlike the book of Amos, which records (if with embellishments and occasional later additions) the actual deeds and words of a real historical figure, the book of Jonah reads like a fable. But there are notable points of contact between the books. Like Amos, Jonah is a prophet of doom. God charges him with informing the inhabitants of the Assyrian city of Nineveh that God intends to destroy them in forty days on account of their wickedness. Just as Amaziah counsels Amos to run off rather than deliver his prophecy of doom, Jonah flees rather than prophesy.

Jonah's flight recalls the final chapter of Amos, wherein Amos speaks of the impossibility of escaping God's wrath (Amos 9:1) and warns: "If they burrow down to Sheol, from there My hand shall take them. . . . And if they conceal themselves from My sight at the bottom of the sea, there I will command the serpent to bite them" (9:2–3). Jonah flees from God by boarding a ship headed for distant Tarshish, but God sends a storm upon the sea. The sailors literally "burrow" (Jonah 1:13)—presumably a reference to hard rowing, but the usage is unique, and strikingly recollects Amos 9:2, which uses the same verb—to escape the storm but cannot, and end up throwing Jonah overboard to appease God. As God in Amos 9:2 commands the serpent to bite those who have fled to the bottom of the sea, so God in Jonah 2:1 furnishes a fish to swallow Jonah.

The resemblances to the book of Amos serve, in part, as a sort of misdirection. As Meir Sternberg has highlighted, the book of Jonah is structured by a surprise ending. We discover, in the final chapter, that the reason that Jonah fled was not, as any reader familiar with the enmity confronted by prophets of doom would have assumed, that he feared that his warning would be received with hostility in Nineveh. On the contrary, he fled because he was convinced that the Ninevites would heed his warning and repent, and thus escape God's wrath. And indeed, the circumstances prove Jonah correct: the Ninevites turn from their evil ways with improbable enthusiasm, and God, in response, relents.

Israel and the Nations in Jonah

It is possible to interpret the book of Jonah—many have indeed so interpreted it—as a critique of Israel executed by putting Israel into relation with other nations, thus not unlike the book of Amos. The starting point for this approach is the fact that the book features two groups of gentiles, the sailors in the first chapter and the Ninevites in the third, both of whom act utterly piously. In the midst of the storm, the sailors make every effort to save Jonah. Even after Jonah specifically instructs them to throw him overboard, the sailors valiantly attempt to row to safety; and when they do finally make ready to cast Jonah into the sea, they pray that God will hold them innocent. Finally, when the seas grow calm and they return to land, the sailors offer sacrifices to the God of Israel. Likewise, the Ninevites respond to the threat of destruction with immediate and radical penance. The king rises from his throne and puts on sackcloth and ashes. He declares a fast not only for the populace but for their animals. The city immediately and comprehensively "turns back" from its evil ways.

In contrast with these paragons of piety, Jonah the Hebrew comes out rather poorly. His first act is to disobey God, and his last is to complain about God's mercy. Although the sailors labor to save Jonah, Jonah seems indifferent to their lives, for during the storm he descends belowdecks to sleep (1:5), even though he likely knows that it is he whom the storm targets. Some have suggested that the book critiques Israel not only through the purportedly representative figure of Jonah, but also by implicitly contrasting the Ninevites, in their readiness to repent, with the Israelites elsewhere in the Bible, who in general seem to ignore the many prophetic warnings that God directs at them.

However, as Uriel Simon and others have observed, this approach to the book of Jonah is ultimately untenable. The major problem with it is that there is no evidence that the book intends a comparison between the gentile protagonists and Israel. While it is clear that Jonah is a Hebrew, the author makes no effort to make him stand for the nation. There is no indication that Jonah's anger stems from the fact that the Ninevites are gentiles, nor does the author gesture contrastively toward Israel's intransigence in its depiction of the Ninevites' repentance. The story would have come off more or less the same if, say, the sailors were from the Israelite tribe of Zebulun, and the sinners resided in the Israelite city of Samaria, or, alternatively, if Jonah were replaced by the gentile prophet Balaam (Numbers 22–24).

But is the choice to feature gentile sailors and Ninevites entirely arbitrary? Here again Simon, citing Yehezkel Kaufmann, furnishes the most plausible answer: The book of Jonah is a meditation on the problem of divine justice. The more famous aspect of this problem, namely, why do bad things happen to good people, is the subject of the book of Job, which we briefly discussed in chapter 2. The other aspect of this problem, which tends to bother us much less (a curiosity to which we will return below), is the subject of the book of Jonah: Why do good things happen to bad people, or put differently, why do bad people enjoy God's mercy? And just as the righteous sufferer of the book of Job is not an Israelite, so the penitent sinners of the book of Jonah are gentiles.

The book of Jonah, like the book of Job, thus makes its protagonists gentiles because this choice allows the biblical author to think about God's nature per se. The author wishes to reflect on the problem of divine justice and divine mercy. If the city in question were Israelite, then an entire covenantal history would come into play in determining God's posture toward it. This history would thus obscure our view of God's nature. Put differently, behind the choice of gentiles as central protagonists in the book of Jonah is the assumption that God's relationship with gentiles reflects who God is in his essence. By contrast, God's relationship with Israel is determined by his long history with this people and its forefathers. The temptation to think of the contrast between Israel and the nations as an important feature of the book of Jonah is an accidental result of the fact that, while the sailors and the Ninevites are gentiles, Jonah himself is an Israelite. But Jonah is not meant to stand for Israel.

This analysis of the Jonah story underscores that gentiles occupy a dual role in biblical literature. On the one hand, they are the non-Israelites, the nations excluded from God's unique, covenantal relationship with Israel. On the other hand, they can, as in the book of Jonah, represent the everyman, the human being as such, a category that encompasses the Israelites as much as anyone else. When God teaches Jonah a lesson about divine mercy, that lesson applies, in principle, to Israel just as much as it applies to the Ninevites.

At the same time, the predication of piety on the gentile actors in the book of Jonah is theologically significant. Even if the book does not intend to condemn Israelite impiety or intransigence, that its exemplars of piety happen to be gentile is important, because it precludes the sort of demonization of the non-Israelite that a particularist perspective might encourage. Compare the story of the sailors in the first chapter of Jonah with a discourse on fear of God from a work called 1 Enoch, which may have been composed not so very long after the book of Jonah. The speaker in the passage in question calls upon human beings to consider "the captains who sail the sea." When overtaken by a storm, "they all fear, and all their good and possessions they throw out into the sea. . . . Do not the captains fear the sea? But the sinners do not fear the Most High" (1 Enoch 101:4–5, 9).[1] It is this concept of the seafarer as sin-fearer that the author of the book of Jonah is adapting, but the book makes the sailors gentiles; and this decision reflects and (insofar as it occurs in a canonical book) reinforces the biblical tradition's willingness to find piety outside Israel.

Mercy and Justice in Jonah

While our main interest is in the figuration of gentiles in the book of Jonah, we would be remiss to bypass any reflection on the book's main topic, namely, the justice of God's mercy, or more precisely, whether it is unjust for God to have mercy on the penitent wicked rather than exacting the due penalty from them. The relationship between God's justice and God's mercy is encapsulated in a list of divine attributes that occurs twice in the Pentateuch in the aftermath of Israelite sins, as part of a process of (partial) forgiveness, first in Exodus 34:6–7

1. The quotation is from George Nickelsburg and James VanderKam, *I Enoch: A New Translation* (Minneapolis: Fortress, 2004), 156–57.

after the sin of the golden calf, and second in Numbers 14:18 after the sin of the spies. This list of attributes describes God as on the one hand slow to anger and abundantly merciful, and as on the other hand prepared to exact punishment. In his oracle against the city of Nineveh, the prophet Nahum cites a version of the list that forefronts divine justice (Nahum 1:2–3), and it is not improbable that the book of Jonah riffs on Nahum's oracle in its decision to reflect on the problem of divine mercy through the vehicle of Nineveh and the list of divine attributes.

The attributes occur in Jonah's mouth in chapter 4:

> He prayed to the LORD, saying: "O LORD! Isn't this just what I said when I was still in my country? For this reason I fled in advance to Tarshish. For I know that You are a compassionate and gracious God, slow to anger, abounding in kindness, renouncing punishment." (Jonah 4:2 NRSV, altered)

God attempts to teach Jonah compassion by putting him in a position to regret the demise of a plant that was providing him shade. If Jonah, God tells him, was so saddened by the death of a plant, on which he expended no effort and which had risen just the day before, "should not I care about Nineveh, that great city?" (4:11).

The book does not give us the impression that we are meant to take Jonah's challenge seriously. It is probably the author's own intention, and not merely our own modern predilection, to cast Jonah as something of a ridiculous figure, a churl. Why is this so? Why are we not troubled by the notion that wicked people can, by repenting and turning to God, escape the consequences of their sins? Why do we think of someone who protests divine forgiveness toward the penitent as mean-spirited?

One might think to critique Jonah with Jesus's famous words (John 8:7): "Let anyone among you who is without sin be the first to throw a stone." But it is notable that God does not respond to Jonah's protest against forgiveness by pointing out that God also forgives Jonah's sins. Rather, he points out that Jonah also regrets loss, or in other words, that Jonah too is inclined to form attachments of the sort that inevitably involve forgiveness. The better comparison, then, is to another famous Jesus logion, from the prayer formula that he recommends: "Forgive us our sins, for we ourselves forgive everyone indebted to us" (Luke 11:4). God teaches Jonah by inverting the prayer: As you forgive (or at least: as you form particular attachments, which are at odds with the distant, universalist, objective perspective characteristic of the strict standard of justice that would preclude forgiveness), so likewise allow me to forgive.

Conclusion

The books of Amos and Jonah limit the consequences of Israelite election in different ways. Amos underscores that God maintains a relationship with the nations beyond Israel insofar as he expects them to refrain from cruelty. More importantly, the book daringly inverts the relationship between election and the universal that emerges from major threads in the patriarchal narratives and that some among the book's audience evidently held dear: God chose Israel, according to Amos, not to except it from the universal but to hold it even more punctiliously to that standard. The book of Jonah casts pious and penitent gentiles in main roles in order to think through one aspect of the problem of divine justice. In this it is no different from the book of Job, but by putting these gentiles in relation to Israel, and to the institution of Israelite prophecy, the book underscores the humanity of gentiles and their engagement with the same moral and theological choices that confront Israel.

For Further Reflection

1. Amos's criticism of the wealthy elite in the kingdom of Israel, beginning with the first critique in Amos 2:6–8, focuses on two charges: abuse of the poor and cultic irregularity. How if at all do these two charges integrate with each other? Consider in particular Amos's remarks on festivals, which are cultic events but also opportunities for conspicuous consumption. See especially 5:18–27.

2. While the biblical prophet is tasked with delivering God's word to the target audience, thus with serving as God's messenger to the people, he also plays a different role, that of the people's representative before God. In this role, the prophet acts as an intercessor who attempts to win God's favor for people. Consider how Amos plays the intercessor in Amos 7. Likewise, we only appreciate the full scale of Jonah's rebellion when we recognize that by refusing to deliver a divine message that might inspire repentance, he casts off not only the role of divine spokesman but also that of intercessor. An insightful analysis of the prophet's intercessory role may be found in the article by Yochanan Muffs in the bibliography below. How do these two aspects of the prophetic role cohere? What do they tell us about the "prophetic personality" (or should we speak of "prophetic personalities")?

Bibliography

Heschel, Abraham J. *The Prophets.* 1962. Reprint. New York: HarperCollins, 2011.

Muffs, Yochanan. "Who Will Stand in the Breach? A Study of Prophetic Intercession." Pages 9–48 in *Love & Joy: Law, Language and Religion in Ancient Israel.* New York: Jewish Theological Seminary of America, 1992.

Paul, Shalom M. *Amos: A Commentary on the Book of Amos.* Hermeneia. Minneapolis: Fortress, 1991.

Simon, Uriel. *The JPS Bible Commentary: Jonah.* Translated by Lenn J. Schramm. Philadelphia: Jewish Publication Society, 1999.

Sternberg, Meir. *The Poetics of Biblical Narrative: Ideological Literature and the Drama of Reading.* Bloomington: Indiana University Press, 1985.

9 | Eden and the Art of Reading

READINGS
Genesis 2:4–4:26; 11:1–9
The Epic of Gilgamesh (see the translation of Benjamin Foster, *Epic of Gilgamesh*)

Introduction

The first eleven chapters of the book of Genesis constitute the Pentateuch's primeval history. They describe a mythic past, a past in which God created the world, then destroyed the world and made it anew, a past in which human beings can live unimaginably long lives and mingle with God and other divine figures. With the story of Abraham and his father at the very end of chapter 11, history emerges out of myth. The Pentateuch's focus narrows from an interest in the universal, in the world as a whole, in the nature of the human condition, to an interest in the particular, in a single man (Abraham) and in the destiny of his descendants (Israel).

The pre-Abrahamic, mythic narrative of Genesis 1–11 leaves almost no imprint on the rest of the Bible: Adam and Eve are not mentioned again, and only occasionally can one catch echoes of the Eden story and of the flood. But the universal perspective of Genesis 1–11 nevertheless stands at the canonical beginning of the Bible, with the privilege of salience that accompanies all beginnings. Centuries after the completion of the Pentateuch, the earliest Christ-followers (Paul first and foremost) would look back to these chapters, especially to Adam, and find in the Eden story one framework for understanding the identity and role of Jesus in universalist terms: Jesus was a second Adam, and a solution to the problem of Adam. Jesus was not merely the Jewish messiah but the savior of all humankind. Rabbinic interpreters, too, would use these chapters to work out their views of human nature and of the ways in which God relates to non-Jews.

The focus of the current chapter is the story of Adam and Eve in the garden of Eden. The name Adam is simply the Hebrew word for "human"; and in our story, the name is always accompanied by the definite article, or in other words, it is not a name at all, but a generic noun. Thus we might speak of him more precisely as "the human." Eve likewise only acquires her name at the very end of our story (3:20). For most of the story she is simply "the woman." Nevertheless, for the sake of familiarity, we shall speak of the protagonists of the story as Adam and Eve.

What Are the Results of Adam's Sin?

For many traditional Christian interpreters, the Eden story describes the birth of original sin: as a result of Adam's (and Eve's) transgression, he becomes "fallen"—less holy, more susceptible to sin—and his descendants inherit this fallen state. Original sin is not itself a sin, but an inherited condition of sinfulness, a condition cured only by Christ. Does this interpretation of the Eden story represent the plain sense of the Genesis narrative?

I wish to claim that the straightforward answer, and the correct one, is no, but that there is another, subtler way in which the answer is a qualified yes. We begin with the straightforward answer, by way of a brief summary of the story. God places Adam in the garden of Eden and tasks him with tending it. He commands Adam not to eat of the tree of knowledge of good and evil, and warns him that on the day that he eats of it, he will die. After Eve is fashioned as a partner for Adam, the serpent persuades Eve to eat from the tree, and she in turn gives Adam of the fruit. Adam and Eve realize that they are naked and sew makeshift loincloths out of fig leaves. God confronts the couple and punishes them, Adam with the pain of agricultural labor, and Eve with labor pangs. Then God speaks, apparently to his (previously unmentioned) angelic council:

> Now that the man [or Adam] has become like one of us, knowing good and bad, what if he should stretch out his hand and take also from the tree of life and eat, and live forever! (3:22)

To foreclose this scenario, God drives Adam and Eve out of the garden and stations guards along the path.

In addition to the punishments of labor, many readers suppose that God also decreed death on humankind, or more precisely, that he rendered them mortal. At least two items of evidence support this view. (For a third, see

"For Further Reflection" below.) First, when God punishes Adam, he refers to his death.

> By the sweat of your brow
> Shall you get bread to eat,
> Until you return to the ground—
> For from it were you taken.
> For dust you are,
> And to dust you shall return. (3:19)

Second, only after Adam and Eve eat from the tree of knowledge does God express concern that they will eat from the tree of life (3:22). Why did this possibility not concern God before? If we interpret 3:19 to indicate that God decreed death upon human beings, then we have our answer: before they ate from the tree of knowledge and received their punishments, Adam and Eve were immortal.

But this interpretation cannot withstand close scrutiny. Genesis 3:19 introduces death only in a subordinate clause ("until you return to the ground"), where the main clause is devoted to the punishment of labor. Surely this is no way to broach so momentous a punishment. But if Adam and Eve were mortal all along, why does God worry about them eating from the tree of life only after they have eaten from the tree of knowledge? The answer is that, just as before they ate from the tree of knowledge they were unaware that they were naked, so they were unaware that they were mortal. God did not fear that they would eat from the tree of life at that point because the tree of life held out no appeal to them. Only after they ate from the tree of knowledge and came to appreciate their mortality did God need to take measures to prevent them from eating from the tree of life.

We may now summarize the consequences of Adam's sin. The immediate result of eating from the tree of knowledge is, naturally, knowledge, evidently knowledge of human nakedness and of human mortality, or in other words, of sex and death. Such knowledge is characteristic of a maturing child, whereas infants happily go about unclothed and unaware that they will die. It seems to us somewhat strange that knowledge of nakedness and mortality should be called "knowledge of good and evil," but the Bible elsewhere (Deuteronomy 1:39) does speak of small children as not knowing "good from bad [or: evil]." We might thus say, in short, that by eating from the tree of knowledge, Adam and Eve transition from infancy to maturity, or, because animals are equally unconcerned with nakedness and death, that they transform from animal-like to human.

Besides this immediate result, two consequences follow on God's part. First, because he forbade them from eating from the tree of knowledge and they disobeyed him, God punishes the couple with labor. Second, because, by learning of their mortality, they will now desire to eat from the tree of life, God is compelled to banish them from the garden.

On this account of the Eden story, it says nothing about original sin, in the sense of a novel inclination to sin. One might find something like original sin in the couple's new consciousness of, and shame about, their nakedness. But the biblical text in no way suggests a link between such shame and sin; it does not mark such shame as bad per se. The larger narrative arc of Genesis 1–11 does acknowledge that people are inclined to sin, that "the devisings of the human's mind are evil from his youth" (8:21, slightly altered). But there is no indication that this inclination is the result of Adam and Eve's eating. This point—that the inclination to sin is not, on the plain sense of Genesis, novel—is important, because the notion that humankind was once better but fell is part of what makes Jesus's task so urgent for Christians who uphold the doctrine of original sin: he comes to restore humankind to its bygone state.

To say that the plain sense of the Eden story does not teach the doctrine of original sin is not to deny the doctrine's validity; recall our introductory discussion of the traditional-canonical method, and especially the poem "Ozymandias." Indeed, many Christian interpreters readily acknowledge that it is only retrospectively, through a christological prism, that the notion that the Eden story is about original sin can surface. The Catechism of the Catholic Church, for example, has the following to say about the Eden story (1.2.1.I.7 [§388]).

> Although to some extent the People of God in the Old Testament had tried to understand the pathos of the human condition in the light of the history of the fall narrated in Genesis, they could not grasp this story's ultimate meaning, which is revealed only in the light of the death and Resurrection of Jesus Christ. We must know Christ as the source of grace in order to know Adam as the source of sin.

For the Church, the notion of original sin, of "Adam as the source of sin," is an interpretation of the Eden story that becomes available only after the Easter events.

We will return later to the question of Eden and original sin, but for now let us consider an urgent problem that arises from the above analysis of the plain sense of the Eden story. Why does God forbid Adam and Eve to eat from the tree of knowledge? How can he wish for them to remain infants or animals, ignorant of their nakedness or of their mortality? The question might be framed somewhat differently: If Adam and Eve were, at the start, like infants or animals, then how could God command them? We do not ordinarily expect infants and animals to follow rules.

In the first centuries CE, a loosely confederated group of Christians (and others) known as gnostics (from the Greek word for "knowledge") thought that the key to understanding God and the world lay precisely in the above question. The reason that "God" forbade Adam and Eve to eat from the tree of knowledge is that he wanted them to remain infants, and he wanted them to remain infants because he is evil. This god, the creator god, is not the highest God but a lower divine force, who created the world precisely to entrap spirit in matter. The serpent, who leads Adam and Eve to the tree, is an emissary from the highest God, sent to save Adam and Eve by bringing them knowledge of their true, spiritual selves.

The gnostic interpretation is obviously counter to the biblical author's intention, but it highlights the challenge posed by the fundamental tension in the Eden story. Indeed, the Eden story itself seems to be aware of the problem. In Genesis 3:5 and again in 3:22, the knowledge of good and evil is characterized as divine, as the sort of thing that makes one godlike. This characterization looks like an attempt to explain why God prohibited Adam and Eve from eating from the tree: the knowledge afforded by the tree is appropriate only for God, not for human beings; and for human beings to desire it is for them to dare to challenge God. But this solution seems inadequate because the content of the knowledge really does mark it as human. Self-awareness about sex and death belongs to the essence of what it means to be human. Of course, we may concede that there is something divine about self-awareness, that this sort of "divine" knowledge is what makes people human rather than animalistic; but it is still problematic for the story to imply that such knowledge should be reserved for God alone.

Eden and Gilgamesh

We can begin to approach a solution to this problem by turning to a text from the ancient Near East, the Epic of Gilgamesh, which contains many motifs familiar from the Eden story. The epic was told and retold over more than a millennium, and survives, to different extents, in multiple versions and in multiple ancient languages. In summarizing and quoting from the text below, I draw from Benjamin Foster's translation, which depends mainly on the standard version of the epic, attested from the seventh century BCE. This version was written in

Akkadian, a Semitic language—thus a relative of Hebrew—that was native to Mesopotamia but also served as a lingua franca of the ancient Near East for much of the second and early first millennium BCE.

The epic centers on Gilgamesh and Enkidu. Gilgamesh is king of the city-state of Uruk, on the Euphrates River. He is famed, according to the beginning of the epic, for building the city's great walls. But Gilgamesh abuses his own people with his boundless strength, and they cry out to the gods, who come to their rescue. The gods create a strong man, Enkidu, who will be Gilgamesh's match and channel Gilgamesh's energies away from his people. Enkidu is formed in the steppe.

> He knew neither people nor inhabited land,
> He dressed as animals do.
> He fed on grass with gazelles,
> With beasts he jostled at the water hole,
> With wildlife he drank his fill of water. (I.108–112)

A harlot, Shamhat, eventually tames Enkidu by tempting him into sex. After coupling with Shamhat, Enkidu returns to the beasts but finds that he can no longer make his home among them.

> When they saw him, Enkidu, the gazelles shied off,
> The wild beasts of the steppe shunned his person. . . .
> Enkidu was too slow, he could not run as before,
> But he had gained [reason] and expanded his
> understanding. (I.197–202)

Shamhat then dresses Enkidu and leads him to Gilgamesh.

Gilgamesh and Enkidu together undertake heroic adventures. First they enter the forests of Lebanon, and, after killing the monster Humbaba, who had been appointed by the god Enlil to guard the forests, they fell a great cedar. Later, after Gilgamesh rebuffs the advances of Ishtar, the scorned goddess persuades her father Anu to send the Bull of Heaven against Gilgamesh. But Gilgamesh and Enkidu together capture and kill the bull. The great gods in council determine that one of the pair of friends must die for their aggressions, and the sentence falls upon Enkidu. When he takes ill and dies, Gilgamesh is shaken. Formerly, Gilgamesh was unconcerned with death, dismissing Enkidu's concerns about the dangers of engaging Humbaba: "Here you are, even you, afraid of death, what has become of your bravery's might?" (II.188–189). But now, confronted with

Enkidu's corpse, Gilgamesh becomes preoccupied with the prospect of his own death: "Shall I not die too? Am I not like Enkidu? Oh woe has entered my vitals! I have grown afraid of death, so I roam the steppe" (IX.3–5).

Our hero therefore resolves to learn the secret of immortality from Utnapishtim, the Mesopotamian Noah, who survived the flood and lives as an immortal in a distant land. Gilgamesh braves various dangers to reach him. Utnapishtim attempts to discourage Gilgamesh from his fool's errand but is finally persuaded to divulge to him the existence of a plant of eternal youth, to be found at the bottom of the sea. Gilgamesh manages to retrieve the plant, but before he can make use of it, it is consumed by a snake, which becomes rejuvenated and sheds its skin. Gilgamesh, resigned to his mortal fate, returns to Uruk to contemplate the city's walls.

The Epic of Gilgamesh is an astounding work of literature, full of subtlety, profundity, and humor. The above summary does not do it justice, but it will do for our limited purposes. The echoes of the Eden story are numerous. As Adam and Eve transition from animal-like to human, newly conscious of their nakedness, which they conceal with clothing, so Enkidu, through sex, comes to abandon his circle of animals and enter human society, newly clothed. Novel consciousness of mortality is thematized through Gilgamesh. After Enkidu's death, he single-mindedly pursues a cure for mortality; but, like Adam and Eve, whom God drives out of the garden and bars from the tree of life, so Gilgamesh ultimately fails in his quest.

These similarities between the Epic of Gilgamesh and the Eden story allow us to appreciate what is distinctive in the latter, and ultimately to explain, if not to solve, the tension inherent in it. The similarities between the Epic of Gilgamesh and the Eden story all align in a single dynamic, in which an animal-like being transitions into a human being and attempts to go further, to become a godlike immortal, only to be stymied. We may visualize this dynamic thus:

Animal → Human ↛ Divine

For the sake of convenience, let us call this the hierarchy dynamic. Human beings in this dynamic are caught between the animal and the Divine. They are superior to animals, but perhaps only to the extent that they, unlike animals, appreciate that they cannot be gods.

What elements of the Eden story does the hierarchy dynamic not account for? The hierarchy dynamic, and the Epic of Gilgamesh more generally, lack something corresponding to the notion of human beings being commanded by God, of confronting a choice whether to obey or disobey, and of enjoying or suffering the consequences of this choice. We may visualize this other dynamic, specific to the Eden story, as follows:

Command → Disobedience ↛ Punishment

This movement—let us call it the command dynamic—is manifested in the Eden story in God's command not to eat from the tree of knowledge, the human couple's decision to disobey this command, and the double punishment of labor through which God responds to their decision. The Epic of Gilgamesh does not incorporate a command dynamic. Though the gods kill Enkidu, they do so not as a punishment for violating a divine command, but because Enkidu has challenged and insulted the gods. Striving against the gods is risky (because the gods can strike back) and futile (because human beings cannot attain to divinity), but it is not an act of disobedience.

Eden as Incomplete Revision

We could easily rewrite the Eden story so that it includes only the hierarchy dynamic, and not the command dynamic. Imagine Adam and Eve, animal-like, or childlike, roaming about the garden. They discover the tree of knowledge, eat from it, and become human, or intellectually mature. They realize they are naked. Perhaps they also have sex at this point. They now appreciate their mortality, too, perhaps when they fall and bleed. So they seek out the tree of life, so as to become godlike. But before they are able to eat the fruit that they have picked, a serpent chances by and eats it. They attempt to pick more fruit but find the way barred.

The Eden story cannot play out this way because it is important for the biblical author that the story of human beings' origins include the command dynamic. The Bible accepts the hierarchy dynamic that characterizes the Epic of Gilgamesh and other ancient Near Eastern myths. But it nuances this dynamic under the pressure of the command dynamic that is distinctively its own. How does the biblical author manage to incorporate the command dynamic? One option would be to have God command Adam and Eve not to eat of the tree of life, and then have them disobey that command. But such a plot would result in human beings enjoying immortality. The biblical author therefore has God command them not to eat of the tree of knowledge, and it is this command that they disobey. But this innovation creates a new problem. Why would God not want the human beings to eat from the tree of knowledge? After all, this knowledge—of nakedness, sexuality, mortality—is quintessentially human. It would be like the gods fashioning Enkidu as a companion for Gilgamesh but then forbidding Enkidu from leaving the steppe.

This basic tension in the Eden story is the one that we isolated above. We have not so much offered a solution to it as explained how it came about. But this is as much as we can do. The story itself leaves the problem unsolved. There can be no coherent, "plain" reading of the Eden narrative precisely because it represents an incomplete transformation of a Gilgamesh-like forebear. It wishes to retain the basic hierarchy dynamic that it inherited, but to superimpose on it a new command dynamic that is distinctively important to it.

Animal → Human ↛ Divine

Command → Disobedience → Punishment

The odd result is that God ends up commanding animals (Adam and Eve before they eat from the tree of knowledge) to remain animals (that is, not to eat from the tree of knowledge).

The important methodological point is this: The above comparison of the Eden story to the Epic of Gilgamesh is a straightforward application of the historical-critical method, which aims to appreciate the Bible as the product of a specific cultural and sociopolitical milieu. But to view the Bible from this perspective is to recognize that biblical texts come into being through the reshaping of traditions available to them or, in other words, to recognize that the Bible is a product of something like the traditional-canonical method. The Eden story looks the way it does because it is reshaping received material. This is the traditional-canonical way: active, creative reception of what has come before—revising, deleting from, expanding on it—in order to make the past a vehicle for new, but not entirely new, insight. Our historical-critical analysis shows that the traditional-canonical process did not begin only with the closing of the biblical canon. Rather, scripture itself arises, in part, by engagement with other texts, either from the cultural milieu (as here) or from elsewhere in scripture.

How does the Eden story's view of the human condition differ from that of the Epic of Gilgamesh? In the perspective of the latter, the human condition is essentially tragic, for two related reasons, both bound up with the hierarchy dynamic. First, as in other epics, the line between human beings and gods is thin but very real. It is entirely reasonable to want to be a god—one can reach out and touch them—but it is also (in almost all cases) impossible: our mortality is our fate. Second, and even more importantly, the gods are defined not by their relationships with human beings but by their superiority to human beings. In a fundamental way, the gods' backs are turned away from human beings. Some gods do care about some human beings, sometimes deeply. For example, in the version of the flood story preserved in the Epic of Gilgamesh, to which we will turn in the next chapter, Belet-ili (goddess of birth) bewails the drowning of humankind (XI.120–126). But the gods have their own circle, and it is what occurs in this circle that is of chief interest to them. The tragedy of the human condition is that we can perceive and desire this circle but cannot enter it.

The Eden story cannot be tragic in this way, again for two related reasons. First, it does not recognize the legitimacy or even the coherence of the desire to be like God. By comparison with the gods of the epic, the biblical God, even in Eden, is so far beyond and so other than human beings that the very notion of wanting to be like God is a kind of foolishness or insanity. (This is so even though the biblical text speaks of Adam and Eve becoming like God, and threatening to become even more so. As I have indicated above, these features of the text are an artifact of its efforts to rework its predecessor. They do not ring as true in the plot, where Adam and Eve are weak, vacillating creatures.)

Second, and more importantly, to not be God does not mean to be on the outside looking in at the divine circle. There is no in, and there is no circle. God instead looks out at us; he is defined by his relationship with human beings. What he does in relation to us, among other things and perhaps foremost among other things, is to issue commands. One who obeys these commands will find success: not the success of being God, but the success appropriate to humans. In short, the hierarchy dynamic does not leave us despairing, because it is moderated and indeed modified by the command dynamic. If there is a tragic aspect to the human condition on the perspective of the Eden story, it is that obedience does not come naturally to us. But to disobey is still a choice, unlike our mortality, which is a natural fact. Even if we disobey and are punished, our lives are not tragic, because their essential features are determined by our choices, not by anything ineluctably intrinsic to us or by fate.

The Tower of Babel

Our reading of the Eden story finds confirmation in the story of the tower of Babel (or Babylon) in Genesis 11:1–9. In the next chapter we will fill in the plot between Genesis 2–3 and Genesis 11; but for now we may simply note that, by this time, human beings have multiplied, but they remain a single group, with a single language. They settle in a valley in the land of Shinar, and there they decide to build a city, with a tower whose top reaches to the heavens, so as "to make a name for ourselves, lest we be scattered over the face of the earth" (11:4, slightly altered). God descends to inspect their handiwork, and voices his concern: "Now, if, as one people with one language for all, this is how they have begun to act, then nothing that they resolve to do will be out of their reach" (11:6, slightly altered). God therefore proposes, evidently to his divine council, that they confuse the human beings' tongues, so that they cannot communicate with one another. After doing so, God scatters them across the earth, and the construction project ceases.

The resemblances to the Eden story are stark. Here too human beings aim to achieve immortality. With the expulsion from Eden, literal immortality is off the table, but the builders seek the quasi-immortality of a "name," or in other words, fame. God expresses concern in almost the same way in both cases: the human beings have already accomplished such and such (eaten from the tree of knowledge, begun to construct the city and tower), and now may do even more (eat from the tree of life, build even higher). Just as such reasoning leads God to expel the first couple from the garden, so now it leads him to divide human beings by means of language and space. Both stories have God act in consultation with his council.

In light of the above analysis, it is clear that the Babel story is constructed around the hierarchy dynamic—or more precisely, the second part thereof—without the command dynamic. The inhabitants of Shinar attempt to attain to the Divine, and the Divine repulses them. God issues no command, and the tower builders cannot therefore be considered in any way disobedient. Nor, for the same reason, is God's response a punishment. The Babel story shows us, as it were, what the Eden story might have looked like without the overlaid command dynamic that determines its fundamental character. In itself, the Babel story is tragic in just the same way that the Gilgamesh story is tragic. The unfinished tower is a symbol of the scope of human ambition and of its inevitable failure; human beings know to reach heavenward, but the gods will not let them get there. God speaks only to his divine council, not to human beings.

In context, however, the Babel story is not tragic. True, the tower builders cannot achieve the "name" for which they long; but a "name" is not, for this reason, altogether out of reach. Immediately after the story of the city and its tower comes the genealogical list that culminates in Abraham. God commands Abraham to leave his Mesopotamian homeland, and promises that, should Abraham do so, God will "make your name great" (Genesis 12:2). The implicit contrast between the Babel story and the beginning of the story of Abraham conveys that human beings can achieve the immortality of a name not by struggling to become gods but by obeying God's command.

According to the appendix to the tower story (Genesis 11:9), the place in which the tower was built acquired the name "Babel" because there God "confused" (NRSV; Hebrew *balal*) human beings' tongues. This unflattering etymology is not the true one; the toponym is from Akkadian, not Hebrew, and signifies "the gate of God." By associating the tower with Babylon, the Bible not only gets in a dig at the contemporary imperial power but also suggests that the hope of immortality through great feats of construction—the hope expressed by Ozymandias—is something alien, something unsuitable for Israel. By contrast, the Epic of Gilgamesh maintains hope in precisely this sort of immortality. It begins with praise of Uruk's walls and ends with Gilgamesh returning to look upon them, and thereby implies that, if Gilgamesh cannot literally live forever, he yet lives through his great deeds and through the poem that sings of them. The tower story rejects this possibility and reserves eternal life for those who heed God.

Conclusion

The Eden story is torn by a paradox: God commands Adam and Eve to remain in their animal-like state. Only by disobeying God do they become mature adults. In this chapter we have suggested that the origin of this paradox is that the Eden story, in typical traditional-canonical manner, revises an earlier account of the human condition, one that we can recover by comparing the Eden story to the Epic of Gilgamesh and to the story of the tower of Babel.

What the Eden story does in revising this earlier account is to introduce the notion that God commands, that the individuals so commanded are free to obey or disobey, and that God responds to their choices with reward and punishment. The Eden story speaks in universalist terms, of human beings in general, but it understands the relationship between human beings and God in the same basically covenantal way that it understands the relationship between Israel and God. Both relationships are defined by the apodictic command and by the choice of obedience and disobedience.

Let us return to the predominant Christian reading of the Eden story, as the genesis of original sin. It does not represent the plain sense, but we have seen that there is no plain sense, that the story is inherently unstable, because it represents an incomplete revision of a Gilgamesh-like account of the human condition. This instability does not license any and all interpretations, but the Christian interpretation is a good one, in the sense that it integrates both of the dynamics in the story—the hierarchy dynamic and the command dynamic—and does so in a way that privileges the command dynamic, which is the distinctive innovation of the Eden story. On the Christian reading, disobedience, a concept from the command dynamic, produces a change in human beings' place in the natural order, the order that structures the hierarchy dynamic. Pristine beings, by disobeying God, become fallen beings.

A common Jewish approach to the Eden story also highlights the presence of the command dynamic but in a different way, a way that hews to the fundamentally nontragic conception of the human condition that is inherent in the command dynamic. This approach begins with the observation in the book of Proverbs that wisdom is "a tree of life to those who grasp her" (Proverbs 3:18). According to rabbinic interpreters, this verse refers to Eden's tree of life, and teaches us that it is nothing other than wisdom, which is in turn nothing other than the Torah. (We will return to the roots of this identification of wisdom with the Torah in chapter 12.) If God bars Adam and Eve from the tree of life, he holds it out to them anew at Sinai, in the form of the Torah's commandments. "I have put before you," says Moses, "life and death, blessing and curse. Choose life—if you and your offspring would live—by loving the LORD your God, heeding His commands, and holding fast to Him" (Deuteronomy 30:19).

For Further Reflection

1. A third argument in favor of the claim that God punishes Adam and Eve with mortality comes from the fact that God tells Adam that on the day that he eats from the tree of knowledge he will die (Genesis 2:17). Adam did not die on that day; hence, goes the argument, it must be that God punished Adam not with death per se but with the capacity to die, that is, mortality. If we do not accept this interpretation, how can we make sense of the fact that Adam and Eve do not die upon eating from the tree of knowledge? Was the serpent (3:4) right?

2. What is the position (or positions) of Genesis 2:4–5:32 on the nature and role of women? Consider, among other things, the story of the creation of Eve in Genesis 2, Eve's role in the Eden story in Genesis 3, and Lamech's wives as audience for his song in Genesis 4.

3. How does the story of Cain and Abel in Genesis 4:1–23 compare to the story of Adam and Eve in the garden of Eden? What do we learn from the similarities and differences?

Bibliography

Abusch, Tzvi. *Male and Female in the Epic of Gilgamesh: Encounters, Literary History, and Imagination.* Winona Lake, IN: Eisenbrauns, 2015.

Anderson, Gary A. *The Genesis of Perfection: Adam and Eve in Jewish and Christian Imagination.* Louisville: Westminster John Knox, 2001.

Foster, Benjamin R., trans. and ed. *The Epic of Gilgamesh.* New York: Norton, 2001.

Jacobsen, Thorkild. *The Treasures of Darkness: A History of Mesopotamian Religion.* New Haven: Yale University Press, 1982.

Kister, Menahem. "The Tree of Life and the Turning Sword: Jewish Biblical Interpretation, Symbols, and Theological Patterns and Their Christian Counterparts." Pages 138–55 in *Paradise in Antiquity: Jewish and Christian Views.* Edited by Marcus J. Bockmuehl and Guy G. Stroumsa. New York: Cambridge University Press, 2010.

Turner, John D., and Ruth Dorothy Majercik. *Gnosticism and Later Platonism: Themes, Figures, and Texts.* 3rd ed. Atlanta: Society of Biblical Literature, 2000.

Zevit, Ziony. *What Really Happened in the Garden of Eden?* New Haven: Yale University Press, 2013.

10 | Priestly Theology and Holy Space

READINGS

Genesis 1:1–2:4a; 5–10

The Epic of Gilgamesh, tablet XI (see the translation of Benjamin Foster, *Epic of Gilgamesh*; the section of text relevant for this chapter can also be found in Benjamin Foster, "Gilgamesh," *COS* 1:458–60)

Atrahasis (see the translation of Benjamin Foster in *Before the Muses,* pp. 227–80)

Psalm 74

Exodus 25:1–9; 39:32–43; 40:17–38

Leviticus 25

Introduction

In the previous chapter we identified some distinctive features of the biblical worldview that emerge through comparison of the Eden and Babel stories to similar ancient Near Eastern narratives found in the Epic of Gilgamesh. In this chapter we undertake other comparisons along the same lines, but introduce a new authorial voice, that of the Priestly school(s), to which we briefly referred in our overview of the Documentary Hypothesis in chapter 3. We will detect this voice first in the flood story, then trace it through other narratives in the Pentateuch. The Priestly school left a decisive mark on the Pentateuch and on a number of other biblical books, and puts forward a view of the relationship between the particular and the universal that we have not encountered to this point.

In between the Eden and Babel stories analyzed in the previous chapter comes the story of the flood. After Adam and Eve are expelled from Eden, they begin to reproduce. Eve bears a son, Cain, and then another, Abel. Cain kills Abel, but Eve bears a third son, Seth. As the offspring of Cain and Seth multiply, humankind becomes corrupted and wicked, to the point that God determines that he will eradicate the world and reestablish it through one righteous man, Noah, a descendant of Seth. God tells Noah that he plans to flood the earth. Noah is to build an ark, and to gather into the ark his family and representatives of all land animals and fowl. Noah heeds God's instructions. The flood comes as foretold, and Noah and the inhabitants of the ark alone survive. After exiting the ark, Noah makes a sacrifice and enters into a covenant with God in which God pledges that he will not again flood the earth on account of human wickedness.

The Ancient Near Eastern Flood Stories

The biblical flood story draws on a long ancient Near Eastern tradition of such stories. In the previous chapter we referred to Utnapishtim, a Noah-like character from the Epic of Gilgamesh. The flood story told by Utnapishtim in tablet XI reworks an older tale in which the hero is a man named Atrahasis. Versions of the poem of Atrahasis are preserved from the classical period of Akkadian literature, between 1850 and 1500 BCE. I again depend on Benjamin Foster's translation in his anthology of Akkadian literature, *Before the Muses* (pp. 227–80).

The beginning of the deluge incident in the poem of Atrahasis closely resembles the beginning of the Noah story. In the former (I.353), "the land had grown numerous, the peoples had increased," and in the latter (Genesis 6:1), "men began to increase on earth." But at this point they sharply diverge. In the Noah story, it is the wickedness of the human population that compels God to flood the earth, and it is Noah's righteousness that spares him. In the case of Atrahasis, the multiplying human population generates noise pollution that disturbs the sleep of the great god Enlil. The flood is his solution to this problem. Atrahasis survives because he is the favorite of Enki, the god who created human beings and who therefore takes pains on their behalf. Enki surreptitiously informs Atrahasis of Enlil's plan. Following Enki's command, Atrahasis builds an ark, into which he gathers not only the animals but also, strikingly, all sorts of craftsmen. He and the other ark dwellers survive the flood, and afterward he, like Noah, offers a sacrifice to the gods.

It is tempting to generalize from the differences between the Noah story and the tale of Atrahasis, and to set apart the moral universe of the Bible, in which the relationship between the Divine and human beings is determined by the latter's free choice between good and evil, from the amoral universe of the ancient Near East, in which gods arbitrarily destroy and save. This temptation should be resisted. We have already noted that the biblical book of Proverbs and other ancient Near Eastern works of wisdom share more or less the same moral assumptions about the governance of the world; and in the preface to the Laws of Hammurabi, the king indicates that his god-given task as king is to bring about justice in the land. In the story of Atrahasis itself, Enlil is rebuked by other gods for his cruelty.

Nevertheless, the comparison between the Noah and Atrahasis stories reinforces some of the basic distinctions between the biblical worldview and that of its ancient Near Eastern neighbors that emerged in the previous chapter. First, and more narrowly, there is probably a link between the craftsmen whom Atrahasis brings aboard his boat and the celebration of human constructive feats by the Epic of Gilgamesh and by the "Babylonians" of the tower story in Genesis 11. The Noah story, insofar as it neglects to devote attention to the problem of preserving knowledge of crafts or skills, shows itself to be at one with the tower story in putting little stock in such knowledge. Second, and more generally, in the Atrahasis story, the gods constitute a distinct upper class, set apart from the human beings who supply their needs. And if, as with any upper class, some of the gods show interest in and even affection for the human lower class, then other gods show considerably less. In the Noah story, there is no divine upper class, only a creator God who is at once both altogether different from his creatures in virtue of his singularity, and at the same time, and for the same reason, utterly bound to his creatures, who are his only companions.

Sources in the Noah Story

A close perusal of the Noah story reveals certain inconsistencies. According to Genesis 6:19–20, Noah is supposed to bring two of each species, a male and a female, into the ark. But only a few verses later, in 7:2–3, God calls upon Noah to convey to the ark a single mating pair from each unclean (ritually impure) species alone; from each clean species, by contrast, he must take seven pairs. In connection with the latter command, God informs Noah that the rain will persist for forty days and forty nights (7:4). Later, in 7:12, we learn that the rain did indeed fall for forty days and forty nights. But soon afterward the Bible reports that the flood endured far longer: the waters swell for one hundred and fifty days (7:24), until "God caused a wind to blow across the earth, and the waters subsided" (8:1). The waters continue to subside for three months, until the mountaintops become visible (8:5). But then, suddenly, the narrator states that "at the end of forty days" (8:6), Noah sent off birds in search of dry land, as though the flood did indeed last only forty days.

How many pairs of animals, then, did, Noah bring on the ark, and how long did the flood last? In chapter 3, on the patriarchal narratives, we noted that many biblical scholars, confronted by, among other things, the puzzling occurrence of doublets, posit that the Pentateuch is the product of the interweaving of multiple sources. The same hypothesis explains the anomalies in the flood story. The flood story as recorded in Genesis is a synthesis of two distinct versions of the story. In one, Noah brings one pair of each unclean animal and seven pairs of each clean animal aboard the ark, and the flood lasts for forty days. The divine speech in 7:1–5 belongs to this version. In the other, Noah saves one pair of every animal, with no distinction between clean and unclean, and the flood persists for far longer than forty days.

In the first version, Noah must have seven pairs of clear animals aboard because after he exits the ark, he will offer a sacrifice from some of those clean animals (8:20). This version of the flood story reads much like the flood story in the poem of Atrahasis, which also ends with a sacrifice. In the verses associated with this first version of the flood story, God is always "the LORD" (*Y-H-W-H*), and this version belongs to J, the Jahwist source. Like Y-H-W-H in the Hagar expulsion story in Genesis 16, Y-H-W-H in the first version of the flood story is an earthy figure, who can express regret about creating humankind (6:5–8), smell the odor of the sacrifice (8:21), and speak to himself (8:21).

In the other version, God is not "the LORD" but "God" (*'Elohim*). This other version does not, however, belong to the Elohist source, E, but to a source that we have not yet examined, the Priestly source, P. (Scholars distinguish between an earlier Priestly source, P, and a later one, H—for "holiness"—but for our purposes I will not distinguish between them.) Priests serve in God's temple, and for the Priestly source, all sacrifice must occur in God's temple. No biblical figure, then, could have offered a sacrifice to God until God's movable temple was built in Exodus, in a narrative to which we will turn later in this chapter. In P's version of the flood story, Noah does not offer a sacrifice, and therefore he need take only one pair of each animal.

The Priestly character of the second version also explains the length of the flood. For priests, the calendar is of cardinal importance, because it determines the temple rites: each new moon, each festival, is accompanied by a different set of offerings and attendant practices. The flood story in P is dotted with calendrical markers. The waters burst forth on the seventeenth day of the second month (Genesis 7:11), and the ark comes to rest on a mountaintop precisely five months later, on the seventeenth day of the seventh month (8:4). The earth dries by the twenty-seventh day of the second month (8:14), or one year and ten days after the flood began. What explains the additional ten days? A lunar year is 354 days. If the year in the Noah story is lunar, then the additional ten days bump the length of the flood to 364 days, the length of a mathematically simplified solar year composed of fifty-two weeks of seven days.

Priests are also intensely concerned with genealogy, because, among other reasons, according to the view that emerges from many Priestly texts, it is genealogy that makes a priest a priest: only a descendant of Moses's brother, Aaron, can serve in God's temple. It should come as no surprise, then, that the genealogical lists that pepper the narrative—in particular, the line of Seth in Genesis 5, and the descent of Noah in Genesis 10—also represent the work of P. In the midst of the genealogy of Seth, we hear of Enoch (5:18–24), who lives a life far shorter than and different from that of his antediluvian compeers. Enoch "walked with God," and lived until the age of 365, "then he was no more, for God took him." What this enigmatic report might mean we cannot here consider, but the story of Enoch is noteworthy in any case for the merger therein of the distinctively priestly topics of genealogy and calendar: the years of the righteous Enoch's life correspond to the number of days in a solar year.

The Priestly Creation Narrative

In the previous chapter we focused on the creation story that begins in the middle of Genesis 2:4. But this creation story is preceded by a different one, a creation story that stretches from 1:1 to the first half of 2:4. The two stories are clearly different and incompatible. In the first, for example, animals are created before human beings (1:24–27), while in the second, God makes the (male) human beings first, and only afterward fashions animals (2:7, 19). In the second story, the creator is "the LORD God," *Y-H-W-H 'Elohim*, a marker of the fact that it originates in the J source (or something like it). The first creation story speaks of the creator as *'Elohim*, and it belongs to P.

J's creation story is plot-driven: there is no vegetation, and so God creates a human being to work the land. But the human being is lonely, and so God creates animals and birds as potential mates for him. But the human being cannot find a mate among them, and so God creates a woman from him. The creation story in P could not be more different: it is monumental, architectonic. At the most abstract level, P's interest in calendar and genealogy reflects a preoccupation with structure and demarcation, and this preoccupation becomes manifest in the basic action of the creation story, namely, separation, and in the intensely organized way in which creation proceeds.

The world before creation consists of a dark, formless sea, the deep. The process of creation is initiated by a "wind from God sweeping over the water" (1:2). On the first day, God brings light into being and separates the light from the dark. On the second day, he produces a firmament—a sky—to separate the upper waters from the lower waters. The third day sees the gathering of the waters into seas, so that dry land emerges. Having created three "spaces" in the first three days, God fills them in the next three. On the fourth day, he populates the first day's celestial dome—by turns dark at night and light by day—with the sun, the moon, and the stars. On the fifth day, the sky and sea from the second day fill with birds and fish. The sixth day introduces animals and human beings, who spread over the dry land that emerged on the third day. After neatly pairing the first three days with the last three days, P ends the creation account with a description of God's cessation from work on the seventh day, the Sabbath.

We may observe, in retrospect, that P's version of the flood story depends on P's creation narrative: the former is a reversal of the latter. In P's flood story, the water comes not from mundane rain, as in J's version, but from the "fountains of the great deep," which "burst apart," and from the "floodgates of the sky," which "broke open" (7:11). The "great deep" in this report is the "deep" of 1:1, the suppression of which is the object of the entire creative process; and the "floodgates of the sky" are the waters that God confines above the firmament on the second day of creation (1:6–8). In P's flood, God undoes creation by letting loose the confined deep and breaking down the firmament barrier. And just as creation begins, for P, with God's wind sweeping over the deep (1:2), so the restoration of the world after the flood, in P's version, begins with a wind from God blowing across the floodwaters (8:1).

Before considering Genesis 1 in relation to other P texts, let us pause to reflect on the fact that the Pentateuch preserves two different, incompatible creation stories. One might interpret this fact as evidence against a claim to historicity: if they are incompatible, then the Bible cannot mean to present both, or either, as historically true, but must instead mean to convey something else. While there is something to this inference, perhaps the more significant lesson from the inclusion of both stories concerns the capaciousness of the process that produced the Pentateuch, and by extension, the biblical canon. Producing a canon can be, indeed almost inevitably is, an excluding move, a move that leaves other texts out, that demotes them to secondary or even heretical status. But it can also be, at least in some cases and to some extent, an inclusive move, one that settles a conflict by not deciding between the two sides. Did God create human beings as a species, male and female, with the mandate to reproduce, as in Genesis 1; or did he first create the male, and only afterward make from him, and for him, a female, as in Genesis 2? The Pentateuch accepts both accounts.

There are other accounts of the creation of the world in the Bible, albeit not in the Pentateuch, and Genesis 1 appears to be in conversation with some of them. Psalm 74, for example, is the prayer of a community under attack from foreign nations who "made Your sanctuary go up in flames. . . . They burned all God's tabernacles in the land" (74:7–8). (The book of Psalms is the topic of chapter 16 below.) In these dire circumstances, the community calls upon God to act by recalling his deeds in creating the world.

> [13] It was You who drove back the sea with Your might,
> who smashed the heads of the sea monsters in the waters;
> [14] it was You who crushed the heads of Leviathan,
> who left him as food for the denizens of the desert; . . .
> [16] the day is Yours, the night also;
> it was You who set in place the orb of the sun;
> [17] You fixed all the boundaries of the earth;
> summer and winter—You made them.

The psalmist alludes to a creation story in which God first destroys the forces of the sea—the sea monsters, Leviathan—and afterward structures the days, the celestial bodies, and the seasons. This sort of creation account goes in biblical scholarship by the German word *Chaoskampf*, the "struggle" (*Kampf*) against the forces of chaos.

In Genesis 1, by contrast, while there is an original chaos, there is no struggle. The creation account in Genesis 1 begins, like Psalm 74, with the sea, and the psalm's "sea monsters" recur therein (Genesis 1:21); but the God of Genesis 1 does not fight against the sea, and the sea monsters are not his primordial enemies but his creations, brought into being in their proper time, on the fifth day. In comparison with the creator God of Psalm 74, the God of Genesis 1 is transcendent, to the point that we can speak of him as supernatural. Even in J's creation account, while God does not confront enemies, he must get his hands dirty, must corral resistant matter into shapes. P's God neither fights nor works, but only speaks and creates.

While Psalm 74 is a biblical text, the Bible obscures and subordinates this creation account by fronting a different creation account, that of Genesis 1, that directly subverts it. This decision has important repercussions for the relationship between the universal and the particular in the Bible. Psalm 74 invokes the *Chaoskampf* tradition to confront a present reality in which Israel struggles against its enemies. The speaker aligns Israel with order and with God, and Israel's enemies with God's own primordial enemies, the forces of chaos. If one's account of creation involves a struggle between God and his enemies, then the creation myth can reinforce a particularist worldview, can indeed root this vision at the very dawn of the world. The creation story in Genesis 1, by contrast, is relentlessly universalist, insofar as it leaves no place for a divine enemy.

Universalism and Particularism in P

But P by no means endorses an uncomplicated universalism. To appreciate how P negotiates between the universal and the particular, we must bring Genesis 1 into conversation with other P texts. Besides the creation of the world, there is one other construction narrative in the Pentateuch: in the second half of the book of Exodus, the Israelites in the wilderness build the tabernacle, a movable temple to house God's presence. Not surprisingly, the tabernacle construction narrative, like Genesis 1, is the work of P. As many scholars have observed, verbal parallels between the ends of the two construction narratives suggest that they should be linked thematically.

Genesis 1:31a; 2:3 (altered): "And God *saw* all that He had *made,* and *behold,* it was very good. . . . And God *blessed* the seventh day and sanctified it, because on it he ceased from all the *work* that God had created for *making*."

Exodus 39:43 (altered): "And when Moses *saw* all the *work,* and *behold,* they had *made* it—as the LORD had commanded, so they had *made*—Moses *blessed* them."

Genesis 2:2a (altered): "On the seventh day God *finished* his *work*."

Exodus 40:33b (altered): "and Moses *finished* the *work*."

Genesis 2:1 (altered): "The heaven and the earth and all their host were *finished*."

Exodus 39:32a (altered): "and all the work of the Tabernacle of the Tent of Meeting was *finished*."

Likewise, in Exodus 40:17–38, as Moses coordinates the erection of the tabernacle, the account is punctuated by a sevenfold refrain about the Israelites doing "as the LORD had commanded Moses." The division into seven recalls the division of the creation of the world into seven days. Finally, as the creative process begins in Genesis 1 with the "wind from God" (1:2), so God fills the craftsman who builds the temple, Bezalel, with a "wind [or spirit; the Hebrew word is the same] from God" (Exodus 31:3), which the verse defines as wisdom.

The connection between the two narratives illuminates both. In the light of the tabernacle construction account, we appreciate that the world created in

Genesis 1 is itself a tabernacle, a place for God to rest his presence. Temples in the ancient Near East housed the image of the god, and Genesis 1 also culminates in the construction of the divine image, in the form of human beings, whom God creates "in His image" (Genesis 1:27). At the same time, the tabernacle, in light of Genesis 1, becomes a microcosm, a world in miniature. There is no divine image in the tabernacle other than the mysterious presence of God himself, but the fact that it is human beings who bear the divine image in the world-as-temple in Genesis 1 encourages us to think of the priests who serve in the temple proper as special or quintessential human beings, perhaps even endowed with the divine image in a special way.

In between the human beings of the world and the priests of the temple comes the people Israel, in the land of Israel. This intermediate category emerges in another text produced by priests, Leviticus 25. This passage details the law of the Jubilee Year. According to Leviticus 25, every fiftieth year is a Jubilee Year, a designation with two major repercussions. First, if an Israelite, having fallen into desperate straits, has sold his ancestral plot, the land reverts to its original owner in the Jubilee Year. Second, if an Israelite, perhaps in even more desperate straits, becomes a slave, he goes free in the Jubilee Year.

These laws obviously protect the poor, and even specifically their freedom, but they also constrain their freedom. An Israelite does not have the legal right to sell his land in perpetuity, nor to sell himself in perpetuity. The reason is that both his land and he himself belong to God.

> The land must not be sold beyond reclaim, for the land is Mine; you are but strangers resident with Me. (Leviticus 25:23)

> [The slave] and his children with him shall go free in the jubilee year. For it is to Me that the Israelites are servants; they are My servants, whom I freed from the land of Egypt. (25:54–55)

The land of Israel is God's land, and the people of Israel occupy it not as owners but as God's servants, resident with him.

Taken together, Genesis 1, the second half of Exodus, and Leviticus 25 indicate that P coordinates between the universal and the particular by means of a spatial spectrum, which one might depict through a map of concentric circles. At the center of the circles is the temple or tabernacle, in which God's very presence rests. Only the priests, the descendants of Aaron, can enter here. Beyond the temple is the land of Israel, God's land, on which his servants, Israel, reside.

Beyond the land of Israel is the world entire, also a temple of sorts, in which God's image is borne by each individual human being.

This way of coordinating between the universal and the particular is very different from the way that emerges from comparison between Proverbs and the patriarchal narratives. In the latter comparison, the relationship between the universal and the particular is fraught, almost antagonistic: insofar as God enters into a relationship of love with a particular people, he does so at the expense of, even in violation of, the universal norms that govern his relationship with the world. The Priestly texts instead align the universal and the particular on a spectrum of proximity. God makes himself manifest, in a personal way, among all people, only more intensely among some than among others. The Israelite priests he draws closest to himself, and after them, nonpriestly Israelites, and after them, all human beings.

What enables the Priestly authors to achieve this synthesis? As we have noted at numerous points, it is history that punctures the universal or, in other words, time in its unrepeatability. While P acknowledges history—the Priestly source evidently included versions of the exodus story, of the Sinai event, and many other revelatory moments—it manages partially to blanch history and time of their particularizing force by means of two interrelated categories. The first is space: the defining Priestly category is the temple, and via the temple, P conceives of the particular and the universal alike in spatial terms. Space figures both in the concentric coordination of the temple, the land of Israel, and the world, and also in P's creation story, which divides the six days of creation into three days devoted to spaces, and three to the things that populate them. This prominence of space comes at the expense of time. Second, the Priestly authors think in mythic terms. To be sure, they rework and even subvert the ancient Near Eastern myths upon which they draw. But the underlying conceptual profile of myth—its structuralist, static, cyclical character—survives in the Priestly texts and serves in them as a bulwark against history.

Conclusion

Many of the things that make the Bible, especially the Pentateuch, alien to the modern reader—the long genealogical lists, the intricately detailed rites and taboos—are the work of the Priestly authors. But these authors also anticipate modernity in their drive to systematize, to classify, to discern and find guiding principles in the world's intrinsic logic. There is, in short, a protoscientific character to P. This character of P's thought has repercussions for one aspect of the particularist/universalist dichotomy. An adherent of the Priestly school associated with P would be inclined to see the boundary between Israelite and non-Israelite as a natural, ontological one: the Israelite is a different sort of being from the non-Israelite. This approach thus widens the gap between Israelites and others.

At the same time, the alignment of the universal and the particular along a mythospatial spectrum in P, a phenomenon described in detail above, generates a certain permeability between the categories. In particular, a non-Israelite can attain to something like Israelite status by taking up residence among Israelites in the land of Israel. Such a person is called a "stranger who resides among you" or a "resident" (Hebrew *ger*), and he is subject, per Leviticus 18:26 and other verses in P, to many of the same laws that govern native Israelite behavior. Indeed, the impression that one gets from some Priestly texts is that the purpose of the Bible's laws is nothing other than to preserve the purity (ritual and moral) of the Israelites so that God can tolerate their presence on his land; and by this logic, there is no compelling reason to distinguish between Israelite and non-Israelite inhabitants of the land. In the postbiblical period, as Israelite identity comes to be dislocated from the land of Israel and reconceived in more transparently religious terms, the *ger* becomes a convert, pledged to the God of Israel, and thus Jewish. The possibility of conversion is a (partial) solution to the tension between the universal and the particular; and it has its roots, in part, in the Priestly coordination of the universal and the particular along a mythospatial spectrum.

We will return to the topic of movement from non-Israelite to Israelite in chapter 14. In the next chapter, as we turn to the dynamic of exile and restoration, we will gain further insight into P's thought through the prism of one of the school's later adherents, Ezekiel.

For Further Reflection

1. The beginning of the story of Atrahasis concerns labor and offers the first literary description of a labor strike. Compare the account of labor in Atrahasis, tablet I, lines 1–247, translated in Benjamin Foster's *Before the Muses* (pp. 229–37), to that in the Eden story (Genesis 2:4–3:24).

2. The conversation between the Priestly creation story, Genesis 1:1–2:4a, and Psalm 74 involves many other partners, both from the Bible and the ancient Near East. The most important conversation partner from the ancient Near East is the Babylonian creation epic, Enuma Elish. Read Enuma Elish—it is translated

in Benjamin Foster's *Before the Muses* (pp. 436–86), under the title "Epic of Creation"—and compare it to the Priestly creation story and to Psalm 74.

3. As noted above, Genesis 1:27 has God make human beings "in His image." The notion of creation in the image of God is familiar from elsewhere in the ancient Near East, but it is typically the king, not human beings as such, who are so created. To characterize human beings as being made in the image of God, then, is arguably to characterize them as kinglike. Is there other evidence from Genesis 1 to support this interpretation?

Bibliography

Foster, Benjamin R. *Before the Muses: An Anthology of Akkadian Literature.* 3rd ed. Bethesda, MD: CDL Press, 2005.

Foster, Benjamin R. "Gilgamesh." *COS* 1:458–60.

Foster, Benjamin R., trans. and ed. *The Epic of Gilgamesh.* New York: Norton, 2001.

Joosten, Jan. *People and Land in the Holiness Code: An Exegetical Study of the Ideational Framework of the Law in Leviticus 17–26.* Leiden: Brill, 1997.

Knohl, Israel. *The Sanctuary of Silence: The Priestly Torah and the Holiness School.* Minneapolis: Fortress, 1995.

Levenson, Jon D. *Sinai and Zion: An Entry into the Jewish Bible.* Reprint. San Francisco: Harper & Row, 1987.

Smith, Jonathan Z. *To Take Place: Toward Theory in Ritual.* Chicago: University of Chicago Press, 1992.

Smith, Mark S. *The Priestly Vision of Genesis 1.* Minneapolis: Fortress, 2010.

11 | Exile and Return: Prophetic Visions

READINGS
Ezekiel 1; 8–11; 36–39; 44:1–16
Isaiah 40–53

Introduction

The crucial historical events behind the transformation of the Israelites of the Bible into the Jews (and eventually also the Christians) of the postbiblical period and beyond are foreign conquest and exile. In the second half of the eighth century BCE, the northern kingdom, Israel, was overrun by the Assyrian Empire. A large portion of the northern kingdom's population—the "ten lost tribes," the search for whom has inspired much mythmaking over the course of the centuries—was exiled to Mesopotamia. Other northerners fled south, to the kingdom of Judah, which, while spared destruction, became a vassal state of Assyria. When Babylonia became the dominant Mesopotamian power in place of Assyria, Judah fell under its sway but vacillated between allegiance to Babylonia and allegiance to its competitor, Egypt. Eventually, the Egypt party won out, and Judah rebelled from Babylonian rule near the beginning of the sixth century BCE. This rebellion was suppressed, and the invading Babylonians exiled the Davidic king of Judah, along with many other Judeans, to Babylonia and destroyed the temple in Jerusalem.

Soon afterward, the Babylonians fell to the Persians, and toward the end of the sixth century BCE, the Persian king Cyrus permitted the exiled Judeans to return to Judah, or more precisely, to the Persian province of Yehud, and to rebuild the Jerusalem temple. This new temple (generally called the Second Temple) would stand for some six centuries, until it was destroyed by the Romans in 70 CE. The scholarly convention is to speak of "Israelites" for the period prior to at least the Assyrian exile if not the Babylonian exile, but of "Judeans" or "Judahites" or "Jews" for the period following the Babylonian exile, because it is from the Babylonian exile onward that the historical record focuses almost exclusively on the inhabitants of Judah.

The impact of these events, especially the Babylonian exile, on the Israelites is difficult to overestimate. As a result, the Israelites came to think of their fate, to an even greater extent than before, in relation to that of the other nations. This development is a natural consequence of the greater exposure to and entwinement with the wider ancient Near Eastern world that came with the incursions of Assyria and Babylonia into the land of Israel and its environs.

A more specific development of immediate concern in this chapter is the advent of a novel orientation toward the future. Before the Israelites were exiled, their temporal consciousness was dominated by the past and present: they lived on the land of their ancestors and practiced rites that reflected this ancestral past. With the exiles comes a preoccupation with the future, with the restoration of a glorious but lost past. This novel orientation toward the future—this horizon of expectation—might not have proved terribly significant. After all, less than a century passed after the Babylonian exile before Jews were permitted to return to Judah and rebuild the Second Temple. One would naturally suppose that with the restoration of Judah, the hope for a better future would itself cease. It did not, however, because the restoration under Persia was not everything that Jews, or at least some Jews, had hoped for.

The return to Judah fell short of expectations in two significant ways. First, some Jews in Babylonia returned to Judah, but most of the exiled population, from the Assyrian and Babylonian exiles alike, remained outside the land of Israel, in a vast diaspora. Second, and even more importantly, despite the restoration of some Jewish rule in Judah, the land remained a Persian province, under the authority of the Persian king. With one limited exception in the second century BCE, to which we will return later (chapter 15), Judah never regained political independence during the Second Temple period. With the demise of the Persian Empire, Judah was controlled by Alexander the Great and his successors, and then it fell under the sway of Rome. No descendant of David ruled as king throughout the entire period. Thus, despite the Persian restoration in the late sixth century BCE, in an important sense the exile never ended. The orientation toward a future restoration thus became a persistent and central feature of Jewish thought, sometimes more prominent, sometimes less. We will take note of another explanation for this development at the end of this chapter.

The orientation toward the future is often called *messianic*, because central to it in most (but not all) of its forms is the hope for an anointed (Hebrew *mashiakh*) Davidic monarch. This posture can also, in some forms, be called *eschatological*, insofar as the hoped-for restoration is imagined not simply as a return to Israel's idyllic past but as in some sense an end (in Greek, *eschaton*) to history, an epochal change in the ways of the world. In this chapter we identify two early patterns in such eschatological thought, a particularist pattern articulated by the book of Ezekiel, and a universalist one preserved in the book of Isaiah. In chapter 15, we will trace the emergence later in the Second Temple period of a distinctive form of eschatological thought called *apocalyptic*, which will prove of decisive importance especially in the emergence of Christianity.

Ezekiel among the Priests

Like Amos, Ezekiel is a literary prophet: rhetoric was central to his prophetic role, and his prophecies were recorded, together with stories about him, in a book that bears his name. A priest from Judah, Ezekiel was among those exiled by the Babylonians to Babylonia just prior to the destruction of the temple. It is in Babylonia that Ezekiel hears of the temple's destruction, and in Babylonia that he appears to take up the prophetic mantle. There were many different groups of priests in this period, and not all of them should be associated with the Priestly school whose thought is preserved in the P source in the Pentateuch, but Ezekiel does share many of P's interests.

Thus, as P's geographical and theological central point is the presence of God in the tabernacle or temple, so Ezekiel's book begins with a tour de force description of God's presence. Stationed "by the Chebar Canal, in the land of the Chaldeans" (Ezekiel 1:3), Ezekiel sees four figures whose appearance gradually becomes clear: they are winged creatures, each with four faces. He looks closer and recognizes that there are wheels next to the creatures. Ezekiel then takes note of a platform above the wings of the four creatures, and on the platform, a throne, and on the throne, "the semblance of a human form," indeed, "the semblance of the Presence of the Lord" (1:26–28).

The true significance of this vision lies—or may lie; the interpretation I advance here is admittedly uncertain—in the fact that the vision does not exist simply in Ezekiel's mind or in a dream. Ezekiel, in Babylonia, has actually seen the chariot of God; this is shocking, because, for the Priestly school that produced P, and with which Ezekiel to one degree or another affiliates, God has no business being in Babylonia. As Benjamin Sommer has clarified, God, for this school, is not omnipresent. God does not, in the first instance, exist in some ethereal way everywhere in the world. He has a body, which occupies a specific space. The native home of the divine body is the heavens; but when the Israelites built a house for God in the wilderness, and then in Jerusalem, God's body took up residence in that house. And there he should yet be, in the Jerusalem temple, in the microcosm that anchors the macrocosm. That he is visible in Babylonia means, then, that he has abandoned the temple. The implication of the opening vision of the book is clarified in chapters 8–11, where Ezekiel experiences himself as being transported to Jerusalem. There he sees the very same "presence" of God that he witnessed in chapter 1. Ezekiel tours the temple and sees the idolatrous rites that have found a place therein. Ezekiel then observes the presence move from its place in the temple and take a position on his chariot. The chariot departs in stages, first to the temple entrance, then to a hill east of the city.

Ezekiel's visions of God clarify a dialectic inherent in the Priestly school to which he belongs. The transcendence of the God of Genesis 1, who need fight no battles and has no equal, is counterbalanced by an impulse toward immanence, or what one might loosely call incarnation. God's image resides in all human beings, and his presence resides very concretely in the midst of his land, Israel, in the temple. If Ezekiel sees God outside the temple, this is because God has left the temple and given it over to destruction at the hands of the Babylonians.

The Restoration according to Ezekiel

In chapters 36–39, Ezekiel describes his vision of Israel's restoration. According to Ezekiel, God exiled Israel as punishment for their sins, which defiled the land, but God is now prepared to restore them. One might imagine that he is prepared to do so because the exile has purged the nation of its sins, or because Israel has repented of them; but Ezekiel takes a decidedly different view: God will restore Israel from among the nations to which he has exiled them because he has no other choice.

> [For] when they came "to those nations," they caused My holy name to be profaned, in that it was said of them, "These are the people of the LORD, yet they had to leave His land." Therefore I am concerned for My holy name, which the House of Israel have caused to be profaned among the nations to which they have come. (36:20–21)

God realizes that by exiling Israel, he has created a new problem. Israel in exile profanes God's name—or in more mundane terms, ruins his reputation—because the nations to whose lands Israel has been exiled assert that "these are the people of the LORD, yet they had to leave His land." The precise meaning of this assertion is unclear. One possibility: the claim is that Israel's God cannot be very powerful, because he could not prevent his people from being forced off his land. The other and more likely possibility: the nations mean to say that God chose his nation poorly, because Israel is so wicked that it could not remain on God's land.

God has thus come to appreciate, according to Ezekiel, that exile is a solution that only exacerbates the problem. Ezekiel says that God will therefore adopt a new strategy. Acting "not for your sake, . . . O House of Israel, but for My holy name" (36:22), God will return the people of Israel to their land and fundamentally change them. He will give them a "new heart" and a "new spirit" (36:26) so that they will not again sin.

Ezekiel's harsh vision of Israel's restoration becomes more intelligible when we appreciate that it represents, in part, a response to an alternative interpretation of the exile that evidently had some appeal within the exilic community. According to this interpretation, for which we will briefly adduce evidence below, the exile means—or might possibly mean—the end of God's relationship with Israel. The destruction of the temple is the concrete correlate of the defunct covenant. Israel should now therefore, on this view, adopt the gods of the nations among whom they dwell. Ezekiel frames the exile in a way that precludes this view. God cannot reject Israel because, having attached himself to them in the past, his reputation is ineluctably bound up with them. To reject Israel after having previously chosen them would only expose God to the calumnies of the nations. One might suggest that Ezekiel prophesies too close to the tragedy to allow the envisioned restoration to rest on God's kindness toward Israel; God's will seems clearly, in the moment, to be aligned against Israel. Only a restoration in which God's hand is forced, against his will, can gain a hearing in the very midst of destruction.

The logic of Ezekiel's vision is fundamentally particularist, in that in it the nations occupy the role of God's enemy. They are inclined to make uncharitable inferences in relation to God. Just as the nations speak ill concerning God's people Israel, so they speak ill concerning God's land; and in this case, too, God is compelled to act, to restore the land's prosperity and indeed improve it.

> Thus said the Lord GOD: Because they said to you, "You are [a land] that devours men, . . ." assuredly, you shall devour men no more. . . . No more will I allow the jibes of the nations to be heard against you. (36:13–15)

The nations' hostility toward God becomes most salient in the final element of Ezekiel's vision of Israel's restoration, in Ezekiel 39. After Israel has returned to its home, a vast assembly of nations under the leadership of the chief prince Gog will advance upon the land to attack Israel. In his characteristically vivid way, Ezekiel prophesies that in this cataclysmic battle, so many among the nations will perish that the house of Israel will have to devote seven months to burying the corpses and will collect seven years' worth of firewood from the enemies' weapons.

Both in devoting such attention to the nations' slander against the land of Israel and in envisioning a cataclysmic battle on that land, Ezekiel perpetuates P's conception of the land of Israel as God's domain. If P can imagine a stable, spatial coordination of the universal and the particular, in which the people of Israel dwell in the land of Israel, around God's templar microcosm, while other peoples dwell beyond the world, in the macrocosmic temple, then Ezekiel, as a witness to the invasion of Judah by Babylonia and to the exile of Judeans to Babylonia—as a witness, in short, to the breakdown of the boundaries presupposed in P's schema—appreciates its instability. And this instability demands a solution.

It is fair to call Ezekiel's envisioned restoration an eschaton, because it involves not simply a return to the past, but a fundamental break with the past: the nations will suffer a crushing defeat that will put an end to their calumnies, and Israel will be transformed in heart and spirit so that it will no longer sin. Another way that Ezekiel frames Israel's restoration in categorical terms is through the image of resurrection, or of a return from death to life. In chapter 37, Ezekiel tells of being brought by the spirit to a valley full of dry bones. At God's instruction, he prophesies to the bones that they will live. Thereupon, and again with the vividness that is Ezekiel's hallmark, the bones join to one another and acquire sinews and flesh. Finally, God's breath restores the bodies to life. God explains to Ezekiel the meaning of this vision: "These bones are the whole House of Israel. They say, 'Our bones are dried up, our hope is gone'" (37:11). Here is the fear that the covenant is now null. But Ezekiel insists that God pledges to "open your graves and lift you out of the graves, O My people, and bring you to the land of Israel" (37:12).

The resurrection imagined in this chapter is clearly metaphorical: no decomposed Israelite bodies will actually rise from the grave. Neither in Ezekiel nor in any earlier biblical book is bodily resurrection portrayed as a possibility to be anticipated. As a general rule, ancient biblical thought appears to have consigned the deceased body to irreversible decay. But, as we shall see (chapter 15), later authors inspired by Ezekiel's eschatological vision or others like it will introduce a general expectation of literal, individual resurrection.

The Restoration according to Second Isaiah

A very different conception of Israel's exile and redemption occurs in the book of Isaiah. The historical Isaiah, a contemporary of Amos, was a literary prophet who lived in the kingdom of Judah in the eighth century BCE, precisely during the years in which Assyria destroyed the northern kingdom of Israel. Isaiah prophesied that God would protect Jerusalem from destruction, and the city was indeed spared. The bulk of the first thirty-nine chapters of the book can be traced to the historical Isaiah.

The next block of chapters comes from some two hundred years later, soon after Persia conquered Babylonia. The decision to join these chapters to the prophecies of the historical Isaiah may have been made by a later editor. Alternatively, the prophet who produced these chapters may himself have taken up Isaiah's mantle and prophesied in his name. Why he would have done so, rather than prophesying in his own name, is not altogether clear. Perhaps he saw in the promise of restoration after the Babylonian exile an echo of Jerusalem's salvation during the Assyrian advance. Such a decision can also be understood as reflecting the growing influence of the notion of a canon, a received set of authoritative books that furnishes the framework within which alone innovation can occur. We will return to this notion at the end of this chapter, and at greater length in the next. At least chapters 40–53 are the work of this other prophet, whom scholars call Second Isaiah (or Deutero-Isaiah). Some scholars attribute later chapters to the same Second Isaiah, and other scholars attribute them to a third prophet, from somewhat later in the Persian period, conventionally called Third Isaiah (or Trito-Isaiah). Our discussion will focus on chapters 40–53.

From the very first word of Second Isaiah, we discern a sharp contrast to Ezekiel: "'Comfort, oh comfort My people,' says your God" (Isaiah 40:1). Second Isaiah imagines God not as a begrudging savior, but as one who aims to comfort. Images of God as Israel's support abound in Second Isaiah. God is, for one, a providential shepherd.

> Like a shepherd He pastures His flock:
> He gathers the lambs in His arms
> And carries them in His bosom;
> Gently He drives the mother sheep. (40:11)

Likewise, God is he "who grasps your right hand, who says to you: Do not fear; I will help you" (41:13, altered). Again, later in the work, God carried Israel at her birth and will carry her afterward: "I was the Maker, and I will be the Bearer; and I will carry and rescue [you]" (46:4).

Alongside these images of intimacy occur numerous grand declarations of God's greatness. Second Isaiah commits, in particular, to two related features of God. The first is his singularity: Israel's Lord is the only god.

> Before Me no god was formed,
> and after Me none shall exist.
> None but me, the LORD;
> beside Me, none can grant triumph. (43:10–11)

> Thus said the LORD, the King of Israel,
> their Redeemer, the LORD of Hosts:
> I am the first and I am the last,
> and there is no god but Me. (44:6)

Second, Israel's God is "Creator of the earth from end to end" (40:28). It is he

> Who created the heavens and stretched them out,
> Who spread out the earth and what it brings forth,
> Who gave breath to the people upon it
> And life to those who walk thereon. (42:5)

The bald assertion that there is no god other than Israel's, or in other words, Second Isaiah's insistent monotheism, is in good measure a novelty in the Bible. Earlier voices tend instead to imagine Israel's God as one among other gods, even if he is the most powerful among them, and/or the only one deserving of worship. While this development has long, preexilic roots, the Assyrian and Babylonian exiles accelerated its acceptance. For if Israel's defeat at the hands of foreign enemies is not a sign of God's weakness, then it must, on the contrary, indicate his cosmic power: having created the world, he directs the fate not of Israel alone but of the whole world. Assyria and Babylonia chastise Israel at God's command, and at God's command, too, Persia brings it comfort.

While Ezekiel would probably not have disagreed with any of Second Isaiah's monotheistic assertions, he does not advance them himself, because they do not serve his immediate needs. By contrast, Second Isaiah uses them to ground an interpretation of Israel's exile and restoration that can be called universalist, albeit in a different sense from the way in which, for example, the book of Proverbs is universalist. Proverbs is universalist in the sense that its worldview has no place for Israel specifically. The subjects whom it recognizes are human beings as such, and the God whom it counsels its subjects to fear is not, in any meaningful way, specifically Israelite. Second Isaiah envisions a salvific plan that excludes no one, and in this sense it is like Proverbs and unlike Ezekiel.

In contrast with Proverbs, however, Second Isaiah insists that all people must worship the God of Israel.

> Turn to Me and gain success,
> All the ends of earth!
> For I am God, and there is none else.
> By Myself have I sworn,
> From My mouth has issued truth,
> A word that shall not turn back:
> To Me every knee shall bend,
> Every tongue swear loyalty. (45:22–23)

This vision of universal worship of God is accompanied by frequent and often parodic denunciations of idol worship, including in the immediate preface to the above passage, where Second Isaiah addresses the "remnants of the nations," who "pray to a god who cannot give success" (45:20). The God whom Second Isaiah calls upon the nations to worship is the aniconic God of Israel, and even as the prophet would have them worship him, God very much remains the God of Israel first: the restoration of Israel is the prophet's first and main concern.

The Servant Songs in Second Isaiah

Much of the rest of our understanding of Second Isaiah's interpretation of Israel's exile and restoration depends on the resolution of obscurities surrounding the so-called Servant Songs therein. For more than a century, scholars have attended with special care to four extended passages in Second Isaiah—42:1–4; 49:1–6; 50:4–9; and 52:13–53:12—in which either a servant is spoken of or a servant himself (or someone who appears to be a servant) speaks in the first person. Some of the boundaries of these passages are ambiguous. More importantly, the servant's identity is not explicitly stated, and we should not assume that the servant in each passage is necessarily the same. But the most likely candidate for the identity of the servant, at least in the passages most immediately relevant to us, is the nation Israel. After all, Second Isaiah explicitly speaks of Israel as God's servant at various points in the book (e.g., 41:8; 44:1–2; 54:17). It is important too in this connection to appreciate, as Benjamin Sommer has well noted, that Second Isaiah draws heavily on the book of Lamentations, which bewails the destruction of the temple; our prophet revises Lamentations' words so as to transform mourning into rejoicing. The central third chapter of Lamentations consists of a long monologue by "the man who has known affliction" (Lamentations 3:1). If the servant in Isaiah, at least in some contexts, represents Israel, it is easy to imagine the servant as Second Isaiah's revision of Lamentations' afflicted man.

In Isaiah 42:6, which may or may not belong to the first servant song, God tells a (collective?) individual, "I have grasped you by the hand." (Compare 41:13, cited above.)

> I created you, and appointed you
> A covenant of a people [?], a light of nations,
> to open blind eyes,
> to rescue prisoners from confinement,
> from the dungeon those who sit in darkness. (42:6–7, slightly altered)

In the second servant song, the same notion recurs.

> It is too little that you should be My servant
> to raise up the tribes of Jacob,
> and the survivors of Israel to restore.
> I will make you a light of nations,
> that my salvation may reach the ends of the earth. (49:6, slightly altered)

Does this verse, which speaks of the servant separately from Jacob/Israel, suggest that the servant is someone other than collective Israel? Perhaps, but earlier in the same servant song (49:3), the prophet explicitly identifies Israel with the servant. These exegetical challenges can hardly be solved here, but we count it probable that Second Isaiah means to assign Israel the role of "light of nations." He seems—but again we are beset by ambiguity—to envision Israel's presence in the exile as somehow leading the nations toward worship of God. A close relative of the phrase "light of nations," namely, "light of peoples," recurs in 51:4, where it refers to the teaching that shall go forth from God. In this context, God addresses "my people," that is, Israel, and perhaps the prophet envisions them as the vehicle through which God's teaching will reach the peoples.

The third and fourth servant songs portray a servant who suffers in patience. In the fourth song, the plural speakers recognize that he suffered for their sake.

> It was our sickness that he was bearing,
> Our suffering that he endured.
> We accounted him plagued,
> Smitten and afflicted by God;
> But he was wounded because of our sins,
> Crushed because of our iniquities.
> He bore the chastisement that made us whole,
> And by his bruises we were healed. (53:4–5)

Who are the speakers? Just before this speech, in 52:15, the prophet refers to the nations and kings who are startled by the servant's appearance, but also by their recognition of something not previously told them. More likely than not, the speakers in the above passage are the nations, and the servant who has suffered for them, of whom they now learn, is Israel in its exile. Just as the first two servant songs assign Israel the role of "light of the nations," the last two have Israel endure afflictions on the nations' behalf.

Conclusion

With the incursions of the Assyrians and the Babylonians, the people of Israel could not but attend in a more sustained way to the question of the relationship of Israel, and Israel's God, to the rest of the world. The exile of the northern kingdom and then the southern kingdom encouraged Israelite prophets to work through this problem within a novel, future-facing orientation, or in other words, within the dynamic framework of (past) exile and (future) restoration.

Ezekiel prophesies in the midst of Judah's destruction, and it is perhaps not surprising that his vision is thus a dark one. For Ezekiel, the exile is punishment for Israel's sins, but Israel's encounter in exile with the nations brings to the surface their underlying hostility toward Israel and toward Israel's God. Confronted by this hostility, God will restore Israel and draw the nations toward their ultimate defeat. Ezekiel's vision is thus intensely particularist. At the same time, the eschatological framework envisioned by Ezekiel is among the most important antecedents of apocalypticism, which, as we shall see in chapter 15, can become universalist in its own way.

The anonymous prophet-exegete whom we call Second Isaiah is active around the time of Judah's restoration under Persia, and his perspective is brighter. Israel's exile is part of God's plan to bring light and perhaps even atonement to the nations, who, with or after Israel's restoration, will come to acknowledge Israel's God as the only god. This monotheistic vision is universalist but, unlike the universalism of Proverbs, Second Isaiah's universalism is objectively intolerant: though God means to bring all human beings to him, the God that does so is specifically Israel's God, and Israel has pride of place now and in the future. I characterize this universalism as "objectively intolerant" to signify that "intolerant" in this context is not a value judgment; it is not necessarily a bad thing to insist that one's own group, and not other groups, has the truth on its side, although this posture comes with dangers, of which the possibility of error is only one.

We noted at the beginning of the chapter that the future-oriented outlook that arose (or in any case, became prominent) with the exile transformed into a fundamental feature of Jewish thought even after the restoration and the reconstruction of the Second Temple under Persia. For this phenomenon we offered a geopolitical explanation: many (most) Jews remained outside Judah during the Second Temple period, and Judah in this period enjoyed little political independence and no Davidic monarch. But there is a second explanation for the survival of the eschatological horizon past the fall of Babylonia: the very prophetic responses to exile that we have analyzed in this chapter (and others that we have not) came to require a certain dissatisfaction with the present, once Jews began to perceive of them as canonical. In the next chapter we will trace the emergence of the concept of canon as a defining feature of Jewish (and later Christian) thought. To reflect on history as a Jew against the backdrop of a canon in which the prophetic promises of restoration loom large is to think of oneself as not yet restored, even if one lives in Judah, in the shadow of the rebuilt temple.

For Further Reflection

1. For those who think of the Bible canonically, thus with the expectation of truth and coherence across all biblical books, how are the tension between the visions of restoration in Ezekiel and Second Isaiah to be worked out? How can both be "correct" in one way or another?

2. Above we noted that Second Isaiah rewrites the book of Lamentations. In *A Prophet Reads Scripture*, Benjamin Sommer offers a detailed analysis of allusions to this and other earlier biblical books in Second Isaiah. How do we make sense of the phenomenon of a prophet "reading scripture," i.e., articulating his vision by means of interpretation and revision of earlier biblical texts? We ordinarily think of prophecy and commentary as two distinct things, one involving com-

munication of novel divine speech and one involving interpretation of prior divine speech; but in this phenomenon, the two coincide.

Bibliography

Blenkinsopp, Joseph. "Second Isaiah—Prophet of Universalism." *Journal for the Study of the Old Testament* 41 (1988): 83–103.

Knibb, Michael A. "The Exile in the Literature of the Intertestamental Period." *Heythrop Journal* 17 (1976): 253–72.

Schwartz, Baruch. "Ezekiel's Dim View of Israel's Restoration." Pages 43–67 in *The Book of Ezekiel: Theological and Anthropological Perspectives.* Edited by Margaret S. Odell and John T. Strong. Atlanta: Society of Biblical Literature, 2000.

Smith, Mark S. *The Origins of Biblical Monotheism: Israel's Polytheistic Background and the Ugaritic Texts.* Oxford: Oxford University Press, 2001.

Sommer, Benjamin D. *The Bodies of God and the World of Ancient Israel.* Cambridge: Cambridge University Press, 2009.

Sommer, Benjamin D. *A Prophet Reads Scripture: Allusion in Isaiah 40–66.* Stanford: Stanford University Press, 1998.

12 | The Consolidation of Judaism: Temple and Torah

READINGS

Deuteronomy 12
Ezra 7
Nehemiah 8
Sirach 19; 24; 36:1–22; 44–50

Introduction

In the preceding chapter we noted the novel salience of monotheism in Second Isaiah. Of decisive importance for Israelite thought on the relationship between Israel and the nations of the world, monotheism is bound up with two other concepts that likewise can be traced to intellectual currents that long predated the Babylonian exile, but came to flourish and eventually predominate around the Babylonian exile and in its aftermath. The first is cult centralization: sacrificial worship of Israel's God should occur in one temple only. The second, to which we briefly alluded at the end of the last chapter, is scripture: all or at least the essence of God's revelation is to be found in a defined set of writings. In this chapter we focus on the development of the concepts of cult centralization and scripture.

Like monotheism, and indeed even more so, cult centralization and scripture represent novel ideas in relation to the biblical Israel of the ancient monarchies. An Israelite from the beginning of the first millennium BCE would almost certainly have supposed that his God (or gods) may and indeed should be worshiped at multiple cultic sites. Nor would our ancient Israelite have thought of a written text as the chief repository of God's will. He might have been familiar with traditions about tablets inscribed with God's word, but such inscribed texts would have functioned mainly as symbols; they would not have served a consultative or pedagogic role. To seek out the will of God, the ancient Israelite would instead have looked to her parents or local elders, the embodiments of tradition, or she would have inquired of an oracle, a priest, a prophet. Divine authority lay first and foremost in people, not in writings.

Judaism as we know it, and as preserved in the Bible in its final form, reflects a consolidation among widely divergent streams of thought around the view that there is a single God, who ought to be worshiped at a single site (on Mount Zion), and whose will is preserved in a single, more or less closed set of books. Each of these three features of consolidated Judaism has a distinct history with considerations specific to it, but together they yield a coherent vision that is objectively "intolerant" in the fashion of Second Isaiah: either one is worshiping the one and only God of Israel, in his one shrine in Jerusalem, and in accordance with the will of God as preserved in Israel's scripture; or else one is, in one way or another, doing something inferior and perhaps even wrong.

Cult Centralization and the Book of Deuteronomy

Between the Decalogue and the Covenant Code, at the end of Exodus 20, God instructs the Israelites in proper cultic worship.

> With Me . . . you shall not make any gods of silver, and gods of gold you shall not make for yourselves. Make for Me an altar of earth and slaughter on it your burnt offerings and your well-being offerings, your sheep and your oxen; in any place where I cause My name to be mentioned I will come to you and bless you. (Exodus 20:20–21, slightly altered)[1]

Verse 21 envisions the cultic worship of God in multiple places, "in any place where I cause my name to be mentioned." A decentralized cult indeed represents the norm in ancient Israel. Some cultic sites were undoubtedly of greater importance than others, whether because of the intrinsic holiness attributed to the location or because of the status of the cultic objects or priestly families at that location; but multiple cultic sites were understood to be perfectly legitimate.

The book of Deuteronomy, parts of which we took up in discussing the Sinai event (chapter 6 above), represents a sharp break from this state of affairs. The book contains multiple editorial layers, but its core likely dates to the reign of Josiah, king of Judah, in the seventh century BCE. As recorded in 2 Kings

1. This follows the division of verses in NJPS. In most English translations these verses are 20:23–24.

22–23, Josiah sponsored a bold project of cultic reform that centralized all cultic worship in the Jerusalem temple and destroyed other cultic sites throughout the country. To what extent Josiah was furthering the work of earlier kings, and what his (and/or his predecessors') motives were, are questions not easily answered. Perhaps centralization in Jerusalem strengthened the hand of the crown or of a Jerusalem priestly elite. Perhaps—and we will note evidence for this hypothesis below—this policy was the corollary, in principle or in practical terms, of a more stringent monotheistic reform. In principle, a multiplicity of cultic sites is suitable to multiple gods, and one cultic site to the only God. In practical terms, centralization would have facilitated the modification and monitoring of cultic practices and the elimination therefrom of polytheistic trappings.

In any case, according to the narrative in the book of Kings, the reform was inspired by the discovery of a "scroll of the Teaching [or: instruction; Hebrew *torah*]" (2 Kings 22:8) in the Jerusalem temple during renovations thereof, a scroll that required cult centralization. This scroll probably represents an early version of our Deuteronomy, and though it purports to represent the words of Moses spoken just before his death, it was evidently composed around the time of or soon before Josiah's reforms. The book addresses cult centralization at greatest length in Deuteronomy 12, which probably stood near the beginning of the original book. Deuteronomy 12 is a window into the new nature of religious authority in seventh-century BCE Judah, and a case study in how to modify cultic law within that authority framework. The chapter does not deny the existence of a decentralized cult, but it delegitimizes it in two ways.

First, it claims that the decentralized cult was a concession to the generation of the wilderness. Moses, speaking to the wilderness generation, tells them that now, here, "every man [does] as he pleases [or: whatever is right in his eyes]," making cultic offerings where he will, but this is only "because you have not yet come to the allotted haven that the LORD your God is giving you" (Deuteronomy 12:8–9). The decentralized cult is appropriate only to a people in motion, without roots; God is, as it were, in motion with the people, circling throughout their camp. Just as the people will find rest on their land, so too will God, and at that point a decentralized cult will make no sense.

Second, Deuteronomy 12 portrays the decentralized cult as, in its essence, a pagan phenomenon, which the Israelites cannot tolerate in their land.

> You must destroy all the sites at which the nations you are to dispossess worshiped their gods, whether on lofty mountains and on hills or under any luxuriant tree.... Do not worship the LORD your God in like manner. (12:2, 4)

The centralized cult thus stands in contrast with the innumerable cultic sites of the Canaanites.

The chapter elsewhere offers different formulations of the centralization law. Of these, the most important for our purposes occurs in 12:13–19.

> [13] Take care not to sacrifice your burnt offerings at any place you like,
> [14] but only in the place that the LORD will choose in ne of your tribal territories. There you shall sacrifice your burnt offerings and there you shall observe all that I enjoin upon you.
> [15] Yet, in accordance with your desire, you may slaughter and eat meat in any of your settlements, according to the blessing that the LORD your God has granted you. . . .
> [16] Yet you must not partake of the blood; you shall pour it out on the ground like water.
> [17] You may not partake in your settlements of the tithes of your new grain or wine or oil, or of the firstlings of your oxen and sheep. . . .
> [18] But only before the LORD your God shall you consume them, in the place that the LORD your God will choose—you and your sons and your daughters, your male and female slaves, and the Levite in your settlements. . . .
> [19] Take care not to neglect the Levite as long as you live in your land. (slightly altered)

As various scholars have noted, the unit has a marked chiastic (ABCCBA) structure, moving from "Take care not" (verse 13; A) to "but only" (verse 14; B) to "yet" (verse 15; C), then back from "yet" (verse 16; C) to "but only" (verse 18; B) to "take care not" (verse 19; A). (Verse 17 has no place in this structure, but we must keep in mind that verse divisions are a modern phenomenon. The composer of this unit may have thought of verses 16 and 17 as a single rhetorical unit.)

The passage not only mandates a single cultic site, "in the place that the LORD your God will choose." It also introduces a permissive corollary: Israelites may slaughter animals in a noncultic way—without offering any of the meat on an altar—in any place that they wish. This license also appears to represent an innovation. In the context of a decentralized cult, there was no such thing as noncultic animal slaughter. If one wished to eat meat, one would have to sacrifice the animal and offer some of the meat on the altar before consuming the remainder oneself. Once Deuteronomy centralizes the cult, it must introduce the notion of noncultic slaughter; otherwise, consumption of meat outside Jerusalem would become impossible.

Scripture and Interpretation

Beyond its substance, on centralization of the cult, what is important to appreciate about Deuteronomy 12 for our purposes is that it does not legislate from scratch. As Bernard Levinson has clarified (building on the work of earlier scholars), the passage draws upon and in a certain sense rewrites Exodus 20:21, the passage quoted above that assumes a decentralized cult. As the Exodus passage immediately contrasts the improper worship of God via "gods of silver" and "gods of gold" (20:20) to the proper worship of God on an earthen altar (20:21), so Deuteronomy 12:2–4, also quoted above, contrasts the illegitimate, decentralized Canaanite cult to the proper, centralized cult.

Likewise, Exodus 20:21 speaks of cultic worship of God "in any place where I cause my name to be mentioned." The words "any place" become the centerpiece of the basic framework articulated in Deuteronomy 12:13–15: one may not sacrifice in "any place," but only in "the place that the LORD will choose"; one may, on the other hand, consume nonsacrificial meat in "any" of the settlements. These verses do not speak of God's name, to which Exodus 20:21 refers, but the formula "the place that the LORD will choose" in Deuteronomy 12:14 is shorthand for "the place that the LORD your God will choose to establish His name"; this formula occurs in Deuteronomy 12:5, 11, and elsewhere in Deuteronomy. Much of the rest of Exodus 20:21 recurs in Deuteronomy 12:13–19. The first two verses of the latter passage speak of burnt offerings, and Deuteronomy 12:17 alludes to sheep and oxen. Likewise, Deuteronomy 12:15 refers to slaughtering and to the blessing of God.

What does Deuteronomy conceive of itself as doing when it reuses Exodus 20:21? Perhaps the simplest explanation is that Deuteronomy means implicitly to claim to offer an interpretation of the Exodus verse. On Deuteronomy's interpretation, Exodus 20:21 includes two distinct laws. The first describes centralized cultic sacrifice on an earthen altar. The second speaks of God blessing Israel in every place. These laws are related, from the perspective of Deuteronomy, because it is the maintenance of the cult in the center that preserves God's blessing upon the peripheries. This is evidently not the original, intended sense of the Exodus passage.

Whatever Deuteronomy's precise intent, what is clear is that Deuteronomy thought it important or even necessary to confront Exodus 20:21. We are witness, in this phenomenon, and in many others like it in Deuteronomy and in contemporary texts, to a growing consciousness of the existence of received, authoritative written texts, of texts that provide access to the revealed will of God, or in short, of scripture. The existence of scripture does not foreclose innovation, but any innovation must in one way or another deal with accepted texts that appear inconsistent with it. In other words, the rise of scripture means likewise the rise of interpretation, or what scholars call *hermeneutics*. This process also operates in the opposite direction: by interpreting Exodus, by as it were tying its fate to Exodus, Deuteronomy makes Exodus more authoritative, even as it undermines its intended meaning.

Deuteronomy itself marks a watershed in the rise of the concept of scripture. Almost uniquely in the Bible, the book of Deuteronomy is self-referential, speaking of itself as "this book of Teaching [or: the instruction; Hebrew *torah*]" (Deuteronomy 29:20) and in similar ways. And the new written text has real-world consequences: as noted earlier, the discovery of the "book of the instruction" (an early form of Deuteronomy) in the temple served as justification for Josiah's reforms. The irony here parallels the irony in the dynamic of enhancing the authority of Exodus through the very act of interpreting it against its plain sense. Scripture is often thought of as a conservative bulwark protecting the old against the onslaught of the new. And indeed, scripture does often function in this way. Moreover, the very concept of scripture depends on the notion of a more authoritative past. But this concept has a history, and at its origin, the concept of scripture is by definition new, and arises in support of a program of innovation. Deuteronomy "invents" scripture because it needs a novel way of appealing to the authority of the past in order to justify its reforms.

Torah and Law: Ezra and Nehemiah

The concept of scripture, first and foremost the Torah (or instruction) of Moses, becomes ever more important in the first centuries of the Second Temple period. Recall that some members of the Judahite community exiled to Babylonia around the destruction of the temple do return to Jerusalem with the permission of the Persian king Cyrus and rebuild the temple. The books of Ezra and Nehemiah, to which we will turn at greater length later (chapters 12 and 14), offer a window onto the province of Yehud (Judah) in the Persian period.

Chapter 7 of the book of Ezra, set in the reign of the Persian king Artaxerxes, introduces the figure of Ezra, a priest and a "scribe expert in the Teaching [or: Torah] of Moses which the LORD God of Israel had given" (Ezra 7:6). Note that, in contrast with Deuteronomy, the book of Ezra refers not to a "book of Torah" but simply to "the Torah of Moses," an indication that this text—whatever it contained, but likely something resembling parts of the five books of Moses that we call the Torah today—was by the time of the composition of the book of Ezra familiar enough that it had a proper name.

Ezra travels from Babylonia to Yehud bearing a commission from the king "to oversee Judah and Jerusalem according to the law of your God" (Ezra 7:14, slightly altered). This verse, together with other evidence, has led many scholars to suppose that it was in the Persian period that Jews came to think of the Torah as law, in a more or less conventional sense, and that the Persian imperial administration may even have supported the production and promulgation of an edition of the Torah for the sake of the governance of Yehud. In any case, the books of Ezra and Nehemiah portray the written Torah as a source of authority for the community. For example, the people gather before Ezra "to study the words of the Teaching [or: Torah]" (Nehemiah 8:13). They find "written in the Teaching [or: Torah]" that God had commanded Moses that the Israelites should dwell in booths (tabernacles) in the seventh month (8:14), and so they do so.

Torah and Wisdom: The Book of Ben Sira

Having risen to prominence, scripture and especially the Torah come to exert a centripetal or coordinating force in Jewish thought: other concepts must be aligned with or defined in reference to them. An example of particular importance for us occurs in the book of Ben Sira. The book was written near the beginning of the second century BCE, around a century and a half after Alexander the Great conquered Persia and Judah fell under the control of Alexander's Hellenistic successor kingdoms.

The author of the book is Jesus son of Sira, or Ben Sira. (*Jesus* is a form of the name Joshua, and *ben* is the Hebrew word for "son." The book is also called Sirach, after the Greek form of Ben Sira's name.) Ben Sira wrote in Hebrew, and his grandson translated the book into Greek. Jews copied the original Hebrew throughout the Second Temple period and for centuries afterward; but the book came to be thought of in Jewish circles as nonscriptural, and Jews eventually ceased to copy it. Today we possess only portions of the original Hebrew, in manuscript fragments recovered from ancient and medieval repositories. But the work became part of the Christian Bible, and so is preserved in full in the Greek translation, from which the quotations below derive.

Ben Sira's book is a work of wisdom literature, in the tradition of and very much influenced by the book of Proverbs. Like Proverbs, it is addressed to young men close to circles of power and warns them against such threats to success as wine, women, and laziness.

A drunken worker will not become rich,
and he who despises few things will fall little by little.
Wine and women will mislead intelligent men,
and he who joins himself to prostitutes will be more reckless.
(Sirach 19:1–2)

A sluggard has been compared to cow dung of dunghills;
everyone who picks it up will shake off his hand. (22:2)

Some aspects of Ben Sira's wisdom teachings, such as his interest in distinguishing genuinely true instances of a category from only nominally true instances, may reflect his Hellenistic milieu; but most of the book's aphorisms would not look out of place in Proverbs.

The major difference between Ben Sira's book and Proverbs is that Ben Sira has an authoritative scripture, including the Torah, the prophets, and other books, that he cannot ignore. While Proverbs is paradigmatically universalist, Ben Sira cannot be: he must situate his wisdom teachings in relation to the teachings conveyed by God to Moses, and to the historical narrative in which these teachings are embedded. Ben Sira does so most explicitly in an extended passage that occupies a privileged position near the very middle of the book, in Sirach 24.

Deeply indebted to Proverbs 8, this passage, like Proverbs 8, has a female personification of wisdom speak of her presence with God before the creation.

I came forth from the mouth of the Most High,
and like a mist I covered earth. (24:3)

But in sharp contrast to Proverbs 8, Ben Sira's Lady Wisdom does not maintain a relationship with the world as such. Rather, she circles the world, seeking a home among a specific people. She travels "in all the earth and in every people and nation," until finally God tells her: "Encamp in Iakob, and in Israel let your inheritance be" (24:6, 8). Wisdom takes up residence, in particular, on Mount Zion, the site of Deuteronomy's one temple. Her monologue ends with a call for all who desire her to come to her. Immediately afterward, Ben Sira resumes speaking:

All these things are the book of the covenant of the Most High God,
a law that Moyses commanded us,
an inheritance for the gatherings of Iakob. (24:23)

While the words "a law that Moyses commanded us, an inheritance for the gatherings of Iakob," represent nearly a direct quotation from Deuteronomy 33:4, the beginning of the verse is more cryptic. Do the words "all these things" refer to Lady Wisdom's monologue? Or does the verse represent a concluding reflection on the entire first half of the book, both Lady Wisdom's monologue and all the aphorisms that precede it? In either case, Ben Sira appears to wish to unify the wisdom tradition and the Torah, despite the fact that the wisdom tradition, in origin, has no place for revelation and situates God at a remove from the world.

How does Ben Sira think of this synthesis? How, indeed, are wisdom and the Torah the same thing? Ben Sira mainly skirts the question. For the most part, he confines the particularist strains of his thought to almost parenthetical set pieces, like the monologue by personified wisdom in Sirach 24. Another interlude occurs later in the book, a prayer at the beginning of chapter 36, wherein Ben Sira acknowledges God as "the god of all" (36:1) but calls upon him to intercede on behalf of "a people . . . called by your name, . . . Israel, whom you likened to a first born" (36:17). The longest set piece is a hymn to great men from the biblical past up until Ben Sira's contemporary, the high priest Simon. This hymn runs from chapter 44 through chapter 50, near the very end of the book, and includes almost no content characteristic of Proverbs. Thus it is fair to say that while Ben Sira asserts the unity of wisdom and the Torah, his integration of the two is relatively superficial.

Torah and Wisdom: Postbiblical Trajectories

We noted above some of the ironies that accompany the emergence of the concept of scripture. Here is another. The book of Proverbs, that paradigmatic expression of universalism within the Bible, is available to us only because it was perceived as scripture, as in one way or another a revelation of God's will. Books that were not so perceived were not studied and copied, and so were lost to history. Yet the very dynamic that preserved Proverbs also made the book very difficult to appreciate on its own terms, because it is universalist, whereas scripture, insofar as it rests on the assumption of an interventionist, revelatory God, is constitutively particularist.

Ben Sira does more to highlight the tension between universalist wisdom and particularist scripture than to solve it. Some two hundred years later, in the Greek-speaking Jewish community of Alexandria, Egypt, a Jewish philosopher and biblical interpreter named Philo attempted to weave together Judaism and Greek wisdom by reading the Torah as an allegorical narrative, more or less

Platonic, wherein the soul undertakes various efforts to perfect itself in virtue and piety, and thus to see God. (For example, when God calls upon Abraham to leave his land in Genesis 12:1, scripture is really telling us that a soul desirous of purification must distance itself from the body, for the body is made of dust, and so can be described as "land.") For Philo, then, the universal largely eclipses the particular: God may have revealed his will to Israel, but his will, read properly, is really nothing other than what wisdom teaches.

Philo's approach enjoyed a long afterlife among some Christian theologians, but rabbinic Judaism in general resisted it, in favor of preserving the particularist character of the Torah as the fundamental expression of Israel's chosenness. Rabbinic Judaism made room for wisdom in a different way. Its foundational legal code, the Mishnah, includes a tractate or volume called 'Avot that collects aphorisms of successive generations of proto-rabbis and rabbis. It is, in short, a work of rabbinic wisdom literature. It begins by constructing a chain of tradition.

> Moses received Torah from Sinai, and transmitted it to Joshua, and Joshua to the elders, and the elders to the prophets, and the prophets to the men of the Great Assembly. They said three things: Be deliberate in judgment, and raise up many students, and make a fence about the Torah. (1:1)
>
> Simon the high priest was from the remnants of the Great Assembly. He would say: On three things does the world stand: upon the Torah, upon the cultic service, and upon deeds of reciprocal kindness. (1:2)

The high priest Simon is the same individual with whom Ben Sira's hymn to great men ends, and from this point tractate 'Avot continues with the aphorisms of successive generations of proto-rabbis and rabbis. The tractate thus positions itself as something of a sequel to Ben Sira. But the chain of tradition with which it begins implicitly offers a solution to the tension between the particularist Torah and universalist wisdom. For the rabbis, Moses at Sinai received not just the written Torah but a wider set of teachings, conveyed orally; he received what 'Avot 1:1 calls "Torah," without the definite article—divine instruction in its fullness—which he transmitted, alongside the written Torah, to his successors. (A written text like the Torah is not the sort of thing that is privately and interpersonally "transmitted"; it is copied.) For the rabbis, then, or at least for the rabbis who produced this text, the antithesis between the Torah and wisdom is solved by a higher synthesis, divine instruction ("Torah"), which encompasses the written Torah but also many things besides.

For Further Reflection

1. Deuteronomy 11:8–21 offers a theological reflection on water and weather that has important resonances in a modern world defined in part by environmental crisis. According to this passage, what are the differences between living in a river-dependent area and living in a rain-dependent area? What conception of the relationship between nature (natural law) and divine intervention is implicit in this passage? See also Genesis 2:8–17; 13:10; Isaiah 51:3; Zechariah 14:17–19.

2. In his book on canon, *People of the Book*, Moshe Halbertal highlights a paradox in the interpretation of canonical texts. On the one hand, one looks to a canonical text for instruction; hence one must be open to changing one's personal view on a given issue to accord with that of the canonical text. On the other hand, a text deemed canonical cannot in any important way be wrong; hence one is inclined to interpret it so that it aligns with one's personal view on the issue. How can a religious interpreter of scripture navigate this paradox authentically?

Bibliography

Fishbane, Michael. *Biblical Interpretation in Ancient Israel.* Oxford: Clarendon, 1985.

Halbertal, Moshe. *People of the Book: Canon, Meaning, and Authority.* Cambridge: Harvard University Press, 1998.

Levinson, Bernard M. *Deuteronomy and the Hermeneutics of Legal Innovation.* Oxford: Oxford University Press, 1997.

Olyan, Saul M. "Friendship in Ben Sira." Pages 87–103 in *Friendship in the Hebrew Bible.* New Haven: Yale University Press, 2017.

Sanders, Seth L. *From Adapa to Enoch: Scribal Culture and Religious Vision in Judea and Babylon.* Tübingen: Mohr Siebeck, 2017.

Toorn, Karel van der. *Scribal Culture and the Making of the Hebrew Bible.* Cambridge: Harvard University Press, 2009.

Watts, James W. *Persia and Torah: The Theory of Imperial Authorization of the Pentateuch.* Atlanta: Society of Biblical Literature, 2001.

13 | Violence and Identity: Joshua and Judges

READINGS
Joshua 1–19
Judges

Introduction

Joshua and Judges, the books that immediately follow the book of Deuteronomy, belong to the Deuteronomistic History, which stretches to the end of the book of Kings. We have postponed discussion of Joshua and Judges until now because our analysis depends in part on an understanding of Deuteronomy and of its historical background.

The book of Joshua describes the entrance of the Israelites into the land of Canaan. They defeat and kill much of its native population, then take up residence, each tribe in its lot. The book ends with the death of the nation's leaders: of Joshua, who served Moses and succeeded him; and of the high priest Eleazar, the son of Moses's brother, Aaron. The book of Judges portrays an epoch of political and theological instability, characterized by a cycle of sin, oppression, and salvation. The Israelites sin, especially through worship of foreign gods, then endure hardship under foreign rule, until God raises up a savior from one or another tribe who unites the Israelites and enables them to free themselves of the oppressors' yoke. After some time, the savior dies, Israel sins again, and the cycle begins anew.

Both books are defined by war and its attendant violence. In the book of Joshua, the invading Israelites attack the cities and villages of Canaan. The violence in the book of Judges is more varied, visited by Canaanite and foreign kingdoms upon Israel, and by Israel upon those kingdoms, and by Israelites upon one another. The violence in these books accompanies the struggles of

Israel to define itself as a nation, in contrast both with other nations (Canaanite and beyond) and with the tribal groups of which Israel is composed. In this chapter we survey the dynamics of violence and identity in these books, and the relationship between violence and identity.

History and Ideology in the Conquest of Canaan

The book of Joshua divides into two main sections. Chapters 1–12 describe Israel's battles against the kingdoms of Canaan. In this section, the nation moves under a single banner, borne by Joshua. With one exception, in the first battle against Ai (7:2–3), the army meets with total success. The warfare takes the form of *herem,* a term perhaps best translated in this context as "annihilative consecration." That is, the victors dedicate their victory to God by taking no captives and typically no spoils; they instead destroy the entire population, man, woman, and child, and burn the spoils or donate them to God's temple. Thus in the nation's first victory, over Jericho, the Israelites exterminate "everything in the city with the sword: man and woman, young and old, ox and sheep and ass" (6:21), and deposit the precious metals in the temple (6:24). Likewise, in Joshua's northern campaign (chapter 10) and in his southern campaign (chapter 11), annihilative consecration occurs at every station, signaled by such phrases as "they exterminated them" and "they let none escape."

The second section begins in chapter 13, with an aged Joshua, to whom God reports that "very much of the land still remains to be taken possession of" (13:1). Following God's instructions, Joshua assigns the tribes their territories and leaves them to conquer whatever peoples still remain in their lots. The process of allotment, settlement, and further war is detailed in chapters 13–21. In this process, each tribe fights its Canaanite enemies independently, with mixed success. We hear, for example, that "the people of Judah could not drive out the Jebusites, the inhabitants of Jerusalem; so the Jebusites live with the people of Judah in Jerusalem to this day" (15:63 NRSV) Or again, the book tells us that the Ephraimites "failed to dispossess the Canaanites who dwelt in Gezer; so the Canaanites remained in the midst of Ephraim to this day, but subject to forced labor" (16:10, slightly altered). There is no reference in this section to the *herem* or to other indicators of total annihilation.

The first two chapters of the book of Judges purport to describe a third stage in the conquest of Canaan, after the death of Joshua. This third stage looks nearly identical to the second stage: each tribe does battle on its own, without deploying the *herem,* and they meet with limited success. Indeed, these chapters highlight precisely the instances in which the tribes (other than Judah, whose failures the chapter is quick to excuse [Judges 1:19] or foist onto others [1:21]) were unable to defeat local peoples. These failures set the stage for the cycle of sin, punishment, and salvation in Judges 3 and forward.

Many scholars have supposed, with good reason, that the Israelite conquest of Canaan did not involve three such neat stages, but rather looked closer to the messy and moderately less violent process described in Joshua 13–21 and confirmed in Judges 1–2: undertaken by individual tribes, with mixed success, and with few instances of *herem*. The portrait of conquest in Joshua 1–12 is, on this approach, the work of a later editor from the Deuteronomistic school who reshaped his source material in light of the imperative in Deuteronomy to "exterminate [the Canaanite nations]; grant them no terms and give them no quarter" (Deuteronomy 7:2, slightly altered). The purpose of this policy, according to Deuteronomy, is to prevent the Israelites from learning these nations' idolatrous ways. The same editor, or a related one, also reshaped the material in Joshua 13–21 to highlight the failure of the tribes (other than Judah, evidently a favorite of the southern editor) to conquer Canaan utterly, by way of explaining the Israelites' lapses into idolatry and God's punishment thereof.

What is the purpose of such an editorial project? It is understandable that the Deuteronomistic editor of Judges 1–2 should wish to highlight the Israelites' failure to destroy the Canaanite tribes, for the aforementioned reasons and more generally in support of the monotheistic reform project initiated (or at least advanced) by Josiah. But why should the editor wish to manufacture a preceding narrative of successful annihilation under Joshua in Joshua 1–12?

An answer emerges when we turn to the book of Judges. The overarching editorial agenda of the book of Judges is clear, and crystallizes in a sentence (in both senses of the term, grammatical and judicial) that recurs thrice (Judges 17:6; 18:1; 21:25), in longer and shorter forms, toward the end of the book: "In those days there was no king in Israel; every man did what was right in his eyes" (slightly altered). The book thus attributes the instability and sinfulness of the period to the absence of a king, and so makes an argument for the necessity of the institution of monarchy, a necessity that the house of David will ultimately supply in the books of Samuel and Kings. The language of the sentence recollects Deuteronomy's demotion of the cultic decentralization as a wilderness practice involving "every man [doing] as he pleases [or: what is right in his eyes]" (Deuteronomy 12:8); this echo confirms the link between the editor of Judges and the book of Deuteronomy.

In light of the editorial agenda of the book of Judges, the purpose of Joshua 1–12 emerges relatively clearly: these chapters advance the implicit claim that the Israelites did successfully carry out the program of annihilative consecration when the nation was under the quasi-monarchic leadership of Joshua. Only in the long leadership vacuum that followed upon Joshua's death did this program fall by the wayside, and the tribes allowed the Canaanites and their idolatrous influence to persist in the land.

Conquest, *Herem*, and the Universal

The conquest of Canaan, on any account, features the Bible at its most particularist. The Israelites invade settled cities and towns, decimate the local populations, and take the Canaanites' homesteads as their own. They do so at God's command and with his approval, in fulfillment of God's promise to the patriarchs. The moral challenge posed by such particularism appears to become rather more acute, morally and theologically, insofar as the invasion involves annihilative consecration, because the destruction then becomes more total (involving not only fighting men but also women and children) and because it then involves God even more directly.

A reader inclined to take the Bible as a moral guide might find some comfort in the fact that the history is not as particularist as the story: the Israelites were likely not, as a whole, foreigners to Canaan, as we noted at the outset of this book; and the *herem*, as noted just above, was probably not as widely employed as the first section of the book of Joshua suggests. But this consideration hardly allays the problem, both because there is indeed history here, and more importantly because the Bible's claim to authority inheres in its story.

Deuteronomy's justification for the *herem*—to preclude the influence of the Canaanites' idolatrous practices—is logical on its own terms, but Deuteronomy does not explicitly weigh the moral cost of its justification, indeed seems blind to the moral cost. A number of passages in the Pentateuch, in Deuteronomy and elsewhere (Genesis 15:16; Leviticus 18:24–29; Deuteronomy 9:5; 18:12), portray the Canaanites as wicked and the removal of the Canaanites as just punishment, but the Bible does not appear seriously to commit itself to this charge; it does not, for example, feature narratives that portray the Canaanites as wicked. In any case, the charge seems too convenient.

One cannot easily justify the conquest of Canaan, and the attendant *herem*, on universalist terms. But one can take cognizance of the role that they play in the formation of Israelite identity. It is clear enough how the conquest narrative constructs an opposition between Israelite and Canaanite, and by extension, between Israelite and non-Israelite. But it is also important to draw out the corollary of the above analysis of Joshua 1–12. This analysis shows that the prominence of the *herem* in Joshua 1–12 is meant also to support Israelite identity in contrast with tribal (and even subtribal) identity, by showing that success is achieved through united, national undertakings, in contrast with local, tribe-specific undertakings.

Tribal Identity and Israelite Identity

Wherein does tribal identity consist? The Bible reflects at length and in various ways on what it means to be Israelite, but has relatively little to say about what it means to belong to one or another tribe or to a family unit within a tribe. The reason for this silence is relatively clear: the Bible's project is, in general, a national one. The major division to which the Bible does, by necessity, devote attention is that between the northern kingdom, on the one hand, centered around the tribes of Joseph, especially Ephraim; and, on the other hand, the southern kingdom, defined chiefly by Judah. But this division most directly expresses itself in the Bible in religious and political terms rather than in tribal terms. We thus have limited access to information about the nature of tribal and subtribal identity.

Yet it is clear that just as Israel works out its identity in relationship to other nations, so it works out its identity in relationship to tribal and subtribal identity. And the latter dynamic of identity formation is important for our purposes, as an understanding of it can provide better purchase on the particularist pole in the particularist/universalist dichotomy that has served as our analytical framework. We turn now to the book of Judges to glean what we can about this dynamic.

The story of Deborah, in Judges 4–5, divides into a prose account of her victory over King Jabin of Hazor and his general Sisera, and a song celebrating that victory attributed by the book to Deborah and her general Barak. As many scholars have noted, the song is earlier than the prose account, and the latter may even be a reworking of the former. In the prose account, information about the composition of Barak's army comes only from one verse in which Deborah instructs Barak to marshal troops from Naphtali and Zebulun (4:6). The poem offers a more complex portrait, heaping praise on Naphtali and Zebulun for their boldness (5:14, 18) but also invoking other tribes and families, some to praise for their support (5:14–15) and others to critique and even curse for sitting out the fight (5:15–17, 23).

Similar tensions occur under the leadership of Gideon, from the tribe of Manasseh. On the one hand, the men of Ephraim confront Gideon for not having called them earlier to join in the battle against Midian (8:1–3). On the other hand, the towns of Succoth and Penuel refuse Gideon's request for food during his pursuit of the Midianites; they mockingly suggest that they will come to his side only after he has won (8:4–9). Upon returning successfully from the battlefield, Gideon exacts vengeance upon them through corporal punishment and execution (8:13–17).

The account of Jephthah has much in common with that of Gideon. Jephthah is from Gilead (11:1), thus closely affiliated with the tribe of Manasseh. He too must respond to the Ephraimites' complaint that Jephthah did not call upon them to join him in the battle against the enemy Ammonites (12:1). Jephthah rebuffs them, and a civil war ensues. Jephthah's men sort out friend from foe by having fugitives speak the word *shibboleth*. A fugitive who cannot properly pronounce the initial consonant in the expected way outs himself as an Ephraimite and is killed (12:5–6). What is especially notable about the Jephthah story is that his confrontation with the Ephraimites is the third of three confrontations, in each of which Jephthah receives an audience and responds aggressively. The first pits Jephthah against leaders of his own tribe (11:4–7), and the second involves the Ammonites (11:12–27). Together, the three confrontations portray a social context riven with potentially violent fault lines, both at the boundary between Israelite and non-Israelite, and within Israel.

Between the accounts of Gideon and Jephthah comes the story of Abimelech, a son of Gideon by a concubine from Shechem in the hill country of Ephraim (8:31). Appealing to "his mother's brothers" and "the house of his mother's father" (9:1), Abimelech manages to persuade them to rid themselves of Gideon's other offspring and assign sole rule over Shechem to Abimelech, because "I am your bone and your flesh" (9:2 NRSV). Abimelech must, in turn, fend off a challenge from a certain Gaal, who appears to make his (ultimately unsuccessful) appeal to the Shechemites on the ground of a connection to the city's pre-Israelite, Canaanite inhabitants (9:26–29). In these struggles, as in Jephthah's, we are witness to the complex interplay—even the overlap—of internal and external boundaries.

Intertribal tension recurs in the story of Micah, an inhabitant of the hill country of Ephraim (Judges 17–18). As Yairah Amit has noted, the story's ideological aims are multiple and include a polemic against the principal cultic sites of the northern kingdom, but our focus lies elsewhere. The protagonist, Micah, produces a molten image, a cultic object, and hires a Levite to minister to it. Everything proceeds smoothly until a troop of Danite men, on the warpath to gain an inheritance for their tribe, encounter the Levite and his image, and persuade him to join them. Micah protests, but can do nothing, for "they were stronger than he" (18:26). Theirs is the might, and no court exists before whom he can prosecute his right.

By far the most violent and editorially perhaps the most complex instance in the book of Judges in which tribal identity figures importantly is the last story cycle, on the near eradication of the Benjaminites (Judges 19–21). The story, which appears to depend closely on that of Sodom in Genesis 19, begins with a Levite from the hill country of Ephraim, traveling with his concubine, a Judahite. When night falls, the Levite is loath to find lodging with the Jebusites, despite their proximity, because "we should not turn aside into a city of foreigners, who do not belong to the children of Israel" (19:12 NRSV, slightly altered). Instead his party enters Gibeah, in the tribe of Benjamin. The locals refuse to take him in, but he is welcomed by a countryman—from the hill country of Ephraim—who happens to have taken up residence in the town (19:16–21). The town's inhabitants press the host to give them the Levite, but he refuses, and the Levite ends up giving them his concubine, whom they rape, leaving her at death's door.

This terrible incident leads to an outright civil war that pits the tribe of Benjamin against the other tribes. The story takes pains to portray this war in terms very similar to the ones in which the conquest of Canaan is portrayed in the books of Joshua and Judges. Just as at the very beginning of the book of Judges, the tribes seek out an oracle of God to determine which tribe should "go up" to conquer its portion first, and the response singles out Judah (Judges 1:1–2), so at the end of the book the oracle tells the tribes that Judah should "go up" first against the Benjaminites (20:18–19 NRSV). The progress of the battle against the Benjaminites—initial failure, tearful consultation of the oracle, then successful ambush—seems to draw from Joshua's battle against the city of Ai (Joshua 7–8). Most strikingly, the tribes nearly eradicate the Benjaminites (Judges 20:48), leaving only a few hundred survivors, and do the same to the inhabitants of Jabesh-gilead (21:11), because they did not participate in the fight against the Benjaminites. In the latter case, the term *herem* is applied to the destruction; the only other instance of the word in the book of Judges comes in Judges 1, in the context of the conquest of Canaan.

The author of the civil war story presumably means to make an argument, through these parallels, for the importance of a king; without a king, the parallels implicitly say, the military energy that ought to be directed outward will instead migrate inward and lead to the spilling of Israelite blood. But this claim depends on the existence of real internal divisions, and the same divisions figure, if with less dramatic consequences, throughout the book of Judges. What can we tell from the above material about these divisions, about tribal and subtribal identity?

Tribal or subtribal identity most often surfaces in the book of Judges in the related contexts of election of leaders and especially the conduct of war.

Family ties can be offered as a self-evident criterion for leadership. Tribes that fight together give expression to and cement bonds, and divisions surface and grow when a tribe is not called to fight or refuses the call to fight. In themselves, tribes and subdivisions thereof are defined in relentlessly genealogical terms. The Jephthah story cycle gives us incidental information about linguistic distinctions among tribes, but otherwise we learn nothing about cultural or cultic differences among tribes. This absence of evidence may be evidence for the absence of such differences; but the book of Judges likely has an interest in suppressing, or at least not dwelling on, such differences, insofar as it projects the ideal of a unified and relatively uniform Israelite nation.

Most likely, the relationship between tribal and national identity is more complex. Tribal identity is intrinsically genealogical, and Israelite identity emerges as an extension of tribal identity, thus likewise as a fundamentally genealogical sort of identity. But precisely this process inhibits the national narrative from acknowledging any aspect of tribal identity other than genealogy. For only genealogy can be easily ramified or scaled up in a way that encompasses and knits together both a larger group and the subgroups therein. Local history, cult, and culture instead serve naturally as sources of division. The Bible does attest to the transference of history from the tribal level to the national level; the exodus story itself may have come to prominence in such a transference, from a preoccupation of the northern tribes to the experience of the nation as a whole; and the same dynamic occurs throughout the book of Judges, in the assignment to all Israel of experiences that in origin implicated only a specific tribe. But that history then becomes lost to the tribe: the experience becomes, in all important ways, that of Israel as a whole, not of the tribe specifically.

Conclusion

If in the Bible, and throughout this book, the chief manifestation of the particularist is the nation Israel, then how does Israelite tribal identity figure in relation to it? One answer, which we developed in the first half of the chapter, is that the division of Israel into tribes justifies reinforcement (often by violent means) of the boundary between Israel and the world. In confronting non-Israelite groups, Israel can suppress its own internal fractures (even if it also runs the risk of exacerbating them). Or in other words, the nation Israel represents an equilibrium in the push and pull between the tribes and the world. A second, related answer, to which the second half of the chapter comes around, is that the tribal structure underwrites the genealogical dimension of Israelite identity. It draws Israel back, as it were, to the book of Genesis, to the nation's familial roots. The next chapter examines aspects of the familial in some late biblical books.

For Further Reflection

1. The book of Joshua is, among other things, a study in the problem of succession; Joshua must fill the imposing sandals of Moses. How does the book address this problem?

2. In his groundbreaking book, *The Poetics of Biblical Narrative,* Meir Sternberg offers Judges 4, on the judge Deborah, as an example of a story with a surprise ending. The crucial verse, on Sternberg's reading, is Judges 4:9. How does this verse set up the reader for a surprise? How is our experience of reading the story different when we appreciate that its ending is a surprise?

3. The most famous of the "judges" is Samson, the subject of Judges 13–16. Samson is also probably the oddest of the judges, blessed with superhuman strength and cursed with all-too-human weaknesses of the flesh. As he is both strong and weak, so he seems both wise and foolish. He is also both Israelite (or at least Danite) and Philistine, Philistine not only in his love for Philistine women but in his resemblance to the other famous strongman of the Bible, the Philistine Goliath (1 Samuel 17). How do these dichotomies operate in the story? Does the editor of the book of Judges want them to convey a message, and if so, what is the message? How do secrets and the revealing of secrets work in the story, and why do they feature so prominently?

Bibliography

Amit, Yairah. *The Book of Judges: The Art of Editing.* Translated by Jonathan Chipman. Leiden: Brill, 1999.

Dever, William G. *Who Were the Early Israelites and Where Did They Come From?* Grand Rapids: Eerdmans, 2003.

Sternberg, Meir. *The Poetics of Biblical Narrative: Ideological Literature and the Drama of Reading.* Bloomington: Indiana University Press, 1987.

Walzer, Michael. "Conquest and Holy War." Pages 34–49 in *In God's Shadow: Politics in the Hebrew Bible.* New Haven: Yale University Press, 2012.

14 | Jews, Gentiles, and Gender: Esther, Ruth, Ezra, and Nehemiah

READINGS

Esther
Ruth
Ezra 4; 9–10
Nehemiah 1–4; 6; 13

Introduction

In the period after the return from the Babylonian exile, in the absence of the independent Jewish kingdom that once gave political expression to the boundary between Jew (or Judean) and non-Jew (or gentile), Jews thought carefully, and with different voices, about how and to what extent this boundary could and should be reconfigured. In this chapter we highlight the importance of women as a lens through which works from the time address these questions. Most of the texts that we will survey—in particular, Ezra 9–10, Nehemiah 13, the book of Ruth, and the book of Esther—center on women who cross the boundary between Jewish and non-Jewish in one direction or another. We will also consider, by way of contrast, a case of male boundary-crossing.

One of the reasons that women feature so prominently as boundary-crossers is that, as Cynthia Baker has emphasized, their status is inherently liminal or in-between. In the patriarchal context of the biblical world, the paradigmatic member of any ethnic group is male. A Jewish woman is therefore, in an important sense, not Jewish in the fullest sense, just as a foreign woman—a Moabite woman, for example—is not Moabite in the fullest sense. Women thus complicate the boundary between Jewish and non-Jewish. But this chapter is not only about gender, and these texts are not only about the problem of women. These texts use women to explore the nature of the Jewish/non-Jewish divide.

Esther, the Jew, and the Agagite

The book of Esther features the one instance in the above texts of a Jew crossing over to the non-Jewish side of the boundary. The story is set in Susa (or Shushan), in Persia, some two generations after the Babylonian exile. The Persian king Ahasuerus, having dispatched his previous queen in a drunken fit, summons all the kingdom's virgins to a beauty contest to find his next wife. In Susa lives a man named Mordecai, a descendant of the community of Jews exiled from Judah by Nebuchadnezzar. He has adopted his close relative, the orphan Hadassah, also called Esther, as his daughter. The names Mordecai and Esther are both Babylonian, while the name Hadassah is Hebrew. That the book provides Esther with two names and Mordecai with only one foreshadows that Esther alone will live a double life. For Esther wins the beauty contest and marries the king; but Mordecai has enjoined her (Esther 2:10, 20) to "not reveal her kindred or her people," that is, to conceal her Judean origins, and she obeys Mordecai's wishes. Accordingly, other than when she is first introduced, the book refers to her always and only as Esther; Hadassah remains concealed.

All this is prelude to the main plot, which begins when a man named Haman rises to become the king's closest advisor. Haman is a descendant of Agag, king of the Amalekites, a famous opponent of Israel (Exodus 17; Deuteronomy 25:17–19; Numbers 24:7; 1 Samuel 15). All the king's courtiers must bow to Haman, and all do, save Mordecai. The other courtiers press Mordecai about his refusal, and he tells them—by way of explanation for his refusal to bow?—that he is Jewish (Esther 3:4). Thus we learn that it is possible in principle for a male Jew, as for a female Jew, to pass as not Jewish; but at the same time, the story sets up a basic contrast: Mordecai is out in the court as a Jew, while Esther's true identity is unknown. The contrast is confirmed by the monikers employed throughout the book, which speaks often of "Mordecai the Jew [or Judean] and Esther the queen" (e.g., 9:31, slightly altered). Esther is never "the Jewess," even after she reveals her identity.

Mordecai's Jewishness immediately becomes the most salient thing about him, as Haman, enraged by Mordecai's refusal to bow, plots to destroy Mordecai's people, the Jews of the Persian Empire. With the help of a hefty gift, Haman persuades Ahasuerus to allow him to carry out this plan. Mordecai, having learned of Haman's intentions, communicates with Esther and attempts to persuade her to intervene with Ahasuerus. Esther expresses reluctance, noting that Persian court etiquette forbids anyone from entering before the king without having been summoned, on pain of death. Mordecai then recalls her to her true self: "Do not imagine that you, of all the Jews, will escape with your life by being in the king's palace" (4:13). Or on another possible translation: "Do not imagine that you can escape from [the fate of] all the Jews by being in the king's palace."

The next verse suggests that Mordecai's conviction that Esther cannot save herself rests not on practical but on theological grounds.

> For if you keep silent at this time, relief and deliverance will come to the Jews from another quarter, while you and your father's house will perish. And who knows, perhaps you have attained to royal position for just such a time. (4:14, slightly altered)

Mordecai implies that God has providentially placed Esther in a position to save her people. As in the Joseph story, to which the book of Esther, as a tale of deceiving and revealing, is deeply indebted at every level, the divine plan for Israel's salvation will be realized willy-nilly, but the human actors touched by this plan are nevertheless free. They can and indeed should discern God's intentions and work to further them; but they can choose not to, in which case they may suffer. Not only Esther will endure God's wrath, according to Mordecai; her father's house will share her fate. The "father's house" serves as a mediating category here between the individual and the people, and Mordecai implicitly suggests that, as Esther is irrevocably bound to her father's house, even after her marriage to Ahasuerus, so likewise does she remain bound to her people.

Moved by Mordecai's words, Esther indeed acts, albeit in her own time and according to her own devices. She hatches a clever plan designed to make the king suspect that there is a bond of affection between her and Haman. With the king already predisposed to suspect Haman of having designs on his wife, Esther turns the screw by revealing that Haman intends to kill her, for her people have been targeted for extermination by him (7:3–4). When Ahasuerus storms off in anger, Haman falls upon Esther's couch to plead for his life. The king, returning to find him in this compromising position, thinks that he means to rape her. Moments later, Haman is executed. (The rape charge that is false but nevertheless has bad consequences for the accused should also recollect the Joseph story.)

The book of Esther offers a complex and partly gendered portrait of the Jewish/non-Jewish boundary in exile. It is possible to pass as non-Jewish and possible to marry a non-Jew, and the book of Esther seems untroubled by these possibilities. But Jews who pass remain tethered to the Jewish people and subject, in some circumstances, to their historical destiny. Esther, as a woman, can pass to a degree that Mordecai cannot, and for the same reason is less "Jewish" than Mordecai is; it is Mordecai and not Esther who is "the Jew," engaged in battle with Israel's ancient enemy, "the Agagite," or Amalek. But Mordecai's success in calling her back to her Jewish identity reveals the practical and normative limitations on the possibility of passing, for male and female Jew alike.

Family and Loyalty in the Book of Ruth

The book of Ruth is set in the period of the judges, between the conquest of the land of Canaan under Joshua and the rise of the monarchy under Saul; but it was composed much later, in the Second Temple period, and paints a nostalgic portrait of King David's Judean ancestors. The story opens with Elimelech, from Bethlehem in Judah, who moves with his wife and two children to Moab to escape a famine in Judah. There he dies, his sons marry Moabite women, and then the sons die. Elimelech's wife, Naomi, remains alone with her two daughters-in-law, Ruth and Orpah.

With the end of the famine, Naomi resolves to return to Bethlehem but urges her daughters-in-law to remain in Moab. Orpah is eventually persuaded to turn back—in Hebrew, the word *'oref*, formed from the same consonants as in Orpah's name, is the back of the neck—but Ruth insists on going with Naomi.

> Do not urge me to leave you, to turn back and not follow you. For wherever you go, I will go; wherever you lodge, I will lodge; your people shall be my people, and your God my God. Where you die, I will die, and there I will be buried. Thus and more may the LORD do to me if anything but death parts me from you. (Ruth 1:16–17)

With this declaration, Ruth affirms her attachment to Naomi and, through Naomi, to Naomi's people and her God. Ruth crosses the boundary between Jew and non-Jew through the vehicle of family, or more precisely, of enduring loyalty to one's family.

Ruth's decision to follow her mother-in-law is an expression of loyalty to her, of course, but the book also construes it as, more importantly, an expression of loyalty to her deceased husband. Because he (and his brother) died childless, Ruth is in a position artificially to restore her husband's succession by marrying a member of her husband's family and bearing a child who will inherit Elimelech's land and become, as it were, the child of the deceased. It is at least in part for this reason, too, that Ruth abandons Moab for Bethlehem.

In the land of Judah, Ruth, assuming the practice of the pauper that she now is, gleans in the field of a man named Boaz and brings food back to her mother-in-law. It turns out that Boaz is a relative of Elimelech and thus of her deceased husband. Ruth asks him to "spread your hems over your handmaid" (3:9, slightly altered), that is, to marry her. The same image occurs earlier in the narrative when Boaz blesses Ruth for her decision to accompany Naomi: "May you have a full recompense from the LORD, the God of Israel, under whose hems you have sought refuge" (2:12, slightly altered).

The implicit analogy between God and Boaz confirms that, for Ruth, affiliation with the people Israel is bound up with her commitment to her family: Ruth's attachment to Naomi leads her beneath God's hems, but her ultimate destination is beneath the hems of her deceased husband's relative, Boaz. Boaz praises Ruth for proposing marriage to him.

> Be blessed of the LORD, daughter! Your latest deed of loyalty is greater than the first, in that you have not turned to younger men, whether poor or rich. (3:10)

Boaz and Ruth marry, and she bears a child, Obed, who would become the grandfather of David.

The word "loyalty" in the above passage translates Hebrew *hesed*, and the word is more precisely if more clumsily rendered as: "the kindness offered against the background of or as the foundation of a relationship." To appreciate how this concept operates in the book of Ruth to bridge the Jewish/non-Jewish boundary, we must turn to Deuteronomy 23:4–5, a legal text that addresses the circumstances of a Moabite wishing to attach himself to the Israelite people.

> No Ammonite or Moabite shall be admitted into the congregation of the LORD; none of their descendants, even in the tenth generation, shall ever be admitted into the congregation of the LORD, because they did not meet you with food and water on your journey after you left Egypt, and because they hired Balaam son of Beor, from Pethor of Aram-naharaim, to curse you.

The expectation that the Ammonites or Moabites should have offered food or drink to the Israelites is probably predicated on the tradition of a familial bond between these nations, perhaps like the one described in Genesis 19:30–38, according to which Ammon and Moab were the children of Abraham's nephew, Lot. According to this text, a Moabite (like an Ammonite) is barred from "the congregation of the LORD"—or in other words, cannot marry an Israelite—because the Moabites failed to provide an expected kindness to the Israelites in the wilderness.

As we will see below, a version of this passage is cited in Nehemiah 13:1–2 as grounds for Jews separating from foreign (and not just Ammonite and Moabite) wives. It is possible to read the book of Ruth as a challenge to the Deuteronomy passage and to the use thereof in the Jewish circles from which the book of Nehemiah emerged. In the book of Ruth, Moab is a source of food when the land of Israel lacks. Even after the famine ends and Naomi returns to Bethlehem with Ruth, Moab remains a source of food, as Ruth the Moabite brings her gleanings to Naomi. And Ruth does the ultimate kindness by abandoning her birthplace and offering herself to the elderly Boaz for the sake of providing a successor to her dead husband. Both Deuteronomy and the book of Ruth link family and kindness, but they move in opposite directions. For Deuteronomy, a foundational failure to do kindness ruptures a familial bond with Israel and constitutes Ammonites and Moabites as outsiders. For the book of Ruth, kindness creates and confirms a familial bond that links Jew and Moabite.

The book of Ruth doubles down on the dynamics of female liminality by constructing the plot around a relationship between two women. Relatedly, Ruth's entrance into the congregation occurs via the gendered category of family. But the book is not just about women. The women of the book serve, rather, to project a world in which the gap between Jew and non-Jew is bridged by relationships, distant or near, forged and reinforced through reciprocal kindness.

Male and Female Foreigners in Ezra and Nehemiah

The books of Esther and Ruth imagine relatively free movement of women between Israel and the other nations. The books of Ezra and Nehemiah put forward a very different vision. The book of Ezra begins with the return of some exiles from Babylonia to Yehud (Judah) under Persian auspices and their efforts to build a second temple. After the temple is built, Ezra, a priest and scribe, makes the journey from Babylonia to Yehud carrying a mandate from the Persian king "to oversee Judah and Jerusalem according to the law of your God" (Ezra 7:14, slightly altered). The book of Nehemiah is the "memoir" of Nehemiah, the Jewish cupbearer to the king of Persia, who, with the king's permission, undertakes a mission to Jerusalem to repair the city's breached walls and otherwise promote the welfare of the community of returned exiles therein. The book describes the repair project in great detail. Within the book's chronology, if not necessarily as a matter of historical fact, Nehemiah comes after Ezra, but relatively soon after, as Ezra reappears as an active figure in the book of Nehemiah (Ezra 8).

A logic of exclusion governs the entire book of Ezra. Both construction projects—that of the temple at the beginning of the book of Ezra, and that of the walls in the book of Nehemiah—occur against the background of hostility from and toward peoples whom the book identifies as foreigners, but who evidently live in and around Jerusalem. In Ezra 4, the "enemies of Judah" hear that the returned exiles are building the temple and seek to participate, because "we too worship your God, having offered sacrifices to Him since the time of King Esarhaddon of Assyria, who brought us here" (4:1–2). According to the book of Ezra, then, the local "people of the land" (4:4) trace their ancestry to foreign nations brought to Judah and its environs by Assyria, under the Assyrian policy of transferring conquered populations. To what extent this is historically accurate—and to what extent, instead, the local inhabitants whom the returning exiles encountered were Judeans who had remained in the land, perhaps intermarrying with other nations, perhaps maintaining native Judean cultural and ritual practices that were different from the practices of the returning exiles—is a complex historical question. In any case, the leaders of the returned exiles firmly rebuff the entreaty of the people of the land, and the latter thereupon make every effort to frustrate the construction project.

Likewise, Nehemiah describes in detail how local leaders, identified by foreign epithets—Sanballat the Horonite, Tobiah the Ammonite, and Geshem the Arab—opposed his efforts to repair the walls of Jerusalem (Nehemiah 2:19). Despite their foreign epithets or monikers, these individuals are evidently deeply entwined with the local Judean population. Thus we learn that one of the high priest's sons is married to a daughter of Sanballat; when Nehemiah learns of this, he banishes this priest (13:28). Likewise, "the nobles of Judah kept up a brisk correspondence with Tobiah, and Tobiah with them" (6:17), and both he and his son married into important Judean families. Indeed, we learn in Nehemiah 13 that in Nehemiah's absence, Tobiah was allotted a room in the temple itself. Against this background, Nehemiah's wall repair project becomes an obvious metaphor for the project of separation: Jerusalem must be walled off against the infiltration of elements deemed foreign. Nehemiah then casts Tobiah out of the temple and gives orders to purify the room that he occupied.

Even as Nehemiah and others labor to disentangle their community from foreign men, they also attend to an enemy within: foreign wives. In Ezra 9, Ezra learns that some Jews have taken women from the surrounding nations—Canaanites, Ammonites, Moabites, and others—as wives. Ezra responds to this news by undertaking acts of mourning and confessing his people's sins before God. He then organizes, in the tenth and final chapter of the book, a public gathering of the community that had returned from the Babylonian exile and manages to get them to commit to separating from their foreign wives.

The language that the book of Ezra employs to describe these intermarriages is cultic, reflecting Ezra's status as priest and the prominence of priests in the community of returning exiles. This community, in Ezra, constitutes a "holy seed" (Ezra 9:2). The nations of the land, by contrast, are marred by menstruant-like impurity (9:11). The returning exiles, by mingling their seed with these nations, have committed a "trespass" (9:2; 10:2), a cultic offense against God.

As the book of Ezra ends with a story of separation from the women among the nations of the land, so likewise does the book of Nehemiah. Such separation occurs at the beginning and end of the final chapter, chapter 13. In Nehemiah 13:1–3, the narrator reports that the exilic community read in the Torah the passage quoted above, Deuteronomy 23:4–5; and as a result, its members separated from their foreign wives. Later, in Nehemiah 13:23–28, Nehemiah learns that some Jews had married women of Ashdod, Ammon, and Moab, so that "half of their children spoke the language of Ashdod, and the language of those various peoples, and did not know how to speak Judean" (13:24 NRSV, altered). Nehemiah subjects these Jews to corporal punishments and recalls to them the example of Solomon, who was led into sin by his foreign wives.

In contrast with Ezra, Nehemiah's objection to marrying foreign women rests less on cultic grounds than on grounds that we might call cultural: unions with foreign women fail to replicate Judean culture, because the children absorb what is literally their mother tongue. It is notable that Nehemiah bothers to note that *half* of the children speak Ashdodite, or alternatively—the Hebrew can be rendered differently—that the children speak *half*-Ashdodite. This observation is likely not merely an objective description: Nehemiah means to condemn the unions with foreign women by portraying their offspring as a hybrid lot, as neither this nor that but something that is in-between and therefore even worse.

The differences between the approach of the books of Ezra and Nehemiah to the marriage of Jewish women to foreign men ("female intermarriage") and their approach to the marriage of Jewish men to foreign women ("male intermarriage") are stark. In the case of female intermarriage, the response is expulsion, presumably both of the foreign man and his Jewish wife. In the case of male intermarriage, by contrast, the response is criticism, exhortation, and coercion of the Jewish husbands, with the aim of having them send away their foreign wives. In the case of female intermarriage, at least from the perspective of the books of Ezra and Nehemiah, there is no real breach of Judah's walls, because the Jewish woman, by her marriage to the male foreigner, has left the Jewish people; she is outside the congregation, with her husband. The husband must be confronted and repulsed, but he is confronted as an outsider. In the case of male intermarriage, by contrast, the foreign woman has insinuated herself inside the congregation. The problem is not one of interloping outsiders but of corruption in the body politic, a circumstance that demands communal self-reflection, repentance, and purification.

Conclusion

All the texts analyzed in this chapter take for granted the categorical distinction between Jew (Judean) and non-Jew. But they take different positions on the permeability of this distinction: the book of Ruth stands at one extreme, and the books of Ezra and Nehemiah stand at the other. The book of Esther positions itself somewhat apart from this contrast, but closer to the book of Ruth. In all four books, the categories of gender and family serve both to constitute and to complicate the boundary between Jew and non-Jew.

It is important to appreciate that the insistence of the books of Ezra and Nehemiah on the nonpermeability of the Jewish/non-Jewish boundary does not imply a total rejection of the universal. On the contrary, for both books, the Persian Empire is a force for good and the Persian king can take his place alongside God himself, as in Ezra 6:14, which reports that the community of returned exiles completed the building of the Second Temple "under the command [*ta'am*] of the God of Israel and by the order [*te'em*] of Cyrus and Darius and Artaxerxes, king of Persia" (slightly altered). Both the priest Ezra and the cupbearer Nehemiah present themselves as loyal servants of the Persian king, and the books give no reason to question the sincerity of these self-presentations. There is no doubt that for the books of Ezra and Nehemiah, the Judean community has a privileged status vis-à-vis the other nations of the world, and those nations win divine favor by favoring God's people; but the attitude of the books of Ezra and Nehemiah toward foreign nations is not per se hostile. Their position, rather, is that good fences, and good city walls, make good neighbors: a positive relationship between the Jewish people and its neighbors depends on the sharp demarcation of the one from the others.

By the same token, neither the welcoming attitude of the book of Ruth toward foreigners nor the book of Esther's lack of anxiety about Esther's marriage to Ahasuerus should be taken as an erasure of the divide between Jew and non-Jew, or of the implicit claim that this dichotomy makes for the superiority of the former. The book of Ruth, however, does come close, if more by what it does not say than what it does say, to a neutral position on the question. In the face of the overwhelming centrality of the family bond in the book of Ruth, national identity recedes to the background, and a kind of universalism emerges that is predicated on the assumption that what makes the person is her commitment to her commitments, her willingness to follow through on the network of relationships that lay claim to her. For the book of Ruth, the political is so much the personal that the former comes close to reducing to the latter.

For Further Reflection

1. Who is the main character in the book of Ruth: Ruth or Naomi? Does the answer make a difference?

2. Rabbinic tradition links Ruth with Abraham. Both leave behind their homes and become something like converts to Judaism. Loyalty and family figure centrally in both departures but in very different ways: Abraham's loyalty is chiefly to God, who promises him a family (a "great nation"), whereas Ruth's is to her deceased husband and his mother, to whose God Ruth pledges herself. What should be made of this difference? Can it be nuanced?

3. While the books of Ruth and Esther both date to the Second Temple period and feature boundary-crossing women, their settings are very different. The book of Ruth takes place mainly in ancient, premonarchic Judah, if also in neighboring Moab. The story of Esther occurs in exile, in the court of a foreign king, and the book's extensive use of the Joseph story, which also centers on a "Jew" who reaches the upper echelons of a foreign kingdom, is a sign of the book's self-consciousness on this score. To what extent does this difference impact the books' representation of Jewish identity?

Bibliography

Baker, Cynthia M. *Jew*. New Brunswick, NJ: Rutgers University Press, 2016.

Koller, Aaron J. *Esther in Ancient Jewish Thought*. New York: Cambridge University Press, 2014.

Ophir, Adi, and Ishay Rosen-Zvi. *Goy: Israel's Others and the Birth of the Gentile*. Oxford: Oxford University Press, 2018.

15 | Apocalyptic: Daniel and the Dead Sea Scrolls

READINGS

2 Maccabees 2:19–12:45
Daniel 1; 7; 10–12
Community Rule (1QS) columns I–IV (see the translation in Florentino García Martínez and Eibert J. C. Tigchelaar, *Dead Sea Scrolls Study Edition,* 1:69–79)

Introduction

This chapter takes us to the (second half of the) latest book of the Hebrew Bible, the book of Daniel, and to two books beyond the Hebrew Bible. The first of the extrabiblical books is a Greek work, 2 Maccabees, composed around the same time as Daniel and deemed canonical by Roman Catholics. The second is a Hebrew text, the Community Rule, composed in the wake of the historical circumstances that yielded Daniel and 2 Maccabees, and discovered around 1950 among the Dead Sea Scrolls (described below). The period represented by these three works was a crucial one for the development of Judaism as we know it, and even more so for the rise of Christianity.

This period began with and was defined by the military campaigns of Alexander the Great in the years around 330 BCE, which transformed the Near East. Starting from Macedonia, just north of Greece, Alexander's armies moved eastward to conquer the Persian Empire and beyond, to the Indus River. At its height, the empire governed by Alexander encompassed Greece, Egypt, Asia Minor (Turkey), Syria, Mesopotamia, Persia, Bactria (Central Asia), and, of course, the formerly Persian province of Yehud (Judah). Alexander's empire fragmented upon his death into smaller successor empires, of which the two most important for our purposes were centered in Egypt (the Ptolemaic Empire) and in Syria (the Seleucid Empire).

In the various regions that Alexander conquered, he founded cities populated by his soldiers, which became centers for the spread of Greek culture. The influence of Greek culture—Greek language, literature, philosophy, political thought, and so on—in the Near East goes by the name Hellenism (*hellenismos*). (*Hellenes* is simply the Greek word for "Greek.") The essential institutions of Hellenism were the Greek city (the *polis*) and the Greek school (the gymnasium, so called because physical training, an essential aspect of Greek education, occurred in the nude, *gymnos*). The best modern analogy to this phenomenon is the spread of Western culture across the globe, in tandem with military conquest. Both Hellenism and global Western culture are syncretistic, meaning that they yield syntheses between the "invading" culture and the local one. Think, for example, of Bollywood, the Indian film industry in Mumbai (formerly Bombay) that intermingles classic Hollywood sensibilities with native Indian ones.

Partly in continuity with the developments traced in the previous three chapters and partly under the novel influence of Hellenism, Jews in the Hellenistic period developed new answers to the question of what it means to be Israel, and of the relationship between Israel and the world. We trace these developments in this chapter.

Second Maccabees and the Beginning of Judaism

The story told in 2 Maccabees begins in earnest in 175 BCE, with the ascent of Antiochus IV Epiphanes to the throne of the Seleucid Empire. At the time, Judah was under its control. In the absence of a Jewish king, Jerusalem in this period was dominated by the high priest and was the site of intense conflict between hellenizing Jews and their opponents. The high priest Onias appears to have been closer to the latter, while his brother and rival to the high priesthood, Jason, was evidently among the former. With the support of Antiochus (2 Maccabees 4:7), Jason gained the high priesthood and ousted his brother. He then built a gymnasium in Jerusalem and "shifted his compatriots over to the Greek way of life," to "an extreme of Hellenization" (4:10, 13).

Amid much further turmoil, Antiochus intervened again to support the hellenizing project, and indeed "to compel the Jews [or: Judeans] to forsake the laws of their ancestors and no longer to live by the laws of God" (6:1). The book reports that the temple was defiled by the worship of foreign gods and by prostitution, and that Jews were compelled to violate the Sabbath and the "festivals of their ancestors" (6:6), to participate in pagan sacrificial rites, and to refrain from circumcising their children, and even, most strikingly, from "confessing themselves to be Jews [or: Judeans]" (6:6).

This last passage demonstrates that for 2 Maccabees, Judean or Jewish identity is first and foremost confessional or religious rather than ethnic. It is an identity that one can leave aside or take up; if it were intrinsic or biological, there would be no sense in forbidding it. The book of 2 Maccabees in fact provides (in 2:21; 8:1 ["Judean faith"]; 14:38) the first known attestations of the word "Judaism" (*ioudaismos*), which likewise, in characterizing Jewish identity as an *-ism*, thinks of it in other than biological terms.

As Daniel Schwartz notes, this book is also the first work (in all literature, biblical and nonbiblical) to use the word *Hellenism* with reference to the Greek way of life generally (rather than the Greek language specifically).[1] The two words are clearly related; 2 Maccabees thinks of the Judean way of life and the Greek as two competing alternatives. And precisely because they are in competition, because 2 Maccabees positions them as alternatives to each other, they must be in a fundamental sense similar. Just as Hellenism, while rooted in a specific place and people, is a way of life that one can adopt, so too is Judaism. Indeed, we also find in 2 Maccabees arguably the first instance of a male—recollect the important distinction between male and female in our previous chapter—seeking to convert, in something like the modern sense, to Judaism: in 9:17, Antiochus, suffering from a grievous injury, pledges that, should God heal him, he will "become a Judean." (God declines the offer.)

But there is a dialectic at work in the construction of Judaism in opposition to Hellenism. On the one hand, as just noted, the opposition implies underlying similarity; and thus Judaism, like Hellenism, must be a "wearable" identity that one can choose to put on or take off. On the other hand, the opposition implies difference; and for 2 Maccabees, the essential fact about Judaism that distinguishes it from Hellenism is that its religious practices—its laws and feasts—are ancestral (as in 2 Maccabees 6:1, 6). For the author of 2 Maccabees, Jews should persevere in their Judaism, because this is how Jews have behaved from of old; and what is old, what is time-honored, is good. This perspective thus roots Judaism in ancestry, in blood. Thus, even as Jewish identity, as "Judaism," becomes detached from Jewish ethnicity, it strikes new roots in Jewish ethnicity through the concept of "ancestral laws." It is important to note that not all Jewish thinkers processed the events surrounding Antiochus's persecution this way. For example, in 1 Maccabees, a retelling of the same events from a very different perspective, the words *Judaism* and *Hellenism* do not occur, and Jewish religious practices are not described as ancestral.

In the wake of Antiochus's persecution, 2 Maccabees reports on instances of martyrdom. In 6:18–31, Eleazar, an elderly scribe, submits to death on the rack rather than consume swine flesh, which the Torah prohibits. The next chapter is

1. Schwartz, *2 Maccabees*, 173.

devoted to the story of seven brothers and their mother who welcome death in the same circumstances. Of particular interest in the latter case is the insistence on the notion that the dead will be resurrected. For example, the second brother declares: "You accursed wretch, you dismiss us from this present life, but the King of the universe will raise us up to an everlasting renewal of life, because we have died for his laws" (7:9).

A revolt among more conservative Jews breaks out under the leadership of a priest of the Hasmonean family, Judah the Maccabee, and he wins a series of battles and thus earns the Judeans a measure of independence and, in any case, relief from persecution. In the aftermath of one of these battles, upon discovering that some of the dead on the Judean side had concealed idolatrous images on their bodies, he arranges for a sin offering on their behalf. The author takes this as evidence that Judah believed in the resurrection of the dead: "For if he were not expecting that those who had fallen would rise again, it would have been superfluous and foolish to pray for the dead" (12:44).

The author's posture indicates that the notion that individuals will be raised from the dead to receive their reward or, alternatively, to be punished was novel and still controversial, for the author takes pains to dramatize it (in the case of the mother and her seven sons) and to find evidence for it (in the case of the episode of the idol-bearing soldiers). We will return to this notion later.

Daniel and Apocalypse

Most of the material in the first half of the book of Daniel, Daniel 1–6, was composed around the beginning of the Second Temple period, probably originally as separate stories. This material concerns the figures of Daniel and his friends, Jewish exiles raised in the court of Nebuchadnezzar, king of Babylonia, to serve among his counselors. Authors living during the time of Antiochus's persecutions supplemented this material with Daniel 7–12. In these chapters, Daniel enjoys a series of visions that describe Israel's historical fate from the Babylonian exile to the rule of Antiochus and just beyond.

Daniel's visions represent one of the earliest examples of an apocalypse. *Apocalypse* comes from a Greek word meaning an uncovering or a revelation; the Greek title of the book of Revelation in the New Testament is *Apokalypsis Ioannou* ("Apocalypse of John"). If we think of an apocalypse as a literary genre reflecting a particular worldview, then we can say that an apocalyptic work is one in which an angelic figure (or figures) communicates previously concealed information to a special human being about the end time or eschaton. In chapter

11 we described the emergence of eschatological thought with the Babylonian exile, as evidenced especially in Ezekiel. One might think of the worldview assumed in apocalyptic texts as radicalized eschatology, in the following senses.

Eschatological thought emerges in a context in which Israel is subject to a foreign power. For the author of an apocalyptic text, the foreign power is not simply an enemy of Israel but a demonic enemy, an enemy that operates as an agent of a supernatural evil force. Eschatological thought envisions an end to—or a decisive transformation in—history; and for the apocalyptic author, that end is imminent. And not only is the end imminent, but much or even all of the past represents a foreordained chain of events leading inevitably to this end. God had fixed and foretold to his prophets that each period of history should be given over to the rule of a particular foreign kingdom, or more particularly of that kingdom's angelic (or demonic) "prince," who governs with little regard for God or God's people. The last of this series of kingdoms is the one that is now, in the lifetime of the apocalyptic author, oppressing Israel. This kingdom will soon meet its end in a great, cataclysmic battle that will usher in a new age of divine rule, a kingdom of God, administered by God's people, Israel. The righteous who suffered death at the hands of the kingdom will be resurrected to eternal life, and the wicked will be condemned to eternal punishment.

The apocalyptic worldview is thus deterministic, mythic, and political. Deterministic, because the entire succession of historical periods—from kingdom to kingdom, until the end—is orchestrated by God. Mythic, because the conflicts and persecutions on earth are mere projections of a drama whose protagonists reside in heaven. Political, because it emerges in response to the problem of foreign rule and projects as its ideal a kingdom of God in which Israel rules as regent.

The authors of the second half of the book of Daniel attempt to make sense of their own circumstances—the indignities of foreign rule and especially the violent persecution under Antiochus—by having Daniel, a figure from the beginning of exile, envision these circumstances as the culmination of an historical series of foreign kingdoms. In Daniel 7:1–8, Daniel has a vision of four beasts, the last of which is most fearsome. An interpreting angel later explains (in 7:17) that these beasts represent four kingdoms, which most scholars think are probably Babylonia, Media, Persia, and Greece (where Greece is Alexander's empire and its successors, most importantly the Seleucid). The last horn of the fourth beast is Antiochus, who "will speak words against the Most High, and will harass the holy ones of the Most High" (7:25).

The fourth beast comes to its death in a judgment scene presided over by "the Ancient of Days," that is, God (7:9). Afterward, a new figure enters the scene.

> One like a human being
> Came with the clouds of heaven;
> He reached the Ancient of Days
> And was presented to Him.
> Dominion, glory, and kingship were given to him;
> All peoples and nations of every language must serve him.
> His dominion is an everlasting dominion that shall not pass away,
> And his kingship, one that shall not be destroyed. (7:13–14)

This figure thus ushers in an end to the series of kingdoms, and thus an end to history. Who is he? The interpreting angel offers an answer at the end of the chapter.

> The kingship and dominion and grandeur belonging to all the kingdoms under Heaven will be given to the people of the holy ones of the Most High. Their kingdom shall be an everlasting kingdom, and all dominions shall serve and obey them. (7:27)

The "one like a human being" is thus not an individual but a collective, the "people of the holy ones of the Most High," presumably Israel, or in any case the righteous among them.

The mythic character of Daniel's apocalyptic visions comes to the fore in Daniel 10. Here the angel speaking with Daniel informs him that he has been battling against "the prince of the Persian kingdom" (10:13) and now enjoys the support of an archangel, Michael, whom he later identifies as "your prince" (10:21), that is, the angelic prince supporting Israel. He also informs Daniel that after battling the prince of Persia, the prince of Greece will "come in" (10:20). The sequence of kingdoms is thus the manifestation of a series of battles between, on the one hand, the princes or angelic figures who correspond to these kingdoms, and, on the other, the angelic supporters of Israel.

Near the end of the book of Daniel comes a vision of resurrection that echoes those in 2 Maccabees. The revealing angel tells Daniel that at the end time, when things look darkest, "the great prince, Michael, who stands beside the sons of your people" (Daniel 12:1), will appear; and Daniel's people, or some of them, will be rescued. Then "many of those that sleep in the dust of the earth will awake" (12:2), some for eternal reward and some for eternal punishment.

Much of the imagery in Daniel's visions is familiar from Ezekiel's vision of restoration, analyzed in chapter 11. Ezekiel, too, construes the nations as implacable foes of God and of Israel, and he also speaks of them meeting defeat in a final, great battle. Ezekiel even envisions resurrection, albeit only of a metaphorical, national sort. The concrete, individual resurrection envisioned by 2 Maccabees and Daniel, like the apocalyptic worldview as a whole, represents a response to the exigencies of destructive and oppressive foreign rule, especially Antiochus's persecutions. If an individual like Eleazar in 2 Maccabees dies not because he disobeyed the law, and not even despite the fact that he observed the law, but rather precisely for the sake of the law, then death must only be temporary, must only be a respite on the way to a more final accounting.

But there is another explanation, vaguer but no less real, for the rise of the notion of individual resurrection after death: the emergence of the individual, in Israel and far beyond it. In the classical biblical period, individuals' identity was apparently more decisively subordinated to that of one's family. In such a context, it makes sense to imagine that a person might reap the reward for his piety in the form of children and grandchildren. One survives and prospers through the survival and prosperity of one's family. But into the Second Temple period and beyond, the individual came to be appreciated as such, and less as a cog in the family unit. In these circumstances, the problem of a successful righteous man who dies cannot be cured through descendants; that very man must receive his reward, if not in life then after death.

The notion of accounting for righteousness and wickedness at the level of the individual rather than at the level of the family represents a certain limitation of Jewish particularism, for the individual is a universal category: one is rewarded or punished on one's own merits, rather than on the merits of one's family, which in the Jewish case is, on the largest scale, nothing less than the people Israel itself. In the next section we turn to another limitation on Jewish particularism that also has its origins in the Maccabean revolt.

Sectarianism and the Dead Sea Scrolls

As an initial matter, the apocalyptic worldview draws the line separating the saved from the damned at the boundary between Israel and the foreign nations, but it can redraw the line further inward, and not only (as in Daniel and in the standard nonapocalyptic worldview as well) to exclude obvious sinners—the murderers, the worshipers of foreign gods, those who forgo circumcision, and so on—but also to exclude other Jews who adopt a different interpretation of what Jewish law is and what it demands. In the decades after the Maccabean revolt, from the second half of the second century BCE through to the end of the Second Temple period (70 CE), we witness such a phenomenon, as small groups of Jews—sects—break off from the mainstream and condemn that mainstream as misled and sinful.

Our best witnesses to this process are the Dead Sea Scrolls. Written between the second century BCE and the first century CE, the Dead Sea Scrolls represent by far the most important archaeological discovery for understanding the crucial transition from the late biblical period to the setting that produced a crystallized postbiblical Judaism, and afterward Christianity. They were discovered in 1947 in a network of caves near the Dead Sea, in the area of Jericho in Israel's Judean Desert. The scrolls had been deposited in jars in these caves by a sect that lived in the vicinity, and there they lay, more or less (but not entirely) unmolested, for almost two thousand years, until three Bedouin shepherds in an area called Qumran discovered the jars. The jars contained hundreds of documents: copies of biblical books, interpretive works, and works produced by the sect itself. A whole, previously unknown library from one of the most important periods in history had been discovered.

This library very likely belonged to a group identified in other sources as the sect of Essenes, which was dominated by priests. The passages below come from the Community Rule (1QS), a text devoted to the organization of the sect.

> And all those who enter in the Rule of the Community shall establish a covenant before God in order to carry out all that he commanded and in order not to stray from following him out of any fear, dread, or testing during the dominion of Belial. (I, 16–18)

> And anyone who declines to enter [the covenant of Go]d in order to walk in the stubbornness of his heart shall not [enter the Com]munity of his truth, since his soul loathes the disciplines of knowledge of just judgments. He has not the strength to convert his life and he shall not be counted with the upright. . . . He will not become clean by the acts of atonement, nor shall he be purified by the cleansing waters, nor shall he be made holy by seas or rivers, nor shall he be purified by all the waters of ablution. (II, 25–III, 5)

> From the God of knowledge stems all there is and all there shall be. Before they existed he established their entire design. And when they have come into being, at their appointed time, they will execute all their works according to his glorious design, without altering anything. . . . He created man to rule the world and placed within him two spirits so that he would walk with them until the moment of his visitation: they

> are the spirits of truth and of deceit. From the spring of light stem the generations of truth, and from the source of darkness the generations of deceit. And in the hand of the Prince of Lights is dominion over all the sons of justice; they walk on paths of light. And in the hand of the Angel of Darkness is total dominion over the sons of deceit; they walk on paths of darkness. From the Angel of Darkness stems the corruption of all the sons of justice. And all their sins, their iniquities, their guilts, and their offensive deeds are under his dominion in compliance with the mysteries of God, until his moment; and all their afflictions and their periods of grief are caused by the dominion of his enmity; and all the spirits of his lot cause the sons of light to fall. However, the God of Israel and the angel of his truth assist all the sons of light. (III, 15–25)

> For God has sorted them into equal parts until the last time. . . . God, in the mysteries of his knowledge and in the wisdom of his glory, has determined an end to the existence of injustice and on the appointed time of the visitation he will obliterate it for ever. (IV, 16–19)

The sect's worldview is apocalyptic, thus deterministic and mythic. God has fixed the arc of history from the beginning and has sorted humankind into two even groups according to their spirits. Those in whom the spirit of light predominates are the "sons of justice," and they fall under the auspices of the Prince of Lights. Those in whom the spirit of darkness predominates are the "sons of deceit," subjects of the Angel of Darkness. The conflict between them will be resolved in the end time.

Unlike the book of Daniel, this passage does not refer to foreign kingdoms. In this sense its apocalypticism is less overtly political than that of the book of Daniel. This difference is a corollary of the passage's sectarianism. The passage redraws the political opposition between Israel and the nations into an opposition between those in the sect—"those who enter in the Rule of the Community"—and those outside it. The latter group, which includes any Jew who "declines to enter into the covenant of God," is condemned to destruction in God's final judgment. As becomes clear from other documents among the Dead Sea Scrolls, those outside the sect are not sinners against Israel's covenant with God in the obvious sense. The sect accuses outsider Jews not of murder or idolatry or the like, but of interpreting the biblical text in such a way as to permit specific practices—marriage after divorce (or perhaps polygamy), for example, or uncle-niece marriage, or certain purification rites—that the sect, adopting a different interpretation of the Bible, prohibits.

The very notion of sectarianism implies inward movement, retreat. The line of the saved becomes drawn more tightly. The vector of sectarianism is thus intrinsically particularist. But if one draws the line ever inward, the next natural stopping point is the individual, a universalist category. The dynamic of sectarianism thus has within it a universalist potential. This is especially so in an apocalyptic framework. For while the political dimension of apocalyptic rests on the distinction between Israel and the nations, its deterministic and mythic dimensions carry in them echoes of the universal. Determinism and myth, after all, hark back to the creation of the world, the paradigmatic expression of the universal. One of the giants of biblical scholarship, Gerhard von Rad, famously claimed that apocalyptic owes a debt to wisdom literature. Whatever the truth of this claim, it owes its plausibility to the presence of these universalist dimensions in apocalyptic.

Conclusion

With the spread of Greek culture and the emergence of apocalyptic and sectarianism at the end of the biblical period, new and complex configurations of the particular and the universal emerge. With 2 Maccabees, the category of Judaism surfaces. It is a potentially universalizable identity—an identity independent of ethnicity—that is, at the very same time, rooted in ancestral practice. This is perhaps the closest approximation of the understanding of Jewish identity in rabbinic Judaism, the predominant form of Judaism today. With apocalypticism, especially in its sectarian form, a particularism emerges that is so circumscribed that it ironically becomes universalist, grounded in creation and in the individual's decision (perhaps predetermined) to choose or reject salvation. This perspective is one that became popular in early Christianity, whose roots lie in Jewish sectarian apocalypticism.

For Further Reflection

1. If apocalypticism is related to wisdom literature, it is also, more directly, a child of prophecy. How does Daniel compare to earlier prophets that we have examined: Amos, Ezekiel, and Second Isaiah?

2. The discussion above briefly described some of the points of disagreement between the Dead Sea sect and its mainstream opponents. The Dead Sea sect

took issue with the mainstream's position on issues related to marriage, among other things. For details see the Damascus Document (CD), columns IV and V. (This document is available in English translation in García Martínez and Tigchelaar, *Dead Sea Scrolls Study Edition*, 1:555–59.) How does the sect defend its positions? What conception of religious law emerges from this passage? On the latter see Aharon Shemesh, *Halakhah in the Making*.

Bibliography

Bar-Kochva, Bezalel. *Judas Maccabaeus: The Jewish Struggle against the Seleucids*. New York: Cambridge University Press, 1989.

Cohen, Shaye J. D. *The Beginnings of Jewishness: Boundaries, Varieties, Uncertainties*. Berkeley: University of California Press, 1999.

Collins, John J. *The Apocalyptic Imagination: An Introduction to Jewish Apocalyptic Literature*. 3rd ed. Grand Rapids: Eerdmans, 1998.

García Martínez, Florentino, and Eibert J. C. Tigchelaar. *The Dead Sea Scrolls Study Edition*. 2 vols. 1997–1998. Reprint. Grand Rapids: Eerdmans, 2000.

Goff, Matthew. "Wisdom and Apocalypticism." Pages 53–68 in *The Oxford Handbook of Apocalyptic Literature*. Edited by John J. Collins. New York: Oxford University Press, 2014.

Levenson, Jon D. *Resurrection and the Restoration of Israel: The Ultimate Victory of the God of Life*. New Haven: Yale University Press, 2008.

Nongbri, Brent. "The Motivations of the Maccabees and the Judean Rhetoric of Ancestral Tradition." Pages 85–111 in *Ancient Judaism in Its Hellenistic Context*. Edited by Carol Bakhos. Leiden: Brill, 2005.

Schwartz, Daniel R. *2 Maccabees*. Berlin: de Gruyter, 2008.

Shemesh, Aharon. *Halakhah in the Making: The Development of Jewish Law from Qumran to the Rabbis*. Berkeley: University of California Press, 2009.

16 | The Israelite at Prayer: The Book of Psalms

READINGS

Psalms 1; 3; 6–7; 18; 30; 37; 90; 94; 102–103; 110; 124; 130–131

Introduction

The book of Psalms is categorically different from almost all the other books of the Bible. While the other books are meant to be received as records of past events and past utterances, the book of Psalms offers texts or scripts—one hundred and fifty distinct scripts—meant for hymnal recitation and prayer. If the Bible, broadly conceived, presents itself as the deeds and words of God, then the book of Psalms, exceptionally, presents itself as the words of human beings to God. The history of the formation and reception of the book of Psalms is, in part, the history of the attempt to overcome this difference, to assimilate the book of Psalms to the rest of the Bible by transforming it into narrative. Thus Gerald Wilson has argued that the psalms in the book were arranged in such a way that they would implicitly tell Israel's history, from the glorious past under David and Solomon, to Zion's downfall and exile, and finally to its hoped-for restoration.

In our treatment of the book of Psalms, we will touch on this and other features of the book through the prism of the following questions: How does the individual Israelite pray in the book of Psalms? How does the praying Israelite implicitly or explicitly express his or her identity? More specifically, does the Israelite present him- or herself before God as a human being (thus in a universalist vein), or as an Israelite (thus along particularist lines), or as both?

The Israelite Community in Psalms of the Community

The name most closely associated with scholarly study of the book of Psalms is a German scholar, Hermann Gunkel. Near the beginning of the twentieth century, Gunkel put forward a form-critical approach to the study of the book as a way of accounting for the dense networks of similarities binding different groups of psalms. On this approach, the first task is to classify the psalms into different forms: the hymn (a song of praise to God), the individual complaint (in which an individual complains to God of the distress in which he finds himself, and prays for deliverance therefrom), the communal complaint (in which the complaining speaker is or represents himself as a community rather than as an individual), and so on. The second and more speculative task is to locate each form in a specific social setting (German *Sitz im Leben,* literally "situation in life"), a set of circumstances in which the form was deployed. Probably the most fundamental formal division among the psalms is that between psalms in which the speaker speaks in the singular, as an individual, and psalms in which the speaker speaks in the plural, as a community.

In communal psalms, the community is inevitably Israel. An example of a communal lament is Psalm 74, which we encountered earlier in our remarks on the first chapter of Genesis (chapter 10 above). The lament emerges against a background of distress: Israel's enemies have attacked and put to fire God's sanctuary (Psalm 74:3–9). The speaker castigates God for his apparent inaction.

> Why, O God, do You forever reject us,
> Does Your anger fume at the flock that You tend?
> Remember the community You made Yours long ago,
> Your very own tribe that You redeemed,
> Mount Zion, where You dwell. (74:1–2 NJPS, slightly altered)

In verses 12–17, the speaker attempts to spur God to action against Israel's enemies by recalling how God defeated the sea and imposed order on the world.

Communal Israel speaks again, this time in the mode of thanksgiving, in Psalm 124, one among a series of psalms (Psalms 120–134) designated as "songs of ascent," perhaps intended for pilgrims ascending to Zion.

> [1] Were it not for the LORD, who was for us—
> let Israel now declare—
> [2] were it not for the LORD, who was for us

when people arose against us,
[3] then alive would they would have swallowed us,
in their burning rage against us;
[4] then the waters would have flooded us,
the torrent swept over us;
[5] then over us would have swept
the seething waters.
[6] Blessed is the LORD, who did not let us
be ripped apart by their teeth.
[7] Our lives are like a bird escaped from a fowler's trap;
the trap broke and we escaped.
[8] Our help is in the name of the LORD,
maker of heaven and earth. (NJPS, slightly altered)

The speaker of the psalm binds his words together by an almost incantatory series of repetitions, especially at the beginning of the verses ("Were it not for the LORD" in verses 1–2; "then" in verses 3–5; "our" in verses 7–8), and offers them for the people to repeat: "let Israel now declare" (verse 1).

The psalm uses different images for the threat posed by the enemy. These images are arranged chiastically, that is, in an ABCCBA pattern. In the very middle of the chiastic pattern (the "C" element), in verses 4–5, the enemy is represented by the raging waters, as in Psalm 74. Around this core, in verse 3 ("alive would they have swallowed us") and verse 6 ("ripped apart by their teeth"), the enemy is a predatory beast (the "B" in the pattern). Finally, bookending these images, in verse 2 and verse 7 (the "A"), the enemy is a person. Verse 2 speaks of "people," in Hebrew *'adam*, the word used for human beings in the creation stories at the beginning of Genesis. In verse 7, the enemy is a fowler, a trapper of birds. Coming at the end of this catalog of the natural world, the closing reference to God as "maker of heaven and earth" is especially compelling: the world entire—watery, beastly, human—is arrayed against Israel, but as the maker of the world, God can protect his people.

The Universal Human in Psalms of the Individual

In the typical psalm of the individual, that individual does not depict himself in specifically Israelite terms. Psalm 6 is an individual lament in which the speaker calls upon God to take mercy on him. The sources of the speaker's suffering in this psalm, as in many others, appear to be multiple, including both physical suffering (Psalm 6:2: "O LORD, heal me, for my bones are shaking with terror")[1] and the assails of an enemy (6:7: "My eyes waste away because of grief; they grow weak because of all my foes"). He depicts himself weeping on his bed: "every night I flood my bed with tears; I drench my couch with my weeping" (6:6). Besides falling upon God's mercy, the speaker offers an argument to support his cry for intervention: "For in death there is no remembrance of you; in Sheol who can give you praise?" (6:5). It is in God's interest, as it were, to save the speaker, because God will thus earn the speaker's acclaim.

Psalm 30 is an individual thanksgiving prayer, precisely the sort of a prayer that the speaker of Psalm 6 promises to offer should God rescue him. Indeed, the speaker of this psalm recollects his past distress in terms that almost precisely match those of Psalm 6. He compares his circumstances to one for whom "weeping may linger for the night" (30:5). Likewise, he reports that he appealed to God and noted that his death would bring God no profit: "What profit is there in my death, if I go down to the Pit? Will the dust praise you?" (30:9). The beginning of the psalm gives expression to this quid pro quo: "I will extol you, O LORD, for you have drawn me up" (30:1). The word for "extol" is literally "raise up": God has lifted up the speaker from the pit of Sheol, and so the speaker now raises up God.

Synthesis: Eternity and History

While the book of Psalms characteristically distinguishes between the praying community, which is Israelite, and the praying individual, who comes before God as a human being, numerous psalms synthesize the individual and the community in numerous different ways. We may begin with Psalm 102, whose synthesis is arguably most striking for the abruptness of its movement between the individual and the community. The first part of the psalm reads just like an individual lament: "Hear my prayer, O LORD. . . . Do not hide your face from me in the day of my distress" (102:1–2). As in Psalm 6, the speaker's complaint ranges from physical illness (102:4: "My heart is stricken") to the taunts of enemies (102:8: "All day long my enemies taunt me"). In his suffering he perceives his mortality: "My days are like an evening shadow; I wither away like grass" (102:11). At this point, the psalm takes a sharp turn:

1. Henceforth in this chapter all biblical quotations are from the NRSV, unless otherwise indicated.

> [12] But you, O LORD, are enthroned forever,
> your name endures to all generations.
> [13] You will rise up and have compassion on Zion,
> for it is time to be gracious to it;
> the appointed time has come.

In verses 14–22, the speaker describes how the nations will praise God in Zion when they gather there to serve him, presumably after God has restored Zion to its former glory. The shift from individual suffering in 102:1–11 to the national narrative in 102:12–22 is abrupt, smoothed only by the contrast of the speaker's mortality in 102:11 to God's eternal fame in 102:12, and by a wordplay between "wither" (Hebrew *'ivash*) at the end of 102:11 and "enthroned" (Hebrew *teshev*) at the end of the first clause in 102:12.

Just as abruptly as the psalm shifts from the individual to the community, it shifts back to the individual: "He has broken my strength in midcourse; he has shortened my days" (102:23). The speaker then returns to the contrast between his mortality and God's immortality: "do not take me away at the midpoint of my life, you whose years endure throughout all generations" (102:24). The loose implicit argument in this verse—that God endures forever and so too, therefore, should the speaker, his follower—is poetically strengthened in the final verse:

> The children of your servants shall live secure;
> their offspring shall be established in your presence. (102:28)

The line depends on a wordplay between "shall live" (*yishkonu*) and "shall be established" (*yikkon*), a wordplay that implicitly suggests that those who dwell with God should by right do so in a firm or enduring fashion.

How does the psalm hold together? Within the framework of what is in essence the prayer of an individual in private distress, how does the fate of the people Israel come into play? There appear to be two steps in this movement. The first involves the association of the speaker's distress with his mortality, which in turn leads to the articulation of a contrast (in 102:11–12, recapitulated in 102:24) between human mortality and divine immortality. The second step involves the association of this contrast with God's kindness toward Israel. God's immortality evokes not only human mortality but also the long history of God's works in the world, in particular the history of his relationship with his people. The God of eternity is also the God of ancient history.

Similar associative links occur in Psalm 90 and again in Psalm 103. Psalm 90 begins by noting how God has always protected "us," presumably Israel: "You have been our dwelling place in all generations" (90:1). As in Psalm 102, God's kindness "in all generations"—a particularist temporal framework, defined by Israelite genealogy—evokes the fact of his endurance across time, that is, the universalist category of divine immortality, in contrast to human mortality.

> Before the mountains were brought forth,
> Or ever you had formed the earth and the world,
> from everlasting to everlasting you are God. (90:2)

The interplay of difference and similarity in the phrases "in all generations" (90:1) and "from everlasting to everlasting" (90:2) gives expression to the complex relationship between the particular and the universal in the psalm.

Psalm 90 continues with an extended universalist reflection on human mortality (90:3–12) that invokes the metaphor of withered grass (90:5) that we already encountered in Psalm 102. The community of Israel, which has remained largely in the background after its initial appearance in 90:1, returns in the final section, which calls on God to turn toward Israel.

> [13] Turn, O LORD! How long?
> Have compassion on your servants! . . .
> [15] Make us glad as many days as you have afflicted us. . . .
> [16] Let your work be manifest to your servants,
> And your glorious power to their children. . . .
> [17] and prosper for us the work of our hands,
> O prosper the work of our hands!

The diction of this conclusion—the parallelism of "servants" and "children," the hope for a firm foundation (*konenah/konenehu*, from the same root as *yikkon* in 102:28)—closely binds it to the conclusion of Psalm 102.

Psalm 103 reprises the same dynamic but adds some new elements. The psalm begins as an individual thanksgiving, wherein the speaker urges his soul to bless God because he "redeems your life from the Pit" (103:4). From here the psalm turns to the communal and the particular—to the Israelite, in other words—with praise of God who "made known his ways to Moses" (103:7). These "ways," as we learn in 103:8, are God's traits of mercy, in which he instructed Moses in Exodus 34:6. In light of these traits, the speaker is confident that God will forgive his people.

> 11 For as the heavens are high above the earth,
> so great is his steadfast love toward those who fear him;

[12] as far as the east is from the west,
so far he removes our transgressions from us.
[13] As a father has compassion for his children,
so the LORD has compassion for those who fear him.
[14] For he knows how we were made,
he remembers that we are dust.
[15] As for mortals, their days are like grass;
they flourish like a flower of the field;
[16] for the wind passes over it, and it is gone,
and its place knows it no more.
[17] But the steadfast love of the LORD is from everlasting to everlasting
on those who fear him.

These verses root God's forgiveness in the gap between the Divine and the human. In the very distance of heaven from earth rests the possibility of mercy, for God, from his exalted station, recognizes human beings as dust, and with this recognition comes compassion. But particularist considerations also underlie God's kindness in this passage. God will forgive not only because of his distance, as the eternal from the ephemeral, but also because of his proximity, as a father to his children.

Synthesis: Israel as Extension

A different coordinative bridge between the universal individual and the particular community occurs in other psalms. One of the songs of ascent, Psalm 130, known from the Latin translation of its first words as *De profundis,* is an individual lament. The speaker calls out to God from "the depths," a location much the same as Sheol or the Pit that we have seen in other psalms of lament. He seeks God's forgiveness, for "if you, O LORD, should mark iniquities, . . . who could stand?" (130:3). The speaker identifies his posture as one of expectant waiting: "I wait for the LORD . . . more than those who watch for the morning" (130:5–6). The psalm concludes with a sharp turn to the particular, by encouraging Israel to adopt the same posture.

O Israel, hope in [or: wait for] the LORD!
For with the LORD there is steadfast love,
and with him is great power to redeem.
It is he who will redeem Israel
from all its iniquities. (130:7–8)

How are we to understand this abrupt introduction of Israel, this sharp turn from the universality of human sin to a national framework? Perhaps, in keeping with the preceding verses, he may mean to express humility: he will come before God not alone, but rather among his people. Additionally, the speaker, by situating himself in relation to Israel, appears to see in himself an instance of and a paradigm for them. The congregation should appreciate that the speaker waits for God not only as a human being but as an Israelite. And Israel, which like him stands in need of redemption, should therefore share his hope.

The next psalm, Psalm 131, manifests a similar dynamic, but through different rhetorical means. The speaker in this psalm of three short verses appears, at first glance, to be different from that in the previous psalm, in that he protests his innocence:

> O LORD, my heart is not lifted up,
> my eyes are not raised too high;
> I do not occupy myself with things
> too great and too marvelous for me. (131:1)

But we immediately perceive that the speaker is claiming not that he is free of sin in general, but that he is adopting the posture of one "from the depths," the posture of one who does not raise his eyes in a gesture of superiority over others who are beneath him, but who instead, on the contrary, acknowledges his infant-like dependence on another: "But I have calmed and quieted my soul, like a weaned child with its mother" (131:2). From this image of contented dependence, the speaker concludes by urging the same upon Israel: "O Israel, hope in [or: wait for] the LORD, from this time on and forevermore" (131:3).

Synthesis: Israel as Sage and Sufferer

A third mechanism for synthesizing the universal and the particular occurs in the Psalms within the framework of the wisdom tradition. Scholars have long noted that many psalms (known as "wisdom psalms") make dense use of vocabulary and concepts familiar from Proverbs. Indeed, some of the most salient chapters in the book count among the wisdom psalms, including the first chapter, Psalm 1, and the longest chapter, Psalm 119. Psalm 1 begins by praising those "who do not follow the advice of the wicked" (1:1) but rather make "their delight . . . the law [or: teaching] of the LORD" (1:2). It contrasts the pleasant fortune of such a man, "like trees planted by streams of water" (1:3) with the wicked, who are "like chaff that the wind drives away" (1:4). Psalm 119 is a massive, eightfold alphabetic acrostic—with eight verses for each letter of the twenty-two letters of the Hebrew alphabet, for a total of one hundred and seventy-six verses—that alternates between praise for the man who heeds God's precepts, and prayers calling on God to teach these precepts. The salience of wisdom in the Psalter has led some scholars to posit that the book's final editors meant to offer it to the reader, as a whole, as something like a book of wisdom.

The wisdom content in the Psalms most faithfully perpetuates the framework of the book of Proverbs insofar as it is universalist. Psalm 1, summarized above, is a good example; it makes no reference to Israel. Another example is Psalm 37, another alphabetic acrostic. The speaker heartens the righteous man who witnesses the success of the wicked and the want endured by the righteous by assuring him that these circumstances are temporary: "The arms of the wicked shall be broken" (37:17), while the righteous man, though he stumbles, "shall not fall headlong, for the LORD holds [him] by the hand" (37:24). The righteous man is one who is "ever giving liberally and lending" (37:26), and "the law [or: teaching] of [his] God is in [his] heart" (37:31). There is no departure from Proverbs in these sentiments, though in this wisdom psalm, like others, there is a preference for the poor—an assumption that the wealthy tend to be wicked, and the poor, pious; that "the meek [or: lowly] shall inherit the land" (37:11)—that is hardly characteristic of Proverbs. This motif has ancient roots, in the book of Amos and elsewhere, but becomes more prominent in later biblical literature and especially in literature of the Second Temple period, including the New Testament.

In other psalms that incorporate wisdom material, this motif becomes a vehicle for the introduction of a particularist element. Psalm 94 offers a good illustration. The psalm opens by calling upon God, as righteous judge, to destroy the wicked: "Rise up, O judge of the earth; give to the proud what they deserve" (94:2). But as the psalmist describes the wicked in more detail, we discover that they prey not on the vulnerable alone, but on Israel specifically.

> They crush your people, O LORD,
> and afflict your heritage.
> They kill the widow and the stranger;
> they murder the orphan,
> and they say, "The LORD does not see;
> the God of Jacob does not perceive." (94:5–7)

What circumstances are these verses describing? If the victims are Israel, then the victimizers should be foreigners; but then why do these foreigners afflict the widow, the stranger, and the orphan specifically? The rhetoric of the psalm maps the distinction between oppressor and oppressed onto the distinction between the nations and Israel, so that the verses convey a double meaning: they condemn both the oppression of the weak by the strong, and the oppression of Israel by the nations.

The same dynamic recurs later in the psalm. The speaker, deploying wisdom categories, expresses admiration for "those whom you discipline, O LORD, and whom you teach out of your law [or: teaching]" (94:12). Such people will not be abandoned in their distress.

> For the LORD will not forsake his people,
> he will not abandon his heritage;
> for justice will return to the righteous,
> and all the upright in heart will follow it. (94:14–15)

Here too the speaker does not hesitate to equate the righteous student of God's teaching with the people and inheritance of God, that is, Israel.

Synthesis: David as the Individual in the Psalter

A final and very important way in which the book of Psalms associates the human individual at prayer with Israel is through the figure of David. Both psalms of the individual with which this chapter began (the individual lament in Psalm 6 and the individual thanksgiving in Psalm 30) feature headings that attribute them to David. Other headings—those of Psalms 3 and 7, for example—identify the specific circumstances in which David purportedly recited the psalm. Attributions to David are pervasive in the book, especially up to Psalm 72. Psalm 72 includes a coda, "The prayers of David son of Jesse are ended" (72:20), that appears to assign all the preceding psalms to David. Despite this coda, some psalms later in the book (among them Psalm 131, analyzed above) also begin with headers that attribute them to David. An attribution of a psalm to David, or at least an attribution that identifies the circumstances under which David recited the psalm, transforms the psalm into a narrative, like other biblical narratives: it no longer constitutes (only) a script, but (also) a transcript, a report on the past.

How did this attribution practice arise? Some psalms refer explicitly to David or to a (Davidic) king. For example, the speaker in Psalm 110 assures the Davidic king that "the LORD sends out from Zion your mighty scepter" (110:2) and enables the king to defeat his enemies. The speaker of Psalm 72 calls upon God to make the king and his son righteous, powerful, and prosperous.

Psalm 18 is especially notable in this connection. It speaks explicitly of David only once, in the very last line of the psalm (18:50), in what may be a later supplement. The body of this long psalm is very similar to the typical individual thanksgiving psalm: the speaker reports that he was in distress, surrounded by enemies, encircled by "cords of Sheol" (18:5), until, in accordance with his righteousness, God rescued him.

But unlike the typical individual psalm of thanksgiving, Psalm 18 refers unambiguously to circumstances of war: "you girded me with strength for the battle" (18:39). The enemies in this psalm are not jeering neighbors or scheming local magnates, but armies of "foreigners" (18:44). The God who appears to save the speaker is a god of war, who "sent out his arrows" (18:14) in support of the speaker. In short, the psalm, despite its resemblance to a typical individual thanksgiving, construes its speaker specifically as the king. Indeed, the psalm heading attributes it to David, who recited it "when the LORD delivered him from the hand of all his enemies." The psalm also appears, with minor differences, in the story of David itself, in 2 Samuel 22, in David's mouth.

But it is precisely the resemblance of Psalm 18 to the typical psalm of the individual that matters to us here. The resemblance explains, in part, why the individual prayers of lament and thanksgiving collected in the book of Psalms, even those that refer to personal rather than political foes, came to be attributed to David (and after them, other psalms); the immediate conditions that motivate lament and thanksgiving are the same in both cases, even if the underlying causes differ. David is an individual like any other, but for the same reason, every individual is a David. In the book of Psalms, then, even the individual speaker who appears to come before God simply as a human being in fact comes before God as an Israelite, a loyal subject and emulator of David.

Conclusion

Through the scripts contained in the book of Psalms, the Bible imagines different ways in which Israelites, as individuals and as a community, enter into God's presence. Even as its speakers enter as mortals before the immortal, they also enter as Israelites before their ancient covenantal partner, and the book of Psalms works in myriad ways to synthesize these personae. Meditation on God's immortality, in contrast with human mortality, can transform into recognition of his role in Israelite history. The individual can gesture to the Israelite community that shares, at a different scale, his hope of and gratitude for salvation. He can praise or take on the persona of an Israelite sage and sufferer. Or he can praise or take on the persona of the Israelite hero and king, David.

For Further Reflection

1. Among other things, the book of Psalms is a powerful if uneven anthology of biblical poetry, one that can be appreciated through literary analysis. One especially bright gem is Psalm 133. It is short enough—only three verses—that it might easily be memorized. How does this poem work? How do its images cohere and convey meaning? See the close reading of this psalm in the final chapter of F. W. Dobbs-Allsopp, *On Biblical Poetry* (pp. 326–49).

2. Many aspects of religious and more generally human experience that biblical narrative takes notice of only in passing figure centrally in the book of Psalms. Consider some of these aspects—for example, joy, pain, mourning, the felt presence of God, the perceived absence of God—as they arise in the book.

Bibliography

Croft, Steven J. L. *The Identity of the Individual in the Psalms.* Sheffield: Sheffield Academic Press, 1987.

deClaissé-Walford, Nancy L., ed. *The Shape and Shaping of the Book of Psalms: The Current State of Scholarship.* Atlanta: SBL Press, 2014.

Dobbs-Allsopp, F. W. *On Biblical Poetry.* Oxford: Oxford University Press, 2015.

Gunkel, Hermann. *An Introduction to the Psalms: The Genres of the Religious Lyric of Israel.* Translated by James D. Nogalski. Macon, GA: Mercer University Press, 1998.

Miller, Patrick D. *Interpreting the Psalms.* Philadelphia: Fortress, 1986.

Sheppard, Gerald T. *Wisdom as a Hermeneutical Construct: A Study in the Sapientializing of the Old Testament.* Berlin: de Gruyter, 1980.

Wilson, Gerald H. *The Editing of the Hebrew Psalter.* Chico, CA: Scholars Press, 1985.

Subject Index

Aaron, 61, 118, 122, 150
Abimelech, 155
Abraham, 11, 38–40, 44, 61, 168
  election, 29–31, 33–35, 110
  righteousness, 32–34
  sacrifice of Isaac, 34–36
Abrahamic covenant, 29–31, 53–54, 56–57, 60–61
Adam and Eve, 100–101, 106, 109, 114
  mortality, 101–3, 106–7, 111, 112
  original sin, 101–4, 111–12
afterlife, 18, 131, 174–75
Ahab, 85–86
Ahasuerus, 160–61, 167
Alexander the Great, 127, 145, 169–70
allegory, 37–38
Amaziah, 88–89, 90
Amenemope, Instruction of, 15, 23
America, United States of, 11–12, 57–58, 59
Amit, Yairah, 155
Amos, 32, 88–94, 98, 188
angels, 172–73, 174, 177
Antiochus IV Epiphanes, 170–71, 172, 173
apocalyptic, 128, 136, 172–75, 176–78
"An Arundel Tomb," 6–8, 9, 69
Assyria, Assyrian Empire, 11, 12, 89–90, 165
  Nineveh, 93–96, 97
  northern kingdom of Israel exile, 126–30, 133
Atrahasis, 115–16, 117, 124
Auerbach, Eric, 34
authority, 3–4, 22
  biblical, 2, 3–4, 27, 34, 143–44, 153
  reason, 2–5, 6, 27

Babel, tower of, 109–11, 116
Babylonia, 11, 12
  Enuma Elish, 124–25
  exile of Judah, 12, 126–30, 133, 135, 136–37, 172–73
  Hammurabi, Laws of, 69–70, 72–75, 115–16
Baker, Cynthia, 159
Bathsheba, 83, 85
Benjamin, 50–52, 156
Ben Sira, 145–47, 148
Bible, scripture, 10–12, 69, 139–40, 143–44, 180
  authority, 2, 3–4, 27, 34, 143–44, 153
  canon, 12–13, 132, 137, 147–48, 149
  Christian, 2, 12, 13, 76, 137, 145
  Jewish (Torah, Tanak), 12–13, 112, 144–45, 146–48, 166
birth, 62–63
Boaz, 162–63

Canaan, 11, 37, 41, 141–42, 143
  conquest of, 150–54, 156

herem, 151–52, 153–54, 156
canon, biblical, 12–13, 132, 137, 147–48, 149
causality, 47–49
chaos, 26–27, 38, 120
Christianity, 2–4, 37, 67, 104, 148, 176
apocalyptic, 128, 169, 178
Bible, 2, 12, 13, 76, 137, 145
Eden story, 101, 103, 111–12
messiah, 78, 86
traditional-canonical method, 5–6
Collins, John, 58
command dynamic, 106–7, 109, 110, 111–12
community psalms, 181–82, 186–87, 190–91
Community Rule (1QS), 169, 176–77
Covenant Code, 66, 69–70, 72–75, 77
covenants, 115. *See also* Sinai covenant
Abrahamic, 29–31, 53–54, 56–57, 60–61
Davidic, 82–83
Cover, Robert, 67–68
creation stories, biblical, 178, 182
Genesis, 23–24
Priestly source, 118–21, 124
tabernacle and, 121–22
creation stories, Near Eastern, 19, 27, 124–25

Daniel, book of, 169, 172–75, 177, 178
David, 80–84, 86–87, 189–90
Davidic covenant, 82–83
Dead Sea Scrolls, 175–79
Community Rule (1QS), 169, 176–77
death, 101–2, 105–6
resurrection, 131, 174–75
Sheol, 18, 36, 94, 183, 186, 190
Deborah, 154, 158
Decalogue (Ten Commandments), 66, 67, 70–72, 75, 76, 77
departure stories, 38–40
Deuteronomistic History, 78, 150
Deuteronomy, book of, 31, 71, 140–42, 143–44
conquest of Canaan, 152, 153
Moses and, 6, 141
Documentary Hypothesis, 40–41, 114, 117–18, 120. *See also* Priestly source
doublets, 38–40, 116–17

Ecclesiastes, book of, 24
echoes, 50–51, 52–53, 110
Eden story, 6, 100–101, 109, 111, 112
Babel, tower of and, 109–10
Christian reading, 101, 103, 111–12
death, 101–2
Epic of Gilgamesh and, 104–7, 108, 110
knowledge, tree of, 101–4, 107–8
life, tree of, 101–2, 107–8, 112
mortality, 101–3, 110
original sin, 101–4
serpent, 101, 104
Egypt, 11, 126, 169. *See also* Joseph
Abraham in, 38, 39
Amenemope, Instruction of, 15, 23
exodus, the, 56–57, 62–63
Jacob, 45, 50–51
wisdom literature, 22–23
election, 29–32, 53
of Abraham, 29–31, 33–35, 110
divine will, 33–36
love and, 31, 37–38
national, of Israel, 63–64, 79–80, 92–93, 98
righteousness and, 32–33
Elijah, 85–86, 90
Enlightenment, the, 5
Enoch, 118
1 Enoch, 96
equality, 74–75, 77
Esau, 30, 31, 32
eschatology, 127–28, 131, 136, 137, 173
Essenes, 176–77, 178–79
Esther, 160–62, 164, 167, 168
Eve. *See* Adam and Eve
exile, the, 12, 126–30, 133, 135, 136–37, 172–73
exodus, the, 56–59, 60–63, 93, 157
Ezekiel, 128–31, 136, 174–75
Ezra, 144–45, 164–67

family, 18, 22, 34–35, 41, 167
identity, 35, 54–55, 175
loyalty, 162–64
structure, 74–75
firstborn, 30–31, 34–36, 61–62
Flaubert, Gustave, 45
flood stories, 109
Atrahasis, 115–16, 117, 124
Noah, 114–17
Priestly, 117–18, 119
Utnapishtim, 106, 115
forgiveness, 96–97, 185–86
form criticism, 181–82
Fox, Michael, 37

freedom, 57–59, 68, 122

gender, 16, 19–20, 28, 159–62, 167
 women, 31–32, 68, 164–67
gentiles (non-Israelites), 48, 91–91, 94–97
 Israel (Jews) and, 157, 159–62, 165–67
Gideon, 154–55
Gilgamesh, Epic of, 104–9, 110, 111, 115–16
gnostics, 104
God, 25–27, 96–97, 109, 133
 causality, 47–49
 chaos and, 26–27, 38
 creation, 25–27, 118–19, 133
 knowledge of, 2–4, 176–77
 fear of, 17, 21
 forgiveness, 96–97, 185–86
 humans and, 109, 111
 judgment, 91–93
 justice, 24–25, 49, 95–97
 as king, 77–78
 love for, 71–72
 love of, 37–38
 mercy, 95–97, 185–86
 Mount Sinai and, 66–67
 nations and, 91–93, 94–97, 98, 129–31, 136
 presence, 44–47, 128–29
 in Proverbs, 21–22
 worship of, 133–34, 135, 142–43
 Y-H-W-H, 61–62
gods, 105–6, 108–9, 110, 115–16
Goliath, 81–82, 158
goring ox, 73–74, 75
Greek Empire, 169–70, 173–74, 178
 Alexander the Great, 127, 145, 169–70
 Antiochus IV Epiphanes, 170–71, 172, 173
 Hellenism, 145–46, 169–71, 178
 Seleucid, 169, 170–71, 173
Gunkel, Hermann, 181

Hagar, 30–31, 38–40, 44, 117
Haman, 160–61
Hammurabi, Laws of, 69–70, 72–75, 115–16
Haran, 43, 52–54
Hellenism, 145–46, 169–71, 178
herem, 151–52, 153–54, 156
hierarchy dynamic, 106–7, 108–9, 110, 111–12
historical-critical method, 6–10, 13, 108, 116–17
history, 21–22, 59, 123, 153, 173
 eternity and, 183–86
 of Israel, 11–13, 24, 63, 180
 salvation, 32, 161
Holy Spirit, 13
human action, 47–49

identity:
 family and, 35, 54–55, 175
 individual, 175, 178, 182–84
 Israelite, Jewish, 153–58, 160–62, 170–72, 178
idolatry, 79–80, 84–85, 129, 134, 140–42, 152, 166
immortality, 101–2, 106, 107, 110–11
 divine, 184–85, 190–91
individual identity, 175, 178, 182–84
individual psalms, 180, 182–84, 186–87, 190–91
Isaac, 30, 34–36, 53–54, 61
Isaiah, 132
Ishmael, 30, 31
Israel / Israelites, 92–93, 126–27. *See also* Judaism, Jews; kings of Israel
 cult centralization, 139–42
 exile, 12, 126–30, 133, 135, 136–37, 172–73
 as God's son, 61–63
 history, 11–13, 24, 62–63, 180
 identity, 153–58, 160–62, 170–71
 idolatry, 79–80, 84–85, 129, 134, 140–42, 152, 166
 Jubilee Year, 122
 land of, 122–24, 129–31
 national election, 63–64, 79–80, 92–93, 98
 northern kingdom of Israel, 12, 30, 52, 58–59, 60, 85, 89–90, 154
 Passover, 62–63
 Persian period, 144–45, 160–62
 restoration, 127, 129–31, 132–34, 136–37, 174–75
 as servant in Second Isaiah, 134–36
 southern kingdom of Judah, 12, 52, 85, 158
 strangers / nations and, 59–60, 124, 162–63, 167–68, 188–89
 tribal identity, 154–58

Jacob, 30–31, 32, 43, 61
 dreams, 44, 45
 Egypt, 45, 50–51
 Laban and, 51–50, 52–54, 52–54
Jephthah, 155, 157

Jeroboam, 58
Jeroboam II, 88–89
Jerusalem, 81, 151, 165, 170. *See also* temple
Jesus Christ, 13, 34, 40, 97
  messiah, 86–87
  as Word, 23–24
Jezebel, 85, 86
Job, book of, 24–27, 38, 95, 98
John, apostle, 23–24
Jonah, 93–97, 98
  as Israel, 94–96
Joseph, 16, 30–31, 43–44, 48–49
  causality, 47–49
  character development, 49–52
  coincidence, 46–47
  dreams, 45–46
  Esther and, 161, 168
  Judah and, 51–52
Joshua, book of, 150–51, 152–53, 158
Josiah, 140–41, 144, 152
Jubilee Year, 122
Judah, 45, 49–52, 54
  southern kingdom of, 12, 52, 85, 158
Judaism / Jews, 126, 127, 140, 169
  biblical canon, 12–13, 147–48
  exile, 126–30, 133, 135, 136–37
  Hellenism, 145–46, 169–71, 178
  identity, 170–72, 178
  messiah, 78, 86–87, 127–28
  Mishnah, 'Avot, 148
  sectarianism, 175–78
  Torah, 147–48
Judges, book of, 150–52, 154–57
judgment, 45, 93, 114–15, 130, 153, 173, 188
justice, 24–25, 38, 49, 92–93, 95–97
Justin Martyr, 2–4, 5, 15

Kaufmann, Yehezkel, 95
Kierkegaard, Søren, 32, 34
King, Martin Luther, Jr., 1–2, 4, 58
kings of Israel, 72, 75, 77–78, 152, 156
  Ahab, 85–86
  David, 80–84, 86–87, 189–90
  God and, 78–83, 84, 86–87
  Jeroboam II, 11, 88–89
  Josiah, 140–41, 144, 152
  messiah, 78, 86–87
  prophets and, 84–86, 88–89
  Saul, 80, 81–82, 87
  temple and, 82–84
knowledge of God, 2–4, 176–77
knowledge, tree of, 101–4, 107–8

Laban, 51, 52–54
Lamentations, book of, 135
laments, 181, 182–83, 186–87
Larkin, Philip, 6–8, 9, 69
Lemuel, King, 22, 23
Levenson, Jon, 35
Leviathan, 27, 120
life, tree of, 101–2, 107–8, 112
love, 31, 37–38, 71–72
loyalty, 34–35, 71–72, 162–64

2 Maccabees, 169, 170–72, 174, 175, 178
mercy, 95–97, 185–86
Mesopotamia, 11, 105, 126
messiah, 78, 86–87, 127–28
Micah, 155–56
Michal, 81–82
miscarriage, 73–75, 76
Moab, 162–64, 168
monotheism, 75, 85, 133, 136–37, 139–40, 141, 152
morals, 2, 6, 17–18, 32, 49–50, 98, 153
  failings, 91–92, 93
Mordecai, 160–62
mortality, 101–3, 106–7, 108–9, 110, 111–12, 184–85, 190–91
Moses, 1–2, 11, 61, 62, 63–64, 121
  Deuteronomy and, 6, 141
  exodus, the, 56–57
  Torah, 13, 148

Naboth, 85–86
Nahum, 97
Naomi, 162–63, 168
narrator, biblical, 44–45, 46
Nathan, 84, 86, 90
nations:
  God and, 91–93, 94–97, 98, 129–31, 136
  Israel and, 59–60, 124, 162–63, 167–68, 188–89
  oracles against, 90–93, 97
Nehemiah, 144–45, 164–67
Newsom, Carol, 25–26, 27
New Testament, 4–5, 23, 34, 40, 172, 188
Nineveh, 93–96, 97
Noah, 114–17
Noahic covenant, 115

non-Israelites (gentiles), 48, 91–93, 94–97
Israel (Jews) and, 157, 159–62, 165–67
norm, 48
violation of, 31–32, 36, 37, 59, 123
northern kingdom of Israel, 12, 30, 52, 58–59, 60, 85, 89–90, 154

obedience, 109
command dynamic, 106–7, 109, 110, 111–12
loyalty and, 34–35, 71–72
obligations, 67–69
Old Testament, New Testament and, 4–5, 23
oppression, 56–58, 63–64, 92–93, 188–89
by kings, 79–80, 83–84
of strangers, 59–60
original sin, 101–4, 111–12
"Ozymandias," 8–10, 111

Pardes, Ilana, 62
particularism, 1–5, 27–28
conquest of Canaan, 153–54
election, 29–32, 33–34
exodus, the, 60–63
kingship, 79–80, 86–87
law codes, 71–72
love and, 36–38
Priestly source, 121–23
sectarianism, 175–78
Passover, 62–63
patriarchy, 31–32
Paul, apostle, 23
Paul, Shalom, 92
Pentateuch, 40, 100. *See also* Torah
Documentary Hypothesis, 40–41, 114
source criticism of, 38–41
Persia, 12, 126–27, 133, 144–45, 164, 167, 174
Ahasuerus, 160–61, 167
Philo, 147–48
philosophy, 2–4, 15, 21
Plato, 2–3, 147–48
Priestly source, 114, 123–24, 128–29, 131
creation account, 118–21, 124
flood account, 117–18, 119
prophets, 3–4, 98, 132, 178
Amos, 88–94, 98
Elijah, 85–86, 90
Ezekiel, 128–31, 136, 174–75
Jonah, 93–97
kings and, 84–86, 88–89
literary, 90, 128
Nathan, 84, 86, 90
nations, oracles against, 90–93, 97
Second Isaiah, 132–37
Prophets, books of, 12–13
Proverbs, book of, 59, 63, 70
cosmopolitan character, 22–23
gender in, 16, 19–20, 28
God in, 71–72
piety, 17–18
retribution, 18–19, 24–25
righteous, the, 17–18, 28
Sirach and, 145–47
Song of Songs and, 36–37
universalism, 21–24, 27–28, 188
wicked, the, 17–18, 28
wisdom, definition, 15–17, 72
Wisdom, Lady, 19–21, 24, 37, 146–47
worldview, 17–21, 48–49
Psalms, book of, 180–82, 186–87, 190–91
laments, 181, 182–83, 186–87
thanksgiving, 181–82, 183, 185, 189, 190
wisdom, 187–89

Rachel, 30, 37, 43, 52
Rad, Gerhard von, 178
reason, 2–5, 6, 27
Rebekah, 30, 31
restoration of Israel, 127, 132–34, 136–37
Ezekiel on, 129–31, 174–75
resurrection, 131, 174–75
retribution, 18–19, 24–25, 47–48
revelation, 37–38, 39–40, 44, 59
righteous, the, 17–18, 28, 36, 118, 174–75, 188–90
Abraham, 32–33
Noah, 114–15
sufferer, 18, 24–26, 27, 95, 173
rights, 67–69
Roman Catholic Church, 103, 169
Ruth, 162–64, 167

salvation, 32, 161, 178, 191
Samson, 158
Samuel, 78, 79–81
Sarah, 30, 31, 38–39
Saul, 80, 81–82, 87
Schwartz, Daniel, 171
scripture. *See* Bible, scripture
sea, 26–27, 62, 120

Second Isaiah, 132–37
Second Temple, 126–27, 137, 164–65
Second Temple period, 67, 86, 144, 162, 172, 175–76, 188
sectarianism, 175–78
Seleucid Empire, 169, 170–71, 172, 173
Servant Songs, 134–36
Seth, 114, 118
Shelley, Percy Bysshe, 8–10
Sheol, 18, 36, 94, 183, 186, 190
shepherding, 43, 50–51, 52, 61, 64, 81, 132
  of God, 132–33
Simon, Uriel, 95
sin, 186–87
  original, 101–4, 111–12
Sinai covenant, 66–67, 130
  Covenant Code, 66, 69–70, 72–75, 77
  goring ox, 73–74, 75
  law code, 35, 57, 58, 59–60
  miscarriage, 73–75, 76
  suzerainty treaty, 70–72, 77
  Ten Commandments (Decalogue), 66, 67, 70–72, 75, 76, 77
slavery, 56–60
society, law and, 67–69, 70, 92
  class distinction, 74, 77
Sodom, 33, 41, 44
Solomon, 22, 36, 58–59, 84–85, 166
Sommer, Benjamin, 128–29, 135, 137
Song of Songs, book of, 36–38, 41
source criticism, 38–41
southern kingdom of Judah, 12, 52, 85, 158
Star Wars, 45
Sternberg, Meir, 94, 158
strangers (foreigners), 59–60, 124
  Haman (Amalekites), 160–61
  Moab, 162–64, 168
success, 16–18, 19, 109
suzerainty treaty, 70–72, 77

tabernacle, 117–18, 122–23
Tamar, 50
temple, 117, 122–23, 151
  Jerusalem, 12, 83–85, 126–27, 128–29, 139–40, 141
  second, 126–27, 137, 164–65
Ten Commandments (Decalogue), 66, 67, 70–72, 75, 76, 77
thanksgiving, 181–82, 183, 185, 189, 190
Toorn, Karel van der, 58, 59
Torah, 12–13, 112, 144–45, 166. *See also* Pentateuch
  wisdom and, 146–48
traditional-canonical method, 5–10, 13, 108

universalism, 1–5
  creation story, 120–21
  Eden story, 100–101, 111
  election, 31–32
  exodus, the, 57–59
  individual identity, 175, 178, 182–84
  kingship, 79–80, 86–87
  law codes, 69–70, 71–72
  monotheism, 136–37
  Priestly source, 121–23
  prophets, 90–93
  Proverbs, 21–24, 133–34
  Second Isaiah, 133–34
Uriah, 83, 85
Utnapishtim, 106, 115

violence, 150–51, 154–57

Walzer, Michael, 60
Western thought, culture, 2, 5, 67, 170
wicked, the, 17–18, 28, 33, 70, 175, 187
  judgment of, 45, 93, 114–15, 130, 153, 173, 188
  penitent, 96–97
wife-sister stories, 38–40
Wilson, Gerald, 180
wisdom, 21, 48–49, 72, 112, 146–48
  definition, 15–17, 72, 121
  Greek, 147–48
  success and, 16–18, 19
Wisdom, Lady, 19–21, 24, 37, 146–47
wisdom literature, 16, 36–37, 115, 145–46
  Joseph story as, 43–44, 48–49
  psalms, 187–89
women, role of, 31–32, 68, 159–62, 164–67
  wife-sister stories, 38–40
worldview, 17–21, 48–49
worship, 133–34, 135, 142–43, 183–84
Writings, 12–13

Y-H-W-H, 61–62

Zion, Mount, 66, 146, 181, 184, 189–90

Scripture and Other Ancient Sources Index

OLD TESTAMENT

Genesis

1 11, 19, 23–24, 27, 119–21, 122, 125, 129
1–11 100, 103
1:1–2:4a 114, 124
1:2 118, 119
1:5–10 114
1:6–8 119
1:21 120
1:24–27 118
1:27 122, 125
1:28 56
1:31a 121
2 112, 119
2–3 109
2:1 121
2:2a 121
2:3 121
2:4 118
2:4–3:24 124
2:4–4:26 100
2:4–5:32 112
2:7 118
2:8–17 149
2:17 112
2:19 118
3:4 112
3:5 104
3:19 102
3:20 101
3:22 101, 102, 104
4 112
4:1–23 112
5 118
5:18–24 118
6:1 115
6:5–8 117
6:9–9:29 41
6:19–20 116
7:1–5 117
7:2–3 116
7:4 116
7:11 117, 119
7:12 116
7:24 116
8:1 116, 119
8:4 117
8:5 116
8:6 116
8:14 117
8:20 117
8:21 103, 117
10 118
11 109, 116
11:1–9 100, 109
11:4 110
11:6 110
11:9 111
11:10–28:9 29
12 33, 34, 44
12:1 33, 148
12:2 110
12:3 29
12:10–21 38
13:10 149
15:16 153
16 44, 117
16:1–2 30
16:4–14 38
16:6 39
16:7 39
17:17 30
18 34
18:9–15 30
18:16–33 32
18:16–19:38 41
18:17–19 32–33
18:23 33
18:25 33
19 156
19:24 44
19:30–38 163
20:1–18 38
20:12 39
21 44

21:1–7 30
21:8–21 38
21:9–12 30
21:11–12 39
21:16–17 30
21:17 39
22 33, 34–35, 36
22:2 33–34
23 41
24 41
25:28 31
25:29–34 32
26:34–35 41
27:5–15 30
27:16 47
27:38 30
27:41 32
27:46 41
28:1–9 41
28:10–17 44, 45
28:10–22 54
28:10–33:20 43
29:6 52
29:7–8 52
29:9 52
29:18 30
29:20 30
29:26 54
29:30 30
29:31–32 30
31:45–47 53
35 43
37–46 43
37:5–11 46
37:10 46
37:11 46
37:12–17 46
37:21–22 54
37:25 47
37:25–28 46
37:26–27 49, 54
37:31–32 47
38 45, 47, 50
38:7 45
38:10 45
39 50
39:5 45
39:7–20 47
39:21 45
39:23 45
40:1–19 46
41:1–32 46
41:33 16
41:38–39 72
41:39 48
42:37 54
43:8–9 54
43:11 47
45:17–19 30–31
46:1–4 45, 46
48–50 43

Exodus

1 62
1–17 56
1:7 56
1:11 58
2 63
2:11 63
2:15 58
2:16–17 64
2:19 64
2:23–25 56–57, 60, 61
4:22 61
6:2–3 61
12:1–2 62
13:4 61–62
15:26 64
17 160
19–24 66
19:1–2 66
20 140
20:2 71
20:7 70
20:20 143
20:20–21 140
20:21 143
21–23 58, 59, 60
21:1 66
21:1–23:33 69
21:2–11 58
21:22–25 74, 76
21:28–32 73
21:31 74, 75
22 59
22:10–11 69
22:21 59
22:22–24 57
22:29–30 35
23 60
23:9 59
23:33 66
25:1–9 114
28:3 16
31:3 121
34:6 185
34:6–7 96–97
39:32a 121
39:32–43 114
39:43 121
40:17–38 114, 121
40:33b 121

Leviticus

18:24–29 153
18:26 124
19:34 59
25 114, 122
25:23 122
25:54–55 122
26:42 61
27:30 80
27:32 80

Numbers

14:18 97
22–24 95
24:7 160

Deuteronomy

1:1–3 66
1:4 66
1:6 66
1:39 102
4:5–6 72
6:4–5 71
7:2 152
7:15 64
9:5 153
10:4 66
10:19 59
11:8–21 149
12 139, 141, 143
12:2 141
12:2–4 143
12:4 141
12:5 143
12:8 152

12:8–9 141
12:11 143
12:13 142
12:13–15 143
12:13–19 142, 143
12:14 142, 143
12:15 142, 143
12:16 142
12:17 142, 143
12:18 142
12:19 142
18:12 153
21:15–17 29, 31
23:4–5 163, 166
24:22 59
25:17–19 160
29:20 144
30:19 112
33:2 66
33:4 147

Joshua

1–12 152–53, 153–54
1–19 150
6:21 151
6:24 151
7–8 156
7:2–3 151
10 151
11 151
13 151
13–21 151, 152
13:1 151
15:63 151

Judges

1 156
1–2 152
1:1–2 156
1:19 152
1:21 153
3 153
4 158
4–5 154
4:6 154
4:9 158
5:14 154
5:14–15 154
5:15–17 154
5:18 154
5:23 154
8:1–3 154
8:4–9 155
8:13–17 155
8:31 155
9:1 155
9:2 155
9:26–29 155
11:1 155
11:4–7 155
11:12–27 155
12:1 155
12:5–6 155
13–16 158
17–18 155
17:6 152
18:1 152
18:26 155
19–21 156
19:12 156
19:16–21 156
20:18–19 156
20:48 156
21:11 156
21:25 152

Ruth

1:16–17 162
2:12 163
3:9 163
3:10 163

1 Samuel

8–10 77
8:4–9 78
8:15 79–80
8:17–18 79–80
9:2 80
9:21 87
10:22–23 87
15 87, 160
16–17 77
17 81, 158
17:4–7 81
17:8–9 81
17:45 81
17:51 81

2 Samuel

5–7 77
6:13–16 81
7:14 86
11 83
11–12 77
12 84
12:9 84
22 190

1 Kings

3:1 58
4:29–34 22
5:13–17 58
9:19 58
10:28 58
11:7–8 84–85
11:40 58
12:4 58
12:28 58
14:21–28 87
16:1–14 87
16:29–21:29 77
18:19 85
18:37 85

2 Kings

3:26–27 35
22–23 140–41
22:8 141

Ezra

4 159, 165
4:1–2 165
4:4 165
6:14 167
7 139
7:6 144
7:14 145, 164
8 164
9 165
9–10 159
9:2 166
9:11 166
10:2 166

Nehemiah

1–4 159

2:19 165
6 159
6:17 165
8 139
8:13 145
8:14 145
13 159, 165
13:1–2 164
13:1–3 166
13:23–28 166
13:24 166
13:28 165

Esther

2:10 160
2:20 160
3:4 160
4:13 160–61
4:14 161
7:3–4 161
9:31 160

Job

1–2 25
1–14 15
29–31 15
38–42 15
38:1 25
38:2–3 25
38:4 25
38:6–7 25
38:9 26
38:26 26
39:6–7 26
39:30 26
40:15 26–27
42:3–6 25–26
42:7–17 25

Psalms

1 180, 187
1:1 187
1:2 187
1:3 187
1:4 187–88
2:7 86
3 180, 189
6 182–83, 189
6–7 180
6:2 183
6:5 183
6:6 183
6:7 183
7 189
18 180, 190
18:5 190
18:14 190
18:39 190
18:44 190
18:50 190
30 180, 183, 189
30:1 183
30:5 183
30:9 49, 183
37 180, 188
37:11 188
37:17 188
37:24 188
37:26 188
37:31 188
72 189, 190
72:20 189
74 114, 120, 124–25, 181
74:1–2 181
74:3–9 181
74:7–8 120
74:12–17 181
90 180, 184–85
90:1 184–85
90:2 185
90:3–12 185
90:5 185
90:13–17 185
94 180, 188
94:2 188
94:5–7 188
94:12 189
94:14–15 189
102 183, 185
102–103 180
102:1–2 183
102:1–11 184
102:4 183
102:8 183
102:11 183, 184
102:11–12 184
102:12 184
102:12–13 184
102:12–22 184
102:14–22 184
102:23 184
102:24 184
102:28 184, 185
103 184–86
103:4 185
103:7 185
103:8 185
103:11–17 185–86
110 180, 189–90
110:2 189
119 187, 188
120–134 181
124 180, 181–82
124:1 182
124:1–2 182
124:2 182
124:3 182
124:3–5 182
124:4–5 182
124:6 182
124:7 182
124:7–8 182
130 186
130–131 180
130:3 186
130:5–6 186
130:7–8 186
131 187, 189
131:1 187
131:2 187
131:3 187
133 191

Proverbs

1 15
1:2–4 15
1:3 17
1:7 17
1:8 22
1:18–19 19
3:18 112
5:3–4 16
6–8 15
6:2 17
6:9–11 16
6:20–35 37
7:10–13 20
7:18–20 20

7:22–23 20
8 24, 26, 27, 146
8:1–5 20–21
8:17–21 20–21
8:22–24 19
8:29–31 19
15–17 15
22:17–23:11 23
22:17–24:22 15, 23
22:20 23
22:22 17
22:23 17
23:10–11 17, 57
23:20–21 16
24:3 146
25–29 28
25:1 22
27:7 23
29:3 21
30–31 15
31:1–9 22, 23
31:10–31 28

Ecclesiastes

1:1 24
2:16 24

Song of Songs

1 29
1:5 36
2 29
2:7 36
5 29
5:7 36
5:8–9 36
8 29
8:6–7 36–37

Isaiah

13–23 91
40–53 126, 132
40:1 132
40:11 132
40:28 133
41:8 134
41:13 132, 135
42:1–4 134
42:5 133
42:6 135
42:6–7 135
43:10–11 133
44:1–2 134
44:6 133
45:20 134
45:22–23 134
46:4 132–33
49:1–6 134
49:3 135
49:6 135
50:4–9 134
51:3 149
52:13–53:12 134
52:15 136
53:4–5 136
54:17 134

Jeremiah

33:26 61
46–51 91

Lamentations

3:1 135

Ezekiel

1 126, 129
1:3 128
1:26–28 128
8–11 126
25–32 91
28:2 80
36–39 126, 129
36:13–15 130
36:20–21 129
36:22 130
36:26 130
37 131
37:11 131
37:12 131
39 130
44:1–16 126

Daniel

1 169
1–6 172
7 169
7–12 172
7:1–8 173
7:9 173
7:13–14 174
7:17 173
7:25 173
7:27 174
10 174
10–12 169
10:13 174
10:20 174
10:21 174
12:1 174
12:2 174

Hosea

2:17 58
11:1 58
12:10 58
12:14 58
13:4 58

Amos

1:3 91
1:3–5 90
1:6–8 90
1:9–10 90
1:11–12 90
1:13–15 90–91
2:1 91
2:1–3 91
2:4–5 92
2:6–7 92
2:6–8 98
2:6–16 92
2:9–10 92–93
2:10–11 58
2:11–12 90
3:1 58
3:1–2 93
3:8 90
5:18–27 98
7 98
7:10–11 88
7:11 90
7:12–17 88–89
9:1 93–94
9:2 94
9:2–3 94
9:7 58

Jonah
1:5 95
1:13 94
2:1 94
4:2 97
4:11 97

Nahum
1:2–3 97

Zechariah
14:17–19 149

NEW TESTAMENT

Luke
11:4 97

John
1:1 23
3:16 34
8:7 97

Romans
5 23

1 Corinthians
15 23

APOCRYPHA

2 Maccabees
2:19–12:45 169
2:21 171
4:7 170
4:10 170
4:13 170
6:1 170, 171
6:6 170, 171
6:18–31 171
7:9 172
8:1 171
12:44 172
14:38 171

Sirach
19 139
19:1–2 146
22:2 146
24 139, 146, 147
24:3 146
24:6 146
24:8 146
24:23 146
36:1 147
36:1–22 139
36:17 147
44–50 139, 147

PSEUDEPIGRAPHA

1 Enoch
101:4–5 96
101:9 96

OTHER ANCIENT LITERATURE

Laws of Hammurabi
I.27–49 70
§209–210 74
§249 69
§250–252 73

Epic of Gilgamesh
I.108–112 105
I.197–202 105
II.188–189 105
IX.3–5 106
XI.120–126 109

Dead Sea Scrolls
Community Rule (1QS)
I, 16–18 176
II, 25–III, 5 176
III, 15–25 176–77
IV, 16–19 177

Justin Martyr
Dialogue with Trypho
1:196 2–3
1:198 3–4

Mishnah 'Avot
1:1 148
1:2 148